Appetite for ACQUISITION

"Eric and Robin have proven their superior expertise time and time again. I have learned so much about the buying and selling processes in this industry and what has shocked me most is how easy it can really be when you use experts like We Sell Restaurants to successfully take care of it for you!"

—Donna Rodriquez, Radio host of *Dishing with Donna,* Atlanta's only food and restaurant radio show

"This book is a must have for anyone buying or selling a restaurant. Eric and Robin are leaders in the industry, and they have written an insightful, informative, and, most important, enjoyable book to read."

—Steve Zuckerman, CPA, board member, Twisted Taco Restaurant Franchise

"When you buy or sell a restaurant, you'll be excited and scared, experience highs and lows, and make quick high-dollar decisions. I've advised in buy-side and sell-side M&A for twenty-two years in many industries. Robin and Eric's book is an excellent roadmap and a wealth of tried and trusted advice for any restaurant owner (or would-be owner). It's also a useful reminder for experienced deal practitioners. If you have questions, buy this book; it's got everything."

—Truc To, Principal Transaction Services, KPMG

"Beginner to expert, anyone interested in entering the restaurant business, I would recommend this book. We Sell Restaurants has the experience and expertise to make your business dreams come true. Their brokers were extremely knowledgeable and took the time to educate me on the process and the restaurant business as well. Those aspiring to be a restaurant operator would be well served to buy this book."

—Tim Walters, Restaurant buyer

"I would highly recommend this book to anyone in the market to successfully buy a restaurant. Eric and Robin are restaurant brokerage professionals. They provide practical advice and time-proven strategies for how to buy a restaurant or bar. The actual stories of buyers throughout this book are real. That alone demonstrates why *no one* should buy a restaurant before reading this book. Their financial explanations are easy to understand and demystify the process of buying a restaurant."

—Jim Moring, Restaurant broker, Principal,
The Commonwealth Company, Founder and
President of restaurantbrokers.info

Appetite for ACQUISITION

The WE SELL RESTAURANTS Guide to Buying a Restaurant

ROBIN & ERIC
GAGNON

Tate Publishing & *Enterprises*

Published by Tate Publishing & Enterprises, LLC
127 E. Trade Center Terrace | Mustang, Oklahoma 73064 USA
1.888.361.9473 | www.tatepublishing.com

Tate Publishing is committed to excellence in the publishing industry. The company reflects the philosophy established by the founders, based on Psalm 68:11,
"*The Lord gave the word and great was the company of those who published it.*"

Cover design by Kristen Verser
Interior design by Stefanie Rane

Published in the United States of America

ISBN: 978-1-61739-814-8
1. Business & Economics, Real Estate, Commercial
2. Business & Economics, Industries, Food Industry
11.01.13

Dedication

To each other, our inspiration. Special thanks to Jim Moring, who was the first to tell us Atlanta needed a good restaurant broker, and Truc To, who agreed to read an early version.

Table of CONTENTS

Appendices

Introduction

Face it. Americans have a love affair with restaurants. We love to eat. We find it irresistible that someone else prepares our meal and delivers it to the table while we put down our plastic or cash and walk away.

The restaurant industry is a $566 billion-dollar industry (2009 estimate).[1] There are nearly one million locations, or one restaurant for every 320 Americans. Six in ten new startup restaurants will fail.[2] It's no wonder that on any given day 20 percent of the nearly one million United States restaurants, bars, and nightclubs are on the market. New restaurants, old restaurants, successful restaurants, and restaurant failures end up for sale in the hands of a restaurant broker. We know because we sell restaurants for a living. For nearly a decade we have worked directly with buyers and sellers in our restaurant brokerage firm. We are industry experts with unmatched education, experience, and knowledge in the restaurant brokerage industry. We have sold hundreds of restaurants firsthand and seen every conceivable challenge served up by both buyers and sellers. Now, we've collaborated on the first book on buying existing restaurants published since 1979.

This is not a dry business book or a pure "how-to." This book includes the real-life stories of restaurant buyers. Their tales could just as easily be your story. Will you be the buyer who threw the keys at the seller and ran after three hours of ownership? What about the one who couldn't figure out how to keep from getting drunk each night after he bought the bar of his dreams? Look for these stories set apart in the text and preceded by the words, "This is an actual story from our experiences; only the names have been changed."

Restaurants are the fabric of our culture. The neighborhood restaurant is where we go on our first date, celebrate a promotion, and gather the family to announce our engagement. In today's society, the neighborhood restaurant or pub has taken over the corner for the place to gossip, hang out, and learn your neighborhood. In a high-tech world, the restaurant is a high-touch environment where we still interact with one another. It is no wonder that buying a restaurant is such a personal journey.

There are lots of books written on launching your restaurant from scratch, complete with advice on everything from kitchen design to menus. These manuals focus on the restaurant startup. What they fail to address is the restaurant buyer who wants better than a 60 percent success rate. This book teaches you how to acquire a restaurant with proven earnings. You will learn the shortest time to market and greatest control over costs comes from buying, not building, your restaurant. We help you analyze your motivation to buy so this personal journey will not end as a lifestyle disappointment. We compare a build-out to a buyout. Instead of unknown costs, uncertain timing, and hoped-for results, we show you how to get certainty and quantified outcomes. You will learn how to buy a restaurant based on the numbers as well as the heart. There are chapters on the correct way to value a restaurant. We will teach you which restaurants have hidden opportunity you can verify by measuring their financial results against industry metrics.

We sell restaurants, so we know how to make you a better restaurant buyer. There are chapters full of worksheets, tips, and ideas. We have pages filled with the mistakes our restaurant buyers have learned over the years. Ultimately, our reader should acquire a restaurant in a way that is less painful, more profitable, and delivers a better return on their investment.

Build-out Versus Buyout

Record numbers of Americans searching for a small business combined with a hunger for all things "foodie" are creating a perfect storm of demand for buying a restaurant. It is no wonder buyers are seeking out established restaurants, since building a restaurant from scratch is such an uncertain prospect.

Six out of ten startup restaurants are out of business by the end of year three, a grim reminder of shattered dreams. Countless restaurants will never get off the ground since the owner capital is all depleted in the build-out phase. Most would-be restaurant owners open their doors cash poor and without resources to advertise, market the restaurant, and sustain it during those critical few months or years it takes to build sales volume and profitability. The belief that "if you build it, they will come" is as improbable in restaurants as it is in baseball. There is no such thing as instant success in the restaurant industry. However, buying an existing restaurant delivers significant advantages over starting from scratch.

Buying an existing restaurant is a streamlined path to restaurant ownership for would-be restaurateurs. Here are the key reasons.

1. *Control over costs.* The single largest cause of failure for restaurant startups is lack of capital. The capital burn rate increases exponentially when a skilled restaurant professional attempts to turn into a building contractor or proj-

ect manager overnight simply because the project is an eatery. Unless you are a general contractor who happens to swing a hammer as successfully as you filet a swordfish, your restaurant will take far longer to build and cost much more than you ever imagined. Any would-be restaurant owner considering a build-out has only to watch one episode of the popular real estate "flip" shows on cable TV to imagine the issues. You negotiate a great lease with three months of free rent, but construction permitting takes four months and rent begins before you open the doors. The special order light fixtures that feature antlers for your steakhouse are delayed, and an electrical inspection turns into a four-week work stoppage. Purchasing an operating restaurant eliminates these issues. The cost to acquire a restaurant is fixed. That means your capital goes into covering expenses in the critical first few months. You are focused on growing market share through marketing and advertising instead of starting out undercapitalized and without money for basics, like payroll and food. What we have seen in years of selling restaurants are countless owners that believe they can build from the ground up and save money. Once they get into the project, they begin ordering the best, moving walls, changing their minds, and generally driving construction costs through the roof. Any second-generation space will always be cheaper.

2. *Time to market.* Time is money in every business. Your great restaurant idea can be operating tomorrow with the purchase of an existing concept. Compare that to six to nine months to permit, build, and open a restaurant from scratch. You can be serving your first sandwich tomorrow to existing customers instead of waiting an average of seven months to open the doors.

3. *Existing sales volume.* An existing restaurant, even a struggling one, has a base of business. Any brand new restaurant has to build the initial dollar of sales volume and every dollar thereafter incrementally. The first $100,000 of sales volume is the toughest to achieve. Without the expense and time spent building from scratch, you can implement marketing plans and operational changes to drive the existing sales line higher. Starting from zero sales is a daunting task no matter how well known you are as a chef or how many customers you believe will visit your store.
4. *Existing cash flow.* Many buyers are in the market for a job, and the purchase of existing cash flow is simple when buying a restaurant. On a comparative basis, purchasing the cash flow of an operating restaurant with good books and records is less expensive than many other business types. The inventory is negligible (approximately 1% to 2% of sales), and cash flow is often purchased for 2.5 times earnings or less. That means someone looking for $100,000 in cash flow can acquire an operating business churning out six-figure earnings for less than $250,000. There are few other investments where placing $250,000 on the line nets you a 40% return in the first year and pays off in two and a half years.
5. *Risk management.* Buying an existing restaurant significantly lowers the risk associated with your new business venture. There are existing sales and profits instead of projected sales on a business plan. This cash flow covers the bills while you make your changes or learn the industry. Even a restaurant that previously failed has significantly lower risk than a startup. You know from the outset that the location meets local and state codes for operation of a restaurant or conforms to liquor licensing requirements. Lastly, your customers know

this location as a restaurant. Customers are creatures of habit. They are used to parking and dining in this very spot. You're asking them to build on an existing habit instead of creating an entirely new one, a much easier marketing challenge.

We often meet buyers that acknowledge all of these reasons but believe it cannot apply to them because they are opening a franchise restaurant. That is incorrect. The same logic applies to both a franchise and independent startup concept. The average franchise restaurant Web site is not shy about estimating build-out costs at $375,000 and up. That is the initial up-front cost before you sell your first premium ice cream cone, latest hamburger concept, or pour your first drink. It is no wonder that franchises require high-income individuals with strong net worth statements to qualify. They know that operators will need lots of capital to survive. Here are the same five reasons why buying is better than building applied to a new franchise unit.

1. *Control over costs.* In a franchise build-out, control over costs transfers from the operator's hands to the franchise. It means nothing to the franchise that you can buy a standard four-top table and chairs for less than $100 each; you are bound by your agreement to adhere to the décor and style guide of the brand. The same table and four chairs are now $400 each, and there's only one vendor in the United States that makes them. If the décor package changes between signup and startup, you can be shelling out money to change to new operating standards before you open. Any cost control is lost in dealing with a franchise. The other requisite issues in dealing with the build-out itself (permitting, plans, inspections, et cetera) are still your problem, and they are layered on top of this.

2. *Time to market.* A new build-out franchise and a new build-out for an independent concept have the same delays reaching the market. You will get slightly more expertise with a franchise. They often offer a project management flow chart or checklist since they are heavily invested in getting you off the ground and generating sales. The work is still yours, and time to market averages six to nine months.
3. *Existing sales volume.* There is not a dollar of sales associated with a new franchise versus a new build-out. The real difference is that when the first dollar of sales occurs, 5–12% of every dollar goes out the door and into the brand's pocket. The franchise gets royalties beginning with the first sale whether or not you are making money.
4. *Existing cash flow.* A franchise built from scratch delivers the same shortfall in cash flow. No cash flow exists since there are no earnings.
5. *Risk management.* We are told by many buyers that they want a franchise because there is "less risk." To be fair, that is a true statement when viewed against independent startups. One well-known study of the restaurant industry conducted by H.G. Parsa, an Ohio State University hospitality management professor, looked at restaurant industry failure rates.[1] He analyzed health department records for around 2,400 independent and chain restaurants in Columbus, Ohio, between 1996 and 1999. His findings showed franchises had a slight advantage with 43% of the chain restaurants still operating after three years. That was only four points better than the 39% of independent restaurants in existence after the three-year mark. However, either number still represents a 60% failure rate and substantiates the purpose of this book. Why buy the risk in either startup

> scenario when you can buy a performing business with substantiated returns already past the three-year mark? Buying an existing restaurant with three years of records ensures that 100% of the time you are buying a viable concept that has beaten the odds.

The last reason, more than any other, demonstrates why the path to restaurant ownership is often a straight line to the purchase of an existing restaurant. Whether you are buying someone else's success or failure, you are buying more certainty than starting from the ground up. You are busy hiring the best staff instead of tracking plumbing orders. You are focused on developing a new special for the menu instead of calling the painter that failed to show. Though there is no guarantee, an existing location delivers historical sales, a defined and customer-tested menu, existing operation methods, and most importantly, cash flow.

Even a restaurant failing in its current state represents a bargain for the new owner if you can understand and adjust for the mistakes in operation. If a restaurant is succeeding, you've purchased a quick path to the lucrative restaurant business without burning your capital. Are you interested? You may be a typical restaurant buyer.

Here is the first of many stories we will share about actual buyers and their experiences; only the names have been changed.

> A buyer with $125,000 in total capital looked at two locations. One would require a menu change and minor update to décor and was doing sales of $20,000 a week. The price was $25,000 for used furniture, fixtures, and equipment. The second location was a closed restaurant space to convert at minimal cost, and he could take it over for free. He continued his search and located a new center where the landlord was eager to make concessions. The landlord offered $125,000 in tenant improvement money and six months of free rent. The buyer thought he won the lottery, assuming he could use the landlord's $125,000 for total build-out and save his own capi-

tal for operations. His plan included opening in four months, giving him two months of free rent and $125,000 in the bank.

We advised against the new space. The cost to build, time to market, and emerging nature of the area were all negatives. He disagreed and went with the new space. Three months later he called. Two separate architects had drawn plans and charged him a total of $30,000, but he could not get them through the city permit approval to begin construction. Did we have a recommendation? We gave him a restaurant architect with contacts in the city building department. Three more months passed, and he called again. He was close to opening (only a few more months). Could we give him the name of an alcohol license attorney? We provided the information. Nine months later, we finally got an invitation to the grand opening.

Within a month he called again. Could we sell the restaurant? His build-out and carrying costs were $315,000, more than two and half times his initial budget of $125,000. He had used up the landlord's contribution, his own funds, and borrowed more. He was averaging $14,000 a week in sales. He was behind in the rent, did not have the money to pay his staff or advertise, and had already burned through all his lines of credit. We told him we could get 20 cents on the dollar for used equipment. He ultimately closed and ended up being sued by the landlord.

Profile of the Typical Restaurant Buyer

After years of selling restaurants, we've encountered every type of buyer. Over time, however, they begin to demonstrate very similar traits. Here's a profile of the most frequently encountered restaurant buyer that we have placed into one of five categories. Look closely, as you may find yourself fitting into one of these categories.

Corporate Refugee Restaurant Wannabe

Our office receives countless calls and inquiries from would-be entrepreneurs trapped in corporate America searching for a way out. On Friday afternoons the agent phones start ringing with disillusioned corporate warriors who are thinking there has to be a better way. They see layoffs and downsizing take place at alarming rates. Their workloads are increasing while cubicles on either side are vacated. They realize that no matter how well they do the job, someone at the top could be making a decision that destroys the company in days. Financial market collapses have convinced many talented people that the only one they can really count on is themselves. They may remember the simpler times of tending bar or waiting tables during their college years when they worked hard and played more and answered to no one. Armed with a severance package, a talent for numbers, and good operation skills honed over decades of delivering for someone else, they imagine themselves in charge of their own little bar or restaurant.

Baby Boomers-The Restaurant Über Consumer

Baby boomers have influenced life in America every step of the way since they were born in record numbers. The impact on restaurants is no exception. The first wave of baby boomers retired in 2007, and the phenomenon will continue for more than a decade. Plenty of those boomers are armed with money and time on their hands. They need something to do after a lifetime of logging more hours than any other workers in the world. They paid their dues and saved their money before many were subjected to dual stock market wipeouts (the dot com debacle in early 2000 and subsequent crash of 2009). They may need a business with earnings to get back on track financially post-retirement. They have worked hard and contributed to some of the greatest economic growth and failures of our lifetime. These boomers have already redefined restaurant habits. This generation displaced the lifestyle where families gathered around the dining room table. The baby boomers are restaurant über consumers, the generation that made eating out at restaurants or picking it up to go a way of life. When considering a business post-retirement (forced or otherwise), it is easy to see how they transition quickly into believing a restaurant could be just the thing.

Top Chef without a Kitchen

Virtually every chef and restaurant worker in the business will tell you they want ultimate control over both front and back of the house. Chefs don't end up in the kitchen overnight fresh from culinary school. Most, including those with or without formal culinary training, have worked their way through almost every restaurant position from waiting tables to sous chef. They have the knowledge and skill to run a restaurant, and they all dream of having one of their own. Many of these talented guys have investors who say, "Let me know when you're ready for your own place." Countless would-be owners are in the kitchen tonight and looking for their own restaurant tomorrow.

Going Galt with a Business of my Own

The changing political climate and distaste for increased taxes have driven some Americans to seek greater control over their earnings. This is fueled by the demonization of those who are the wealthiest, defined by an arbitrary cutoff of earning $250,000 or more annually. When weighed against a tax code that allows the greatest flexibility and expense write-off for those who own their own business, it's not unusual to encounter a physician, engineer, or corporate executive searching for a restaurant to buy. He accepts that his income will be lower, but he understands the control he will exercise over his destiny.

Those "Going Galt," a reference to *Atlas Shrugged*,[2] want the opportunity to expense their way out of tax consequences.

Ultimately they see restaurant ownership as a business with a relatively low cost of entry and something they are familiar with.

Unemployed and Buying a Job

Unemployment levels unmatched since the Great Depression have left highly qualified executives unemployed or underemployed for the first time in their lives. Many have spent entire careers earning six figures while heavily recruited by headhunters for their next position. Now they are shocked at the difficulty of replacing their income and finding another job. Armed with strong capital resources—though they are quickly burning through these without cash flow—they are faced with buying themselves a job. Restaurants are high return and good leverage properties, attractive to this group.

Current Owners with an Eye on Expansion

Operators or investors that have already successfully mastered the industry are another large group of buyers. They are seeking their second, third, or tenth location to grow their business.

Top Ten Reasons to Buy a Restaurant

It's easy to see yourself identifying with one of these groups. Are you already imagining the lifestyle choice you'll be making when you are master of your own restaurant domain? Our clients do. Over the years they have given us their reasons why buying a restaurant is the right decision for them, and as you read the next section carefully, you'll begin to understand their motivation. Owning a restaurant fills a need on many levels as you consider your career path. Here are the top ten reasons our clients tell us they want to buy a restaurant. One of these may align with your own needs. These are the most commonly shared criteria by our buyers as their incentive to buy.

Job Security

Downsizing has convinced us that nothing is forever, especially a job. In the last decade, Americans have changed jobs at an unprecedented rate, and layoffs are a way of life. Compare that to your father's or grandfather's generation that stayed in the same firm for decades. Lifetime pensions and loyalty to companies have evaporated, along with the belief that the CEO or anyone else has the company's best interest at heart. Cynical Americans share stories from corporate survivors who see their retirement in company stock and pension plans disappear under poor corporate governance. All this teaches us that the only person looking out for number one is you. Owning your own business puts the responsibility for keeping your job in your hands, not in the political landscape of corporations where nepotism or favoritism may guide who survives the cut.

Quality of Life

In corporate America, he who logs the most hours wins. Though buzzwords like *flex time* and *work balance* are bandied about by the human resource team, the reality is very different. Americans work more hours than any other country in the world. The tightening economic environment has every company pushing employees to do more with less or, put simply, do more. This is one reason cited for an eventual jobless recovery as economists look at large productivity gains despite the economic downturn. The advent of technology has only increased stress on time off because of the incessant "Crackberry buzz," cell phone ring, urgent text message request, and the "tweet" that requires your constant attention whether you're in church on Sunday morning or attending your child's piano recital. The point of all this technology is to keep you tethered to your office, where it is still a badge of honor to be first one in the morning or last one out behind the janitor at night. When you own the restaurant, the hours logged are your own to decide. Each hour worked in your own business serves to benefit only one entity, you and your family.

Tax Benefits

Whether it was immigrants chasing dreams across an ocean or pioneers heading west for land, capitalism and entrepreneurship are as much a part of the American heritage as baseball and apple pie. This legacy was rewarded in the tax code and, despite populist outrage over tax benefits for big corporations, the small operator also sees real benefit from the tax system. Legitimate tax deductible expenses like health insurance, auto expense, office supplies, home office deductions, and more are part of a tax code that advantages the small business owner. When you work for someone else, you pay the highest possible tax rate and have the lowest potential to protect your income from taxes through legitimate expenses. Ever-increasing tax burdens are being passed to those in the top percentiles of earnings. It is small wonder some would rather take home less money and legitimately flow expenses that directly benefit their family. A certified public accountant (CPA) can help you understand the tax benefit for a corporation that consists of as few as three people—me, myself, and I. This delivers dollars to your pocket versus the government.

Pure Love of Food

Those TV food ratings and best-selling cookbooks exist for a reason. The pure love of all things culinary draws buyers from every industry into the one where cuisine is front and center.

The success of Food Network, prevalence of television cooking reality shows, and best-selling cookbooks all fuel the passion for the novice or experienced would-be restaurant owner.

Money

When you are in business for yourself, there are no annual raises based on a politically charged situation and the company bell curve. You are in charge of your own raise, and there is no ceiling. That is good news for the super-performer. Corporations have a "manage to the middle" mentality, with standard 3% raises across the company. There's no such thing as incredible incentives for extraordinary performance.

When you own the shop and make brilliant changes to the marketing that drives sales results, money comes back to you and your family. You get all of the benefit. For those who are superstars, this is the reason to go into business on your own. Read the best-sellers on self-made millionaires, and you'll find most have a common trait as entrepreneurs. They own businesses from which they have maximized their wealth and that of their family. Business owners make money, and they make a lot of it.

Retirement Funding

At some point, everyone has to stop, slow down, change gears, and figure out how to pay for it. As a restaurant business owner, there is an opportunity to fund your retirement differently than contributing a capped amount to a company plan. You can create your own 401K plan with the help of the right advisors. You can also fund SEP (Self-Employed Persons) Individual Retirement Accounts at a rate often higher than the one available to you as a "highly compensated" individual for a large corporation. Lastly, there is the option to invest in the real estate where your company operates, building another asset that you can pay for with restaurant earnings and cash out when you are ready to retire.

Restaurant ownership affords you the ability to build assets today that can sell tomorrow. You are taxed a lower rate on the income you get because you depreciate the physical assets and get a better rate from the income you are receiving. Then you end up with an asset that is worth more based on appreciation over time. That is a very different from being locked into the company plan at a capped level or percentage and then being levied maximum taxes on your income.

Control Over Your Own Destiny

Control is often cited as a reason to buy from corporate warriors shopping for a restaurant. Any worker that has sat through mindless meetings that achieve no real results can appreciate the control your own business delivers. Those transferring from restaurant workers to restaurant owners have ideas they have been trying to implement for years without the influence to make it happen. Buy your own restaurant and the control shifts directly to you.

Performance Reviews

When you are in business for yourself, there is one performance review, and you control the outcome. The restaurant profit and loss statement is the quantitative measure of your success. Of course, you are also gauged on your performance every night when customers tell you the special was delicious and they have recommended the restaurant to their friends. Ultimately, however, all the satisfied customers along with excellence in operations and control over the food costs and control you've shown over food costs feed to this single point of analysis. The satisfaction you derive when the bottom line performance is 15% earnings on $1.2 million in sales far exceeds what you get in the corporate world from growing someone else's profits.

Intellectual Capital

When it is your business, there is a direct return on a good idea. You get 100% of the reward. There is virtually no one in business today that has not put forward a brilliant idea only to have it echoed from the top without being acknowledged. Managers forget that recognition can triumph over money for many. Is it any wonder that the truly talented are ready to jump the corporate ship and become captains of their own destiny? In your own restaurant, keep bringing the good ideas, and the payoff, both financial and emotional, belongs to you.

Friends and Family

Your restaurant is a place where you make friends. Repeat customers begin to feel like family. When you stop by the table to see how things are going, you become a participant in all the special occasions of your customers' lives. They are in your restaurant to celebrate their birthdays, anniversaries, promotions, and college graduations. They, in turn, watch your children grow up, tell you when a server is in a bad mood, and share advice (some welcome and some not so much). The connections, human contact, and just plain joy you derive from this experience provides ultimately a very satisfying way to live. From biblical times until today, nothing on earth has connected people to one another like the act of breaking bread. Your restaurant becomes the catalyst for this human contact, and you share in the experience.

These are ten great reasons compiled by our clients over the years to get into the restaurant business for yourself, and one of them may resonate with you. But that is only one half of the story. Read the next section carefully as we share the reasons our clients have also given for not pursuing their restaurant dream.

The Top Ten Reasons You Should Not Buy a Restaurant

It's easy to fall in love. We have all experienced the glow that comes from shopping for a new home, a shiny new car, or even a new pair of shoes. As with everything for sale in the world, the first time you inquire about a restaurant, optimistic and excited over the prospect of doing your own thing, you are convinced this is the business for you. You fondly remember seeing your wife for the first time at the college bar where you both waited tables and think, *This is not that hard.* Take a time out. Read the top ten reasons you should not buy a restaurant before you leap head first into something you regret. Remember, owning a restaurant is a lifestyle, not a job. If these reasons sound familiar, that is because every decision in life has a corresponding and alternate possibility. Understanding both sides of the coin is part of your commitment to owning a restaurant.

Job Security

While corporate America can lower the boom at any time, the only security when you own the restaurant is belief in yourself and the guts to stick it out. It is not for everyone. You must understand the level of risk you are comfortable with. Clients approach us with 100% funding for their purchase from a 401K account. Forget Las Vegas; these are truly high rollers. No matter what business you buy—restaurant or otherwise—there is inherent risk. If you value the security of that paycheck, owning a restaurant may not be for you. That does not mean you should never buy a restaurant, but you should thoughtfully develop a plan that might lessen the risk.

Ways to minimize the risk including bringing partners into the deal so you do not have the full financial burden. You can postpone your plan while you carefully fund a savings target that gives you security to pursue the purchase. You can get a commitment from your spouse that he or she will go back to work or be the major breadwinner for a predetermined period of time so money pressures will not kill your dream before you are started. If you are risk averse, find a way to diminish the risk before entering the restaurant business and shore up your financial picture.

Quality of Life

When you own your own business, you are on 100% flex time. The hours are yours to dictate rather than the other way around. What you should not expect early on in the ownership cycle is to work less. You should plan to work more. In case you believe we just did a little bait and switch on you, know that at some point in the ownership cycle of the business you should absolutely be able to bring balance to your life. You just cannot plan on doing it day one.

The first crucial months as you take over a business require you to learn every job in the restaurant. If the bartender calls in sick, you're on the hook to tend bar. If the chef takes off for Key West for the winter, you have to cook up whatever is on the menu. If the servers all call out because they don't like the new uniform policy, you will be serving food or turning away customers. You have to learn every role in case you have to cover it, not because you will be doing it long-term. Along the way, you will discover efficiencies or small process changes that will save the restaurant money. Consider these first years your crucial business degree to ensure that you will generate the correct return on your investment.

We often field inquires from would-be buyers for restaurants that operate "absentee." This is a risky move and rarely successful. The majority of the restaurants successfully operated in the country are run hands-on by the owner. Consider that new restaurant to be like a child. For the first days and months of their life, no one could pry that infant from your arms. This is your money. This is your livelihood. This is your investment.

This is your child. Do not allow someone to rob you by staying distant from the business early in the transfer. That can happen later.

Tax Benefits

You should not own a restaurant for the tax benefits bestowed upon you by Uncle Sam, especially if your primary concern is the size of your paycheck. That is like buying a house more expensive than you can afford because you get to deduct the mortgage interest. Despite the fact that plenty of people in America took this path, which ended in the sub-prime mortgage crisis, it is not a responsible approach. Only Washington leaders are naïve enough to think the only solution to tax problems is to spend more. Review the tax benefits against the cash flow implications of owning your own business. You may be comfortable paying more taxes and holding on to security.

Love of Food

Think long and hard about this one before buying your own restaurant. Loving something and having the skills you need to run a business are two very separate things. Make no mistake. This is a job. It is a serious commitment of time and effort. You can dream of spending your days trying new recipes and conducting menu tastings, but the reality is you will be arguing with suppliers to get your delivery on time and making sure the valet service shows up. Do a gut check on this one before moving forward.

Money

No one should enter the restaurant business for the money. If you do not have a passion for the business, then the money will never follow. You have to be willing to fail, risk the money, try another idea, fail again, and then do it all over again to be successful. This takes passion. It takes commitment and a strong belief in self. If you can cut through a profit and loss statement in the blink of an eye and zero in on the problems, you might not have a future in this business. The restaurant business requires strong financial skills, but it also requires a strong disposition and the ability to think outside the box with great ideas. If you buy a restaurant earning a six-figure income today and stay status quo for the next five years, your investment will deteriorate. While you're standing still, the restaurant down the street will be on top of the next great trend.

In order to succeed you have to stay current; in order to stay current, you have to visit the competition, introduce new menu ideas, try new marketing techniques, greet customers, read about the industry, work with vendors, and the list goes on. That requires passion. That means doing it for more than the money. If you are passionate, the money will come.

Retirement

If the only reason to buy a restaurant is to fund your retirement, visit some very savvy investment strategists. That is a better choice than buying a restaurant. Better yet, buy the building occupied by a restaurant that's paying a return on the lease. The restaurant business is full of risk. You do not want to spend your retirement money to fund the purchase of a restaurant, and you do not want a restaurant to be what you are counting on to fund yours. Think in terms of a diversified portfolio. If your holdings are sufficient enough that an investment in a restaurant would be only 15% to 20% of your total portfolio, then see your financial advisor and have a discussion before proceeding. Do not bet the family farm on a restaurant. It is a great strategy to buy an asset to hold until retirement, but it is not a place to invest all those precious retirement dollars.

Control

Spend time considering how much control you want over your existence before proceeding. Can you handle the control you would have? How would you manage a staff of ten? How do you manage now? Have you led a team this size before? Jack Nicholson made a movie line famous when he said, "You can't handle the truth." For some would-be restaurant operators, you simply cannot handle the control. It is better to know up front if you are really just more comfortable behind the scenes rather than leading the charge. In your own business, you are the one and only leader everyone's looking to for answers.

Performance Reviews

Make sure you have the discipline to handle ongoing profit and loss reviews, your version of a performance review. Monthly or, at a minimum, quarterly meetings with your accounting firm are a required part of running a successful business. If you prefer to stick your head in the sand and ignore the advice of others (especially people you're paying, like attorneys and accountants), then the restaurant business may not be for you. Only a monthly review of your profit and loss statement will tell you the truth about how you're performing, and if you don't like hearing both the good and bad news, buy some strong performing restaurant stocks instead. You can throw your stock statements in a drawer and forget about them.

This is an actual story from our experiences; only the names have been changed.

> Derrick was a successful banker in his firm until he was downsized in a corporate layoff. He had a nice stock settlement from his layoff and decided to buy a small seafood grill and bar. In theory his financial and management skills should have been a slam dunk for operating a restaurant. The restaurant was doing more than a million in sales and earned a net

profit of about $105,000 in total owner benefit the year before the purchase. However, about six months into his ownership, we got a call from the CPA firm we had recommended to him.

They asked if we knew why Derrick kept cancelling his P&L review meetings. We told the CPA we weren't sure but would check in with him at the restaurant. To our surprise, we found the former banker, who had lived by the rules in his former life, couldn't handle the lack of oversight and "no rules" of business ownership. He made friends with the bartender and though he knew he was stealing, kept him on staff. He drank every night in the bar instead of managing the restaurant. Intellectually, he knew the business wasn't doing well since it needed cash infusions, so he just cancelled the P&L review meetings. Derrick could not make the transition from all controls, all rules, all the time, to a man in charge of his own destiny. After two years the restaurant closed, and he lost his investment. He went back into banking with a structured environment, where he was once again quite successful.

Intellectual Capital

The opposite of good ideas are the ones that fail, and plenty of them will fail. The music in the bar that you think is such a great idea will drive off your early diners who want a quiet place to talk. The wine tasting event will cost more and deliver less than you predicted. You get 100% of the rewards for your ideas and intellectual capital, but you also get 100% of the failure. If you are the kind of person who brushes off the seat of your pants and jumps back on the horse, this industry could be for you. If disappointments cripple your soul and erode your self-esteem, think again before buying.

Friends and Family

Buying any business is a family affair. Friends and family need to understand your commitment to the restaurant up front. If your mother expects you for a week at Christmas and every single family occasion or you'll be struck from the will, consider staying in your current job if she is loaded. If you are a newlywed with a wife and two toddlers, working in a nightclub until 3 a.m. every morning will never earn you the daddy of the year award. Owning your own business will mean disappointing the ones you love because the buck stops with you. When all else fails, this restaurant will need you at exactly the same time your family wants you around. If you cannot handle the emotional toll that will take on yourself, your friends, or your family, consider another profession.

If you have finished reading both sides of the coin and still think buying a restaurant is for you, there is hope. The next chapter will take you through a simple exercise to help you narrow down your search. We call it the Restaurant Assessment Tool.

Chapter Summary-Key Points

* Independent startup restaurants fail 43% of the time versus new build franchise restaurants, which fail 39% of the time after three years.
* The five key reasons to buy an existing restaurant rather than building from scratch are: control over costs, time to market, existing sales volume, existing cash flow, and risk management.
* A typical restaurant buyer fits a profile of Corporate Refugee, Top Chef, Going Galt, Baby Boomer, and Unemployed in Search of a Job.

* There are ten reasons to buy a restaurant, and all ten are also reasons you should not buy. They include: job security, quality of life, tax benefits, love of food, money, retirement, control, performance reviews, intellectual capital, and friends and family.

Sizing Up the Restaurant for You

Before you begin your search, it is important to define both what you want and which type of restaurant fits your personal lifestyle. Our Restaurant Assessment Tool takes you through a series of questions designed to answer these questions. This is vital to the buying process and a step that most buyers overlook. If you are honest in your answers, you will be prepared to begin your search. This survey helps you rule out the wrong restaurants and zero in on the right ones.

Today's restaurant buyer relies on the Internet as the prime source of restaurant listings. This has contributed to a condition we term the "Restaurant Buyer Internet Dating Approach." The typical confused restaurant buyer visits the half-dozen most popular sites, clicking away to send inquiries, and before you know it has expressed interest to five different brokers on six different listings. The same client requests information on everything from Irish pubs to fine dining Italian restaurants. Though the buyer believes he is doing a little anonymous research, odds are he could be damaging his chances at the best listings.

The unsuspecting buyer may not realize that the same broker or firm represents several restaurant listings. In most instances, the buyer is sending multiple inquiries to a single source who can tell at a glance that he has not prequalified his interest and has no idea what he is looking for. The Restaurant Buyer Internet Dating Approach generating simultaneous inquiries can look like this to the broker:

> Buyer John Inquiry 1: Please send me information on this nightclub open until 4 a.m. earning $200,000.
>
> Buyer John Inquiry 2: I'm interested in this asset sale sandwich shop open Monday through Friday for breakfast and lunch on the market for $25,000.
>
> Buyer John Inquiry 3: Need more information on this fine dining French restaurant with real estate on the market for $1.5MM.

It is hard to be taken seriously by a broker when your inquiries are this broad in price point, lifestyle, and operations. A broker can tell at a glance that you have not begun to personally qualify your needs and are very confused about what type of restaurant you are pursuing. In the example above, one listing requires that you go to work at 8 p.m. and finish at 4 a.m. In the second inquiry, the same buyer is saying he wants to work from 5 a.m. to 2 p.m. running a breakfast and lunch business. The price point in all three varies widely, and while it's not uncommon to find inquiries on $25,000 listings, it is a rare individual that would be simultaneously interested in something requiring a cash commitment under $30,000 and one that requires $1.5 million. The broker will correctly assume that you don't know what you're looking for. Brokers are human, and given the choice between the buttoned-up buyer who knows what he's looking for and one that's all over the board, he'll concentrate his effort on the focused buyer.

Restaurant buyers can avoid this easy trap by using the Restaurant Assessment Tool. This is a ten-question survey that leads you to answer:

1. What type of restaurant am I looking for?
2. What type of restaurant delivers what I need for myself and my family?
3. What am I willing to sacrifice to obtain this restaurant (money, time, lifestyle)?

This tool is built for buyers to help you align your lifestyle, financial, and business requirements with the type of restaurant listings where you should focus your attention. Successfully complete the Restaurant Assessment Tool and you will be equipped to meet sellers and brokers with a clear strategy for your own success. Thoughtfully consider each question and read both the questions and the notes for each potential answer. Begin by filling this out in pencil. Place notes in the margin for any questions you want to return to or you are not sure about yet. You will probably want to revisit the Restaurant Assessment Tool over the course of the book as you learn more about the search to further define the business of your dreams.

Restaurant Assessment Tool Exercise

Question One:

What does my earnings requirement force me to focus on?

a. An operating restaurant—profitable earnings

b. A turnaround situation—low to no profit

c. A closed restaurant—I have my own concept

d. Franchise restaurant resale

e. New unfinished space for my own concept—I'm *Bob the Builder* in my spare time

This question asks you to define your required earnings. This question has the most implications for yourself and your family. If you need black and white earnings, then an operating restaurant with profitable earnings is the only acceptable answer no matter how good something looks. If you have good management and marketing skills along with a supply of capital to keep you going, than a turnaround restaurant without profits can fit your lifestyle. It will take between six and twelve months in a good economy for a strong operator to perform a restaurant turnaround. A startup in a good location may be on the hook for twelve to eighteen months of capital before seeing break even or approaching profitability.

Many restaurant buyers start out looking for earnings but fall in love based on an emotional response to how the restaurant looks. This leads them to good-looking restaurants that are not making money. It is an industry certainty that the best-looking restaurants are shiny, new, gorgeous ones built at costs that far exceeded the budget and are not delivering a return. They have little hope of making money since there is no capital to drive marketing and build the business. These are the listings you see advertised as "Gorgeous build-out. Owner spent more than $500,000 to create. Seller will sacrifice for $250,000." What the ad doesn't tell you is that this restaurant is not making a dime.

The restaurant that is generating $1.8 million in sales will look a little worse for the wear. It will not be shiny and new. The kitchen equipment will be darkened from use, and the bar area will carry the lingering smell of cigarette smoke and a few alcohol spills. The books, however, will be a thing of beauty. The gross profit margin will be north of 55%. The net earnings to the owner will exceed $250,000 on average, and it will all be spelled out in black and white without any references to "potential."

Answer c, a closed restaurant space, affords the buyer a good opportunity to pick up someone else's build-out at a good price but again will force you to lay out operating capital for the period of time it takes to see earnings. You're also starting at zero sales.

A franchise restaurant resale (answer d) can be either profitable or nonprofitable depending on the concept and staffing and can often also be acquired at good pricing. This allows you a hybrid of a developed system to rely on if you're inexperienced. Our chapter on franchises will teach you the Rule of Three that should be applied to franchise resales in order to acquire a moneymaking concept.

Lastly, think hard about taking on a new unfinished space (answer e). This requires the most commitment of capital and the highest level of experience. You are starting with no concept, no menu, no pricing, and no customers. It takes the longest amount of time to launch and thus delivers the greatest risk to performance. This book is about buying restaurants, a process we believe in, not startups.

Question Two:
What type of lease or purchase situation do I want?

a. Restaurant and real estate

b. Restaurant only—I'll lease the space

c. Real estate only—I'll convert

Most restaurants are leased, not owned. That helps a new operator since he won't have to come up with the cash for a down payment on real estate and instead will have only a deposit on a lease space. Consider whether you want to be your own landlord or become another landlord's tenant. It is most common in the restaurant industry to lease space from a landlord. Restaurants thrive in strong commercial districts where the price of real estate may be prohibitive as a startup. Landlords will require both good credit and a personal guarantee on most leases. Conversely, if you decide to buy, you may be able to leverage the real property with a lender. Leveraging the real estate means that with a down payment (20% or so of the purchase price), the bank will loan against the property. All risks associated with doing a build-out are present in the purchase unless you are buying a restaurant that is ready to go, sometimes called a turnkey property. If you're purchasing real estate to convert, it is going to take a lot of capital, and again, time to market will be extended dramatically.

Question Three:

What kind of restaurant do I want?

a. Upscale/fine dining restaurant
b. Barbeque restaurant
c. Pizza/Italian restaurant
d. Sports bar/Bar/Club
e. Fast casual
f. Asian restaurant
g. Deli/sandwich restaurant
h. Franchise restaurant only—I want someone else's menu
i. Takeout/delivery only restaurant

What type of restaurant do you want to operate? Early in the process restaurant buyers will often say, "It doesn't matter as long as it's profitable," but that is clearly not the case once the search begins. A sports fanatic will be better off in a franchise sports bar restaurant than a white tablecloth upscale concept. A night owl will be much happier in a nightclub getting home at 2 a.m. than a catering operation that has to have orders loaded and delivered by 9 a.m. every day. Think through this question carefully and examine your own background and experience. You may have personal values or religious beliefs that would conflict with certain concepts, or you may be the ultimate entrepreneur who wants no oversight. That rules out franchises. This may also change during the course of your search depending on what the market delivers in terms of opportunities.

What you should understand is what you are willing to compromise up front. We have had buyers that inquire about sports bars with 55% alcohol sales and then tell us their religion prohibits them from serving alcohol. We have buyers that request information on franchise pizza concepts but want to ask the franchise to eliminate ham and change the pizza toppings to all kosher. Thinking through this logically up front eliminates the most obvious issues with your choices.

This is an actual story from our experiences; only the names have been changed.

> A recent buyer inquired about a franchise barbeque concept. The listing had the earnings he was looking for to qualify for an E-2 visa as well as excellent books and records. He made an offer that was accepted and started the process of taking over the business. He went to discovery day for the franchise, where he received his franchise disclosure document and learned about the chain that focused on barbeque pork. We negotiated the lease, and he began franchise training. A few days into training, the problems began. This gentleman's religion prohibited him from eating any type of pork. This was a fact he had failed to mention to the broker, the franchise, or the seller. The franchise required that he train and taste the product he was preparing to ensure it was cooked to their standards. After several days of wrangling with the franchise over alternatives, they denied him franchise approval. His time was wasted. The seller was crushed. Whether or not the franchise was correct in denying him a franchise over the issue is another matter, but from a practical perspective, a buyer should focus on concepts where he can thrive.

Question Four:
How much money do I need to make to support my family?

a. I'm independently wealthy and don't need an income

b. Earnings of under $50,000

c. Earnings of between $50,000 and $99,000

d. Earnings above $100,000

e. Earnings above $200,000

As the net income of a restaurant increases, the purchase price goes up. Expect to require cash of about two and a half times earnings for both the purchase price and to get established (landlord deposits, inventory purchases). We'll cover earnings and valuation in detail in later chapters, but cash is king. Consider your total cash available to be the combination of investor financing, personal funds, or other financing that would represent your total stake to acquire. Lending in the last few years has been virtually nonexistent for restaurant borrowers.

Question Five:

How much restaurant experience do I have?

a. I do not have any restaurant experience
b. I have restaurant experience as an owner or manager
c. I have experience as a manager for a franchise
d. I have restaurant experience in back of house (kitchen)

Whether or not you have restaurant experience can impact your ability to get a lease with some landlords. It is also very relevant to the lender and often a condition of an SBA guaranteed loan or some owner financing. It is not unusual for landlords, franchises, or lenders to turn away candidates without background and experience.

It is our opinion that experience is overrated as a predictor of success in the industry. We have seen hugely successful operators take over restaurants and destroy them while complete novices take over other businesses and thrive. Lack of experience may factor in choosing certain concepts over others. Some restaurants are simply easier concepts to learn. A quick service burrito restaurant will be a simpler undertaking for someone without experience than a fine dining French restaurant.

Question Six:

If I'm in charge of my own destiny by owning a business, what days and hours do I want to operate?

a. Open for breakfast and lunch
b. Open for lunch and dinner until early evening (9 p.m.)
c. Open late nights midnight–2 a.m. including weekends
d. Open until early morning hours (2 a.m.–4 a.m.)
e. Monday through Friday only
f. Seven days a week including weekends

This question affects your future lifestyle and time with your family. It is a good one to discuss with your significant other before you begin looking at sports bars open until 2 a.m. each night. If you have three children under the age of five and a working spouse, late hours could be an issue. Are you a night owl or an early bird? Do you live for the weekends and time with your family?

Question Seven:

What is the alcohol level I'm comfortable serving?

a. Low alcohol/high food
b. Mid alcohol/mid food
c. High alcohol (bar levels)/low food
d. No alcohol

The highest profit margin in a restaurant, bar, or nightclub is made on alcohol sales. The alcohol ratio will drive the net profit on the restaurant up or down significantly, depending on the proportion between food and alcohol. Nightclubs are all alcohol, along with high profits and inherent risks (underage drinking, ID checks, need for security to name a few). Local and state restrictions on the type of alcohol licenses generally dictate a ratio between food and alcohol. If you have religious or moral convictions that preclude the service of alcohol, recognizing this up front will eliminate a large portion of your search.

Remember that if you are buying a restaurant for cash flow, you are buying based on the current and prior year results. If you intend to make a dramatic change to the business, like eliminating alcohol sales, you should concentrate on businesses that meet your criteria up front. The future earnings of the business change dramatically with any alteration of the alcohol service.

Question Eight:

What's my relationship status?

a. Single—I can work any time.

b. Married or committed relationship but no kids or responsibilities for others. My significant other has a "regular" job.

c. Married or committed relationship with toddlers through school-age children.

d. Married or committed relationship; my significant other is my partner in this business.

A restaurant acquisition is a lifestyle choice that significantly affects your family. It is easier to understand this up front rather than waiting until you've bought a business to figure it out. Each category of commitment to another person will alter how you approach restaurant ownership.

If you are young and single, congratulations, your time is your own. Just remember you will be dropping out of the dating scene on Friday and Saturday nights since you will most likely be working in the restaurant. DINKS—the double income, no kids demographic group—will find that the restaurant consumes nights and weekends. If your spouse has a regular job like banking or teaching, your time together will be limited.

Are you married with toddlers or school-age children? The restaurant business could give you a chance to see them during traditional school hours, but forget the Friday night football game. Are you married with a partner that will join you in the business venture? You will definitely see each other, but can you handle working together? All these decisions should be considered by the family entering the restaurant business since, ultimately, it is never a decision made alone.

Question Nine:

How far am I willing to travel from my home to my restaurant to work each day?

I am willing to travel _____ miles from my current home to my new restaurant.

This question is also important to your family and should be considered before you begin the search. Sellers often fall in love with the description, earnings, and photographs of a restaurant or bar only to learn it is located more than eighty miles from their home. Unless you are ready to relocate, you can minimize your search and time spent communicating with brokers if you tell them up front, "I'm not interested outside this area."

Decide in advance how far you will travel or if you will move to acquire the right restaurant. Changing your children's school is a family decision. The right business in the wrong location may not be an option for you. If you are moving to an area, never buy the house first and the business second. There are a lot more houses available on the market than businesses that will meet your needs.

This is an actual story from our experiences; only the names have been changed.

A buyer called on several listings stating that she and her fiancé were moving to the metro area. We provided her with several listings in her price range, and she chose one for a site location on Saturday morning. The buyer arrived about half an hour late for the viewing. She loved the restaurant. It had all the right elements except she wished it had a bar. She was ready to make an offer. Then she began to apologize for her delay to the meeting. She and her fiancé had rented a house forty miles away, and she had not realized how far it was. On a Saturday with no traffic, it took her almost an hour. We asked why she had rented already, and she said it was the same town her aunt lived in and they needed help with their infant daughter. We explained to her that it would take her twice as long to travel to the business (an hour and a half both ways) on a normal weekday. In the meantime, we had a small bar and grill in the same town that was five minutes from her rental home. We hadn't previously shown her this listing since it was not in her target area. She bought the second listing and closed two weeks later. This was an extremely lucky circumstance. Most buyers should get the restaurant first and the housing second if they are relocating.

Question Ten:

Where am I going to get the capital for my restaurant?

a. I will not require financing or capital.

b. I have loans or investors secured up to __________.

c. I need the owner to finance ____% or $______, but I have $__________ to put down.

d. I have little money to put down, but I have great credit.

The first question to ask yourself before you go shopping is what you can afford. You would never shop for a house without a preapproval or a budget, and you should not start shopping for a restaurant without the same. Who is paying for the business? Will you need financing? Are you looking for owner financing? In recent years, the availability of financing from traditional sources has all but dried up, so finding alternative funding sources or leveraging the purchase has become a bigger challenge for would-be restaurant owners. We have an entire chapter on financing your restaurant dreams, but at the outset, you should understand that traditional financing has transitioned from limited to nonexistent in recent time.

After this exercise, you should be able to consolidate your answers into exactly what you're looking for simply by listing your responses and writing them into a paragraph. Here is an example from a buyer that answered the Restaurant Assessment Tool as follows:

1. a = profitable
2. b = restaurant with lease
3. c = fast casual
4. d = earnings above $100,000
5. d = restaurant experience, back of house
6. c = late nights, weekends okay
7. c = high alcohol
8. d = married, committed relationship who will be partner in the business
9. Twenty-mile commute, will not move
10. c = I will not require financing or capital.

These answers look like this when combined into a paragraph:

> I want a profitable restaurant with earnings above $100,000. I prefer a fast casual restaurant and am comfortable with late nights, weekends, and high alcohol. My wife is going to join me in the business. I am experienced in kitchen operations of a restaurant. We will not move, so it needs to be no more than

> twenty miles from my home. I will not require capital, and I have more than $250,000 in cash for the purchase.

The answers to the questions above indicate this buyer prefers fast casual, but the mutual acceptance of high alcohol and late nights indicates that in addition to fast casual, he would also be a great fit for a sports bar concept.

Use the space below to capture your own answers to questions 1–10 and combine the answers into a brief paragraph describing your ideal restaurant situation. Flesh out your answers with your personal beliefs or situation until you have something that reads like the examples we provide. Then you should be able to easily identify the ideal restaurant opportunities.

Other Examples

Example 1:

I need to earn at least $75,000 a year from a restaurant, and I have $100,000 to put down. I don't have restaurant experience, but I'm a bartender and I've worked in clubs for three years. I'm willing to work nights and weekends, and since I'm single, I'll relocate next to the right business location.

You are an ideal candidate for a nightclub or sports bar.

Example 2:

I can make it without any income from the restaurant. I'm not into late nights, so a breakfast and lunch spot no more than fifteen miles from my home would be ideal. My wife and I are strong members of our local community and don't want to move. I have about $50,000 to put down, excellent credit, and experience in management.

You are an ideal candidate for an office building cafeteria that operates Monday through Friday or a small catering business where you can leverage your community contacts to expand the sales.

Example 3:

I have $300,000 to spend on my concept, but whatever I buy must match up to my religious beliefs that do not include the use of alcohol. I'm not into super late hours because I've managed a buffet concept that closed at 9 p.m. for the last five years.

You are an ideal candidate for a fast casual or buffet franchise operation with standard practices, high volume, and no alcohol sales.

You can see that by working through the Restaurant Assessment Tool before you begin your search, you can cut down on the Restaurant Buyer Internet Dating Approach. This creates advantages for you over other buyers in your search. Your broker knows exactly what type of restaurant you are seeking. You are identified as a serious buyer ready to move on the listing first. This saves you time in the search, and time is money. Lastly, it will keep you from procrastinating when the perfect opportunity comes your way.

This is an actual story from our experiences; only the names have been changed.

> Jim, an out-of-state buyer, approached us in his restaurant search. He began as an Internet shopper with fifteen ad

> inquiries. We prequalified his ability to buy and worked with him to narrow his focus. Jim had no interest in committing to one type of cuisine, one level of earnings, or even a single state. He looked at everything from franchise pizza concepts to independent sports bars. He was determined that he wanted to see everything before he could make a decision and since he had cash available to buy he would "know it when he saw it."
>
> Jim spent three weeks and four conference calls to review the plus and minus of all fifteen businesses. He reviewed financial data and did site visits on four restaurants. Finally, he narrowed it down a franchise pizza restaurant. He interviewed the franchise, the seller, and the seller's broker. He spent another two weeks asking for additional information from the listing broker. After this exhaustive search, Jim was able to make an offer. He was five days too late. Another buyer entered the marketplace, knew exactly what he wanted, saw the business, and had the restaurant under contract within twenty-four hours.

Use the Restaurant Assessment Tool to understand what you want before you go shopping so that when you hit the marketplace you are positioned to put in an offer and wrap up your ideal concept. As the story of Jim shows, time is your enemy. We have listings sit on the market without activity for days, but once someone's interested they heat up to red-hot almost immediately.

If you complete the Restaurant Assessment Tool now and continue to update your answers as you read this book and learn about the industry, it will help you define your search. You will be able to see whether your ideal concept is a reality in the marketplace. Often there is a gap between your ideal situation and available listings. It is best to learn that early in the game as well. If you have $25,000 to put down and are looking for earnings of $100,000, you'll be disappointed by a shortage of funding to leverage your purchase. Likewise, if you think you want a franchise but want to rewrite the menu, you will quickly see that franchise systems aren't interested in accommodating your creativity. Understanding what you want so you can measure this against available listings is the first step in the process of becoming a successful restaurant buyer. It is much less expensive to learn this before you acquire a business than after the fact.

This is an actual story from our experiences; only the names have been changed.

> A mutual contact introduced Rob, a sports bar buyer. We learned he wanted a sports bar within ten miles from his home. He needed an income of around $75,000 a year to meet his obligations. He had a total of $72,000 he could use for the purchase, and that was the sum total of his net worth. We had a sports bar that met all his criteria except the listing was on the market for $139,000 and the landlord required a net worth of at least $300,000 on the lease. Rob looked at the sports bar anyway, and he was in love. It was perfect, and he had to have it. Two problems: he couldn't afford it, and the landlord wouldn't approve him. Despite the issues, we tendered his offer for $70,000 down and the balance owner financing. We also submitted him for approval with the landlord. Both parties said no. Meanwhile, a full price offer with no financing surfaced that the seller accepted.
>
> Eight months later Rob called again. His situation had changed. He now needed to buy a business with no money down that was earning $75,000 a year. He said his entire $72,000 nest egg was seized by an out-of-state agency for past due child support. He proceeded to tell the agent it was the broker's fault his money was seized because if he had worked harder to get the seller to take his offer eight months earlier, those funds wouldn't have been available for the child support agency to garnish.
>
> This buyer's story illustrates the gap between some buyers' thinking and the reality of the marketplace. We were gracious with the buyer and indicated that if we encountered a listing

with no money down and no requirement on the lease that was earning $75,000 a year, we'd be in touch. We hope he is not holding his breath somewhere.

Chapter Summary-Key Points

* You won't be taken seriously as a buyer if you participate in the Restaurant Buyer Internet Dating Approach.
* Buying a restaurant is a lifestyle choice for yourself and your family that has far-reaching consequences to consider.
* The Restaurant Assessment Tool exercise helps you identify the right restaurant concepts to fit your lifestyle and skills.

The Team You Need to Buy a Restaurant

You have made it through the first two chapters. You may have seen yourself in the profile of a typical restaurant buyer or found one of the top ten reasons to be exactly why you are ready to buy a restaurant. Finally, you are armed with specific knowledge about the type of restaurant that will fit you and your family's lifestyle. Now it is time to build a first class team to make your restaurant acquisition a reality.

There may be five to ten players on your support team before you are done. Each one plays a critical role in the deal. There is no reason to line them all up before you begin, but you should understand the role each will play. Finding the first team member, the business broker, typically makes the rest fall easily into place. Every team member should be focused on your success and working toward closing on your behalf.

The critical first step is finding a reputable business broker to represent your interest in the search. This is the single most important act you will take in acquiring your restaurant. The right business broker can both guide you through the process and provide you with resources to assist you in the purchase. Picture the restaurant broker or business broker as the quarterback on your team. He or she is calling the plays to get you into the end zone. If you choose wisely, he can provide you with an infinite array of resources to help you buy your restaurant.

The graphic below displays some of the team members you may assemble before your restaurant search ends in the purchase. Some buyers use only one or two team members in addition to their broker. Other buyers rely on extensive expertise, especially if they don't have a restaurant or financial background. The choice is entirely up to the buyer. We'll explain each team member's role and how they contribute to the process of buying a restaurant.

Starting Your Restaurant Search

While it is theoretically possible to represent yourself in buying or selling a business, the stories, worksheets, and information provided by this book demonstrate why the broker is critical to the transaction. There is an old attorney's credo that a man who represents himself has a fool for a client. You would never go through an IRS audit without your CPA or represent yourself in court without an attorney. Restaurant brokers bring specific skills and knowledge about the industry that are vital to protecting your interests in the search. As this book unfolds, you'll see why buying a business requires the skills and knowledge of a professional. Here are a few ways the broker adds value to the transaction.

Representation without Cost

The services of a broker are almost always paid by the seller, not the buyer, so using a broker is just good business sense. It is a rare business transaction that allows you to draw upon the expertise and knowledge of a professional without any cost to you. A strong restaurant broker knows the market. He or she knows which businesses have recently sold and for how much. They get the first calls from other brokers when a new listing surfaces. The broker has specialized financial knowledge and access to comps to justify pricing and advise you on offers. They know which landlords require what information so that your lease application is approved on the first pass. Strong ones have time-tested asset purchase agreements that strictly limit the liabilities you are purchasing and secure the assets you want.

Some people are just cheap. They think they can get a better deal if they go direct to the owner and there's no commission involved. Brokers get daily e-mails from buyers that don't realize they are representing a seller asking what the price would be if there was no commission involved. If you approach a seller and have them perform a dishonest (and illegal) act by breaking a contract to sell direct to you and cut out the business broker, how trustworthy do you believe this seller will be with you? Past performance predicts future behavior.

Compensation is provided by the seller and is offered in the form of commission for a consummated deal. Business brokerage commission levels are varied. They can range from 5–12% on average, though generally speaking, the smaller the transaction the larger the commission. For most restaurants that are sometimes referred to in the industry as "Main Street" businesses with revenues of between $100,000 and $1,000,000, commissions range from as low as 10% to as much as 15%. That can lead to less experienced firms attempting to conduct restaurant brokerage despite a lack of training, education, knowledge, or skill. Commissions are paid by the seller and negotiated between the seller and the broker. They are normally paid at closing. There are some instances whereby a flat fee is imposed instead of a percentage.

Closing the Transaction

Connecting the buyer to the seller and reaching agreement on price is often the easiest part of the transaction. The follow-up work after the contract is written and getting it to the closing table requires knowledge, resources, hard work, and experience. Less than 50% of contracts written between individuals get to the closing table while those represented by good brokers will close more than 90% of the time. Deals fall apart between signature and closing for countless reasons, but a good broker knows how to overcome the standard issues. It is business as usual for him to set and reach agreement on all the elements of the transfer like training, inventory, tax clearance letters, tax liens, employee issues, liquor license transfer, and more. Attempting this on your own is a high risk game.

Even if, especially if, you are only doing a lease, we strongly recommend you use the services of a business broker. Why? A broker who is experienced can save you many times the fee on the lease (paid by the landlord at no charge to you), and he will be the person who has you best interest at heart.

This is an actual story from our experiences; only the names have been changed.

John from Pasta Crazy purchased a two-store concept without the help of a business broker and wanted to expand. We met with John and told him we could find additional locations and handle the lease negotiations. John could not understand why he would need a broker. We explained that unlike the landlord's representative who is working for the landlord or the attorney who is looking at lease language, the broker would be working the business terms of the deal. We would negotiate based on prevailing rates and set up an exit strategy in case everything goes wrong. Fresh from his success in acquiring the business, John was certain he could save money (even though there was no cost to him) and get a better deal on his own.

Ultimately, John opened four stores. All went well until year two. Two of the four stores were losing money. He called us to sell these stores, but there wasn't enough time before he had to simply close all four locations. He had not used a broker's advice to set exit terms in the leases. His personal guarantees were for millions. Ultimately, he ended up in bankruptcy court with liens against his personal assets. When we met to sign listings on the stores, he said the dumbest move he ever made was to not take advantage of someone who knew what they were doing in lease negotiation. John thought he would save money if the landlord did not have to pay his broker a commission. Ultimately, it cost him everything.

Contracts and Contacts

Relationships and documents that cover all contingencies are another benefit of a restaurant broker. Strong business brokers have contracts for business transactions with specific steps and measurable consequences for moving the deal to the closing table. They write the contract. They move it through due diligence. They can provide you with business attorneys familiar with asset agreements to transfer the sale of a business without acquiring its liabilities. They can help you find the other team members you need, including liquor license facilitators, equipment inspectors, and food suppliers. They are educated, licensed, professional, and working for you. Of all the steps you may be tempted to skip, this shouldn't be the one. The contract itself is so critical to the transaction that we have an entire chapter on this topic.

Experience Matters

An experienced business broker specific to the restaurant industry is worth his weight in gold. A strong industry expert will specialize in restaurants, bars, and nightclubs at the exclusion of other businesses. If someone approaches him to handle a dry cleaner, you will not find the listing on their roster. A broker that tells you he can sell you a restaurant, an auto supply store, or a day care is not a specialist in restaurants and will probably fail at being a generalist in many things.

A restaurant broker's knowledge puts him in contact with every element of the restaurant business. Call him to ask about an equipment inspection and you can be confident he will have two numbers in his cell phone. Ask who services an Ansul (fire) System, and he will know what it is and who can be there within a day. Ask who is doing food safety training, and in the blink of an eye, he will forward a list of dates. His services are covered by the commission paid by the seller, so use him frequently without charge. It is like having a free consultant on call. Buying a restaurant is a once or twice in a lifetime effort for the average person. It's a once a week phenomenon for the best restaurant brokers. Why would you not take advantage of this experience, especially when there is no cost to you?

Finding a Reputable Business Broker

Your search for a business broker should begin online and end with interviews. Do an online search for restaurant listings on the large online Web sites like www.bizbuysell.com, www.businessbroker.net, and www.bizilla.com. See which brokers have multiple restaurant listings. Restaurant brokers advertising on these sites generally have links to their own Web sites, which contain even more listings and information.

Use popular search engines to look for restaurant business brokers. Visit the broker's Web site and spend time reading the content. Is it a compilation of listings, or does he also include articles, advice, and real information? Evaluate his overall web presence and how highly he ranks on the search engines when you search. Look at the number of listings he has online. Is he specialized in restaurants, or do his listings include lots of other types of businesses? Spend time looking at both the text and the description of the listings. Do his listings contain hard data—gross sales, net income or owner benefit, lease terms, lease amount—or are they fluff with no substance? Is he affiliated with a residential real estate firm, or does he truly specialize in restaurants, bars, and nightclubs? How easily can you contact the broker? Does he list a phone number, e-mail address, and other easy means to reach him?

One new broker decided to specialize in restaurants and overnight posted twenty-five listings online with a popular listing Web site. The only problem was the entire listing consisted of a headline, "Great Pub for Sale—High Earnings," and a price. Beyond that, he had the exact same data for every single listing.

> Gross Sales: call for details
> Net Income: call for details
> Square Footage: call for details
> Rent: call for details
> Operating Hours: call for details
> Owner Financing Available: call for details
> Employees: Full Time/Part Time: call for details
> Year Established: call for details
> Indoor Seating: call for details

If a broker does not have the basic listing details ready and available for entry into a Web site listing, do not waste your time calling. He's either not a restaurant specialist or he doesn't really have a listing at all and is just fishing for buyers to shop other broker's listings to.

The advent of social media marketing can provide a buyer with another strong indication of whether someone is actually an expert specializing in restaurants. Social media marketing covers the spectrum of blogs, Twitter, Facebook, LinkedIn, YouTube, and all other online media communicating with the masses. Check to see where your prospective broker shows up. If he has a bare chest shot on his Myspace page but appears buttoned up and professional everywhere else, use your own judgment to decide whether he is right for you. If he is tweeting everything from dry cleaner listings to block parties for residential showings, it is pretty clear he is not a specialist in the restaurant industry.

Pay the most attention to his blog. What is he blogging about? A true authority will be writing about relevant trends, industry happenings, and restaurant news. What is he tweeting about? New listings, restaurant news, and industry information should lead his tweets. What is his professional image on Facebook or LinkedIn page? Is he on YouTube? If he can't be found online beyond a Web site, it could simply be he hasn't made the leap into social media marketing, but real industry experts won't be hiding online.

Read any potential broker's online biography carefully to understand his background, professional affiliations, education, licensing, and more. What you cannot do is rely upon state or federal licensing to test and weed out the unqualified. Unfortunately for the consumer, there is no business brokerage licensing process. There are just fourteen states that require business brokers to have a real estate agent license. Those states are: Alaska, Arizona, California, Florida, Georgia, Idaho, Michigan, Minnesota, Nebraska, Oregon, South Dakota, Utah, Washington, and Wyoming. Even in those states, there are frequently brokers operating and advertising listings for sale that do not hold that state's real estate license. They are clearly operating illegally.

Look for state business brokerage organizations. Virtually every state has organizations with bylaws that stress integrity, professionalism, and ongoing training for their members. Visit the appendix to this book for a list of business broker organizations for each state as well as national organizations like IBBA, or the International Business Broker Association. The IBBA does have a certification process for business brokers called the CBI, or Certified Business Intermediary designation. If a broker does not have equivalent experience or education (banking, finance, or business degree), then a designation as a CBI assures you that he has undergone valuation training and an intense course of study.

Finally, after going through this research, the same names should begin to surface again and again. You will have begun to narrow down the brokers in a geographic area that specialize in restaurants that could be a good fit for your business. The next step is to call and interview that broker over the phone. If you have not already learned the answers to these questions from your online research, here is a list of questions you should ask any broker.

1. How long have you been a business broker? You do not want to work with a residential agent that is just learning to broker businesses.
2. What was your business background before you began selling restaurants? Look for someone with a financial background like banking or accounting or holding a business degree or MBA.
3. Are you licensed? Remember, only fourteen states require a valid real estate license to act as a business broker, and these are subject to change. Every state that requires

licensure allows you to verify the status of a license online. You should do this. You wouldn't hire an unlicensed contractor to build an addition to your home; why would you hire an unlicensed person to represent you? Go online to the Real Estate Commission for the given state and check the status of their license. A complete list for the states requiring licensure is provided in the appendix of this book.

4. Do you have references or testimonials for restaurant buyers and sellers you've worked with in the past? Most brokers post this on their Web site.
5. Give me the name of three restaurant people you have worked with in the last year.
6. What is your educational background? It's not a requirement that someone have a formal education to sell businesses, but given the choice between someone with an MBA and someone that didn't complete trade school, which do you think will bring the most to the table in financial due diligence?
7. How many restaurant listings do you have now?
8. How many restaurants have you sold? One firm came into a major market as a restaurant specialist and got lots of listings quickly because they would list at any price. Six months after launching, they still had not sold a single restaurant.
9. Do you have prepared contracts for purchasing a business? The answer here should be yes, as you don't want to pay an attorney to develop a contract for your purchase.
10. What other resources do you have available to assist me in the purchase of a restaurant? Do you have contacts and resources for construction, insurance, liquor licenses, and all the other items that can surface after the sale?

11. Do you belong to any state organizations? Most states have strong organizations for both business brokerage and restaurants. A competent professional is probably a member of both. The business brokerage associations generally include an ethics component and experience or education requirements to join. For restaurant associations this is not the case as they accept for membership anyone paying the dues. There is a complete list of every business brokerage organization and restaurant association by state in the appendix of this book.
12. Do you belong to any national organizations? The IBBA, or International Business Brokers Association, is one of the largest in the industry.

The next step is to call the broker. See if he answers his phone or return calls promptly. No matter how slick an online presence, the number one reason to work with someone is that he is available and working for you. If you labor nine to five and your search has to be conducted off hours, he is not the broker for you if the phone rolls to voice mail when your search period is beginning. See if he answers the phone at 7 p.m. Send an e-mail and see how quickly you receive a response. Test a broker by inquiring on a listing. Go through their confidentiality agreement process and request a package.

Review the broker's package. A listing presentation should be a combination of marketing fluff and photographs along with factual data and financial results. What are the numbers? What's the history of the business? How does it compare to industry standards? What are industry standards? A good broker should be able to quickly and easily share all this information with you in a standardized format for any listing.

Restaurant business valuation is a science. It presents specific challenges and requires industry knowledge. Make sure the broker you are working with has the appropriate education and background to represent your interests in the transaction.

Categories of Brokers to Avoid

There are some categories of brokers you should definitely avoid in the purchase of a restaurant. Asking the questions above should help you weed out those individuals that do not have the expertise you need for representation. In general, the representation you should steer clear of falls into four important categories.

Category 1–Residential Real Estate Agents Masquerading as Business Brokers

You may encounter residential real estate agents that want to represent you in buying a restaurant. Holding a valid real estate license may technically allow an agent to assist in a sale (in some states) but does not qualify his ability to assist in buying a restaurant. The skill set and business knowledge required for selling residential real estate versus selling a business is completely different. Unfortunately, even states requiring real estate licensing do not require a separate license for business brokerage. You have to do your own due diligence on this topic. Ask questions about the type and number of listings held by the person you choose to represent you in buying a business. If his listings consist of residential listings, he is not a business broker, and you would be better served having him refer you to a specialist.

The entire educational requirement for real estate agents is a focus on real property. Real property is a term virtually synonymous with real estate. Real property includes land, land improvements, and property rights. More than 90% of all restaurants are sold as asset sales under asset purchase agreements without any real property (or real estate). Assets are strictly defined in accounting terms as things of value that can be readily converted into cash.

There are two classifications of assets: tangible assets and intangible assets. Tangible assets are the hard items for sale in the business such as furniture, fixtures, and equipment. The stoves you cook on and the chairs where you seat customers fall into this category. Intangible assets are nonphysical resources and rights with value because they give the company some kind of advantage in the marketplace. Strict accounting examples of these are goodwill, copyrights, trademarks, et cetera. For a restaurant, that goodwill may derive from the menu, recipes, established location, and clientele. The required protections to transfer ownership of real property (something the typical real estate agent is familiar with) versus transfer of assets (something only a qualified business broker would understand) are as different as night and day.

This is an actual story from our experiences; only the names have been changed.

> We listed an inexpensive deli for $25,000 where the sellers just wanted out of the lease. A residential agent approached us with a client for the listing at full price. We asked if she had handled business closings in the past. She insisted she was fully capable of handling the commercial transaction.
>
> Two days passed, and we did not receive the contract from the broker. We contacted her, and she said she was having trouble figuring out which state real estate form to use for the contract. We explained that there is no such thing as a standard form for this transaction since the state forms available for agents only cover residential or commercial sales for real property. Finally, she broke down and just asked us to write the contract for her client. In the interest of the deal, we agreed to write it and move forward.
>
> Two days before closing, she called in a meltdown because her client was screaming at her. The due diligence phase of the contact had passed, and they had failed to get an equipment inspection or extend the contract. All this occurred because she wasn't a business broker familiar with the process or the forms. Luckily, there were no issues with the equipment and the sale moved forward, but her lack of knowledge placed her client in a very dangerous scenario.

A business broker is a specialist. He will generally have strong financial and business skills. He will be able to analyze a profit and loss statement for "add-backs" (we'll discuss this topic more fully in the chapter on restaurant valuation). He has access to business comps or "comparables" for other businesses that have sold. A residential agent won't be able to find comps for business sales, as the data is confidential.

Business brokerage requires a very different contract than real property. A residential agent is typically tied by his company or state law into the use of preprinted contracts that only address real property and don't have the exhibits, addendums, and forms required to handle representations and warranties from a seller, non-compete agreements, and the countless other details required in the transfer of a business. If your aunt Mary is a residential agent and says she wants the commission for helping you, tell her to do both of you a favor and refer the business to a broker for a fee instead. You'll both come out way ahead. Go for the restaurant brokerage specialist, not the residential specialist.

Category 2–Commercial Real Estate Agents

A commercial realtor also has a different kind of expertise. He typically has a strong understanding of land values, market capitalization rates on investment properties, and the availability of ground leases. He typically has very little knowledge related to the sale of an ongoing business. Like residential agents, they rely on preprinted forms from their area's commercial board of realtors that focus on real property, not asset transfer. Most commercial brokers are too busy in their field to go after business brokerage but occasionally will show up to represent a client. They will experience the same issues as a real estate agent when attempting to transfer assets in a business brokerage transaction.

Category 3–Leasing Agents

A leasing agent represents a shopping center owner or developer. He will work hard to show you that developer's properties. He will have good information about traffic counts and demographic information for the centers he shows to you, but his duty of loyalty is to the person writing his check—the landlord.

Generally, you will get a vanilla box—or cold, dark shelf—from this type of agent. That requires that you do the build-out to finish the space (all interior walls, furniture, fixtures, and equipment). Remember that when you are dealing with a leasing agent, he represents the *landlord,* not you. His duty of loyalty is not to the person contacting him about space; he wants the best deal for his boss. For that reason, you should still contact a restaurant broker to aid in this situation. It is a myth that you will save money on the transaction if you don't use a broker. The landlord has a set commission on the property. If you don't use a tenant representative, the landlord's representative gets 100% of the commission as well as 100% control over the deal. With no net difference in cost to you, why would you give over 100% control to someone that has 0% vested interest in your success? We have an entire chapter devoted to landlord representation and issues titled "The landlord is not your friend." This goes into landlord issues in great detail.

Here's the easiest way to think of the commission: A landlord has a set amount of commission dollars allocated to each space. The chart below shows what happens when those funds are allocated between two representatives (one representing you and one represening the landlord). It also shows the interest being protected by both parties when there are two representatives verus one. Essentially two representatives means the landlord has to split commission and has someone fighting against him for your interest. When there's one representive, the same commission pays out to the landlord's representative, and only the landlord is protected. You can easily see why the landlord's representative has no interest in working with a buyer's agent.

SCENARIO A No Buyer's Representative	SCENARIO B With Buyer's Representative	
LANDLORD REP	**LANDLORD REP**	**BUYER'S REP**
100% Commission $5000	50% Commission $2500	50% Commission $2500
100% Representation for Landlord	100% Representation for Landlord	100% Representation for Buyer
0% Representation for Tenant (Buyer)	0% Representation for Tenant (Buyer)	100% Representation for Tenant (Buyer)

The focus of this book is the transfer of an existing restaurant, but some operators do seek out spaces they can build from the walls in. In addition to the example above that shows there are no savings and potential liability in not using your own agent, a strong restaurant broker brings a lot of knowledge to the table to assist in these negotiations. He can tell you average costs for build-out of basic items like a grease trap and hood. He can negotiate everything from tenant improvement money to the amount of air-conditioning you need for the space (restaurants require more than retail space, and landlords will not volunteer extra air-conditioning for free). Most specialized restaurant brokerage firms also perform site location.

If you want a closed restaurant space represented by a landlord's representative, we still recommend you use the services of a business broker. Landlords typically contact strong business brokers with their closed restaurant space as soon as they suspect it's going to be available. This closed space is typically sold as "assets only" for pennies on the dollar or simply to take over the lease, and they move very quickly. If you find a space that's been sitting, it could be an indication there's a problem with the location.

Category 4–General Business Brokers

It is very difficult to be all things to all people. If someone lists themselves as a restaurant specialist, look at his listings to be sure that's where his real focus lies. If he sells everything from dry cleaners to convenience stores, find someone else. This is still a better choice for you than the other types of agents covered in categories one through three; however, the ideal situation is to have someone helping you with specialized knowledge and resources. Financial parameters vary significantly by industry, and while a labor ratio of 12% may be appropriate for a convenience store, dealing with someone who looks at only restaurant profit and loss statements can take one quick glance and tell you if a number's in line without having to do the research.

Remember, the business broker is the most important member of your team. Hire the best resource you can find in the industry where you want representation. Once you have identified the right broker, it is time to assemble the rest of the team.

Other Team Members

There are other team members important to your restaurant acquisition. If you have located a qualified and reputable business broker, the rest of the team is easier to assemble since your broker will have recommendations. Make sure you ask your broker whether he receives any compensation for referring resources. Most licensed real estate agents must disclose whether they are compensated. Our firm has always avoided any compensation, but it is always best to ensure there is no conflict of interest in the advice provided. If you are in doubt, ask for a minimum of three in each category of service and make your own selection. Not all team members will be required for all transactions, and some may not come into play at all until the due diligence period. Here are some of the other potential roles you would need when buying a business.

Attorney

Both the broker and the attorney will protect your interest in the purchase of a business. The important thing to remember about this team member is very similar to the advice provided on finding a restaurant broker—use a specialist. The attorney that drafted Uncle Arthur's will or the last closing attorney you used to buy your house is not the right choice when buying a business. Like brokers, good attorneys specialize in certain types of transactions. There are individual nuances associated with buying a restaurant that require explicit knowledge. A good attorney may be able to learn this quickly and get up to speed, but do you really want him to learn on your transaction? Here are some of the items a business brokerage attorney must understand to process the transaction:

1. *Asset purchase agreement* to buy *only* the assets of a business. While we are not attorneys and this is specifically not legal advice, it is important to understand the distinction between buying a corporation and buying the assets of a business. When you buy a corporation, you get it all—assets and liabilities. If there is an old pending lawsuit against a corporation, you now own it. If there is an old unpaid bill from seven months ago that's not discovered before closing, you owe it. In most instances you do not want to buy a corporation, but a good business brokerage attorney that sees many of these transactions on an annual basis can give you advice on this.
2. *Sales tax clearance letters.* Death and taxes are certain facts of life. The other almost certain fact is that business owners are sometimes slow to pay them. Before you acquire a business you have to be sure the taxes are paid, or this pesky little thing you need called a liquor license could be withheld. Good restaurant brokers and attorneys understand this. Early in the transaction they are getting a power of attorney from the seller to make sure

all taxes are cleared before closing. They have strong contacts and relationships developed in the state tax offices to make sure progress is taking place on the clearance letter. If something is owed, they know how to get it cleared quickly so the closing can stay on schedule. Uncle Arthur's estate attorney will still be stuck in "dial 1 for payoffs, dial 2 for tax liens" while the experienced guy has it figured out.

3. *Liquor license.* If you want to be in the restaurant business, you have a sense of how important the sale of alcohol is to your business. The sale of alcohol can contribute 45% of sales while delivering 60%–65% of the business profit. Above all, you have to be able to serve alcohol without interruption when you transition a business. Liquor license laws vary by state, by city, and by county. Some states sell liquor licenses that can be moved from location to location (Florida for example). Other states renew a license each year, and it is tied to a specific location (like Georgia). There is an appendix to this book with a list of Web sites for each state's liquor licensing rules. These are very complicated for the novice to comprehend. This is one place it doesn't pay to skimp. Good attorneys know how to draft the correct documents that legally allow for the use of the prior owner's license or the application of a new license so the all-important topic of a liquor license is covered.
4. *Costs.* Closing attorneys that routinely handle business brokerage transactions know how much time they take and will quote you an all-in closing fee. If you go to an attorney that doesn't specialize, he or she may bill you by the hour, and before you know it, attorney fees are costing you thousands of dollars. An attorney that specializes does not have to research the answer to your question (and bill you for the privilege); he knows the response off the top of his head.

5. *Deal makers versus deal breakers.* There is a type of attorney that wants to wrap his or her client into a Kevlar® vest of protection from any risk, real or imagined. These attorneys get lost in the argument of a single small point that costs the entire deal. Good attorneys know they may lose one battle to win the restaurant for their client, not the other way around. Locate a good attorney that knows how to manage your rise, not eliminate your risk, or you may never come to terms on a restaurant deal.

These are only some of the reasons having the right attorney on your team is essential to purchase of a restaurant. Here's how you find one. First and foremost, ask your business broker. If he specializes in restaurants, bars, and nightclubs, he has a network of attorneys that understand the parts of the transaction. He can provide you with a list of recommendations. Second, research attorneys listed as affiliate members for business brokerage state organizations listed in the appendix. They typically specialize in this work if they are active in state level business brokerage organizations. Finally, contact your state bar association and ask for attorneys that specialize in business brokerage transactions. This is the least favored method, and if you're going to go this route, be prepared with a list of questions when you call the attorney recommended by the bar association to be sure he can properly represent your interests. That list of questions should include:

1. How many transactions of this size have you done this year? This will give you a good indication of whether the fit is correct. Clients using high-powered law firms that specialize in mergers and acquisitions can end up with $12,000 in attorney's fees on a $175,000 purchase. Good expertise is available at fair pricing. You are buying a small restaurant business; you are not buying Ford Motor Company.

2. How many restaurant closings have you done this year? Remember, the intricacy of a liquor license requires specialization. If he has not done multiple closings on restaurants, keep calling.
3. How much will you charge? Consider another attorney if he quotes you an hourly rate. You should be able to get a closing fee all-in so you can bank on what your expense will be.
4. Can you handle the liquor license? How much will you charge? How many successful liquor licenses have you handled this year? If he gives you a low number, hire someone else to handle the liquor license. You do not have to use the same attorney for your liquor license that you use for your closing attorney.

Banker

Finding someone who says he will finance your dream will be easy; making it happen is much more difficult. You can find sources of business lending with your current banking relationships. If you do not already have strong existing relationships with a banker, talk to your business broker. He or she will be able to recommend lenders to you that specialize in restaurant transactions. We will cover everything required to finance a restaurant in a later chapter on financing your restaurant dream.

Equipment Inspector

Between contract and closing is a due diligence period. During this time someone comes to the restaurant, inspects the equipment, issues a report, and provides you with costs for repairs. Typically the seller repairs these items prior to closing, or you can arrange a credit at closing for the cost of repairs. Strong restaurant brokers typically have a list of individuals they have worked with in the past that can do this inspection. Plan to pay about what you would pay for a house inspection, $300–$500. Do not use a house inspector. This is an equipment inspection, not a real estate inspection. The inspector should be knowledgeable and pay particular attention to the HVAC system, refrigeration, and freezers since these are the most costly repairs.

Equipment inspections typically take place in the off hours either before or after opening hours of the restaurant. Make sure your inspector knows that he may be scheduled at midnight or 8 a.m. and that he may have to pretend to be someone else, i.e. an insurance inspector or potential maintenance contractor. The inspector typically goes alone and reports back to the buyer. Multiple people wandering through the kitchen are a pretty clear indication the restaurant is for sale. Make sure the inspector knows the transaction is confidential. Until the deal closes, you are still operating under the terms of the confidentiality agreement and are responsible in most cases for what you relay to others.

This is an actual story from our experiences; only the names have been changed.

> We had a contract for an historic property including both the restaurant and real estate. The inspection was set for 9 a.m. on a Tuesday morning. The buyer did not warn the inspector to keep his intention undercover, and his first act upon walking in was to greet the chef he knew from a prior working relationship and say, "So what do you think about this place being sold?" Needless to say, the chef, kitchen staff, and everyone else were in a panic and called the owners. The seller responded by calling the broker with threats to sue the buyer. By the time the entire group calmed down, it was several days later.
>
> Fortunately, the sale was consummated, the staff stayed on, and no harm was incurred. Otherwise the buyer could have faced serious legal consequences from failing to advise his agent (the inspector) of the confidentiality of the transaction.

Liquor License Facilitator or Liquor License Attorney

In addition to a good attorney, buyers often need a specialist in liquor laws, such as a liquor license facilitator or separate attorney specializing in liquor licenses. The sale of liquor is covered by a complex set of laws that vary by state, by county, and by city. Most restaurants, bars, and nightclubs need both a state license and a city or county license. Laws vary immensely by geographic area. Some counties allow you to pour alcohol until 3 a.m. while others stop at 1 a.m. Some cities require a nightclub license if you serve limited amounts of food, and others allow liquor by the drink as long as food is more than 51% of your total sales.

Your restaurant broker will not be the authority on liquor licenses. A complete list of state alcohol licensing authorities and their Web sites can be found in the appendix. Only the licensing authority can provide you with specifics on the process and laws for your location. You must do the investigation for yourself or rely on the services of a license facilitator. Your restaurant broker should be able to provide you with the names of liquor license facilitators or permit specialists you can contact. Expect to pay several thousand dollars between facilitation fees and application fees to obtain a liquor license in addition to the acquisition cost of the business. Here is a list of questions for your liquor license facilitator.

1. How much will you charge for your fees?
2. What is the application fee that must be paid to the city, county, or state in addition to your fees?
3. After the cost of the initial license, what is the cost and process for subsequent renewals?
4. Does your process allow for uninterrupted flow of alcohol pours at the restaurant between the prior owner and my new operation?

5. What do you need from me? Do you have a checklist of required documents? He should tell you he needs a clean background check. If he doesn't, go ahead and confess any transgressions in your background whether you believe they are expunged or not to make sure there's no issue getting a license in your name.
6. How many liquor licenses have you obtained this year? It should be more than a dozen if he really knows what he is doing, or find another expert.
7. How long will it take before my license is available?

CPA or Certified Public Accountant, or Accounting Firm

You will need a strong accounting firm, but do not expect forensic level accounting information on a restaurant acquisition. Annual profit and loss statements are customary. Monthly profit and loss statements are rare unless the business is doing more than a million annually in sales. Cash flow statements are practically nonexistent and, as you'll learn in the chapter on due diligence, virtually worthless based on add-backs.

Make sure the accounting firm you use has experience in restaurant accounting. All numbers are not the same, and accounting for comps and understanding the flow through from the POS (point of sale) system is best left to someone who handles restaurants on a monthly basis rather than someone specializing in travel agencies. We recommend they have a minimum of ten restaurant clients in their client base. Here's a list of questions:

1. How many restaurant clients do you have currently? The answer needs to be ten or more.
2. Have you worked with reports from the most common restaurant POS systems (Aloha, Micros)?
3. What's a reasonable range for labor costs in restaurants? Test this against what you learn in this book in subsequent chapters.

4. Which add-backs do you include? Look for this to match with add-backs listed in subsequent chapters of the book.
5. What do you need in order to validate the restaurant books?

Business Coach

Some buyers are investing in business coaches early in their acquisition strategy. This is an individual that is compensated for providing advice and information about growing a business. Someone transitioning from the corporate world to the restaurant industry is sometimes more comfortable with an additional consultative source on his side. You can search online for national organizations with local ties or ask your business broker for recommendations. Business coaches are frequently affiliate members of state or national level business brokerage organizations that can be found in the appendix. Be careful about the use of this resource, as we frequently find the coach hired on to a restaurant acquisition has far less experience and knowledge than strong restaurant brokers. They are often highly compensated for their services, and an experienced broker is available to you usually at no charge.

Friends and Family

If you fully completed the Restaurant Assessment Tool exercise, you see how family implications weigh into the decision to own a restaurant. We have worked with buyers countless hours on restaurant acquisitions only to be told, "You know, my wife just doesn't want me in the restaurant business; she's afraid I won't have enough time for the family." This is information you should learn up front. Make sure the journey you are embarking on has the support and agreement of everyone in your family, whether it's rich Uncle Joe who says, "I'll cut you out of the will if you do that," or your wife. This is a long journey, and it is not fair to waste everyone's time going down the path if you haven't fully committed your family first to the idea. Remember, you are buying more than a job or a business. You're investing in a lifestyle that has long-term consequences for you and your family.

Here is one last but very important note on the team you assemble to buy your restaurant. Each player has a specific and independent role in the transaction. Stick to that role when working with your team. It's easy to get caught up in taking a poll on the business with each party, but ultimately this will lead you down a path of total confusion. Do not ask your business broker to offer a legal opinion. He is not qualified and, in most states, can be charged with a practicing law without a license if he attempts to do so. The informed business broker will do the correct thing and refer you to a lawyer. If you ask anyone else in the deal his opinion on a topic for which he is not qualified, i.e. "Mr. Attorney, what do you think about my location?" or "Mr. Accountant, what should I put in the lease for an out clause?" you'll generally get exactly what you ask for—lots of opinions. Unfortunately for you, they are in areas where these parties don't have the substantive experience or knowledge in restaurant transactions. You will end up incredibly confused and doubting your original decision. This same statement holds true for friends and family. They have to believe in your decision to purchase a restaurant, and second-guessing each decision, while human nature, places incredible pressure on you.

Make sure that once the team is assembled, you use each party for his specific role. Trust that each will deliver on his responsibility. This is critical if you want the transaction to move forward. Remember that your business broker is the quarterback running the plays. There may be a last second or audible call that everyone has to react to. Having trusted team members in place allows the transaction to continue smoothly.

Chapter Summary-Key Points

* Finding a reputable business broker is the most critical part of your restaurant search.
* There are four categories of brokers to avoid in your restaurant search: residential real estate agents masquerading as business brokers, commercial real estate agents that don't specialize in business brokerage, leasing agents, and general business brokers.
* The team you need to buy a restaurant can include your restaurant broker, attorney, banker, equipment inspector, liquor license facilitator, CPA, business coach, and friends and family. Make sure each sticks to his independent role to avoid taking a poll on every decision.

Preparing Yourself for the Search

There are several steps you can anticipate when buying your restaurant. This chapter teaches you the fundamentals so you are prepared as you encounter the following:

- Confidentiality agreements
- Personal financial statements
- Proof of funds
- Credit check
- Criminal background check

After you've chosen your broker, it is time to prepare yourself for the purchase. Remember the lessons drawn from the Restaurant Buyer Internet Dating Approach. You will not be taken seriously if you call a broker asking about everything from a $3.5 million-dollar business with real estate to an asset sale at $69,900. The broker immediately knows you have not done your homework and cannot define what you are looking for. The best brokers are incredibly busy. They hold the best quality listings and work hard to put those in front of qualified buyers. They will want to qualify you up front as a buyer. If you are not prepared to follow through on that process, they may choose not to work with you.

Refer back to the Restaurant Assessment Tool exercise you completed in the earlier chapter and refresh this based on your current thinking. If you have completed that exercise, you should be able to confidently state to a broker exactly what you are looking for in terms like these:

"I am seeking a business with earnings in the $80,000–$100,000 level. I want a high alcohol based business (sports bar or nightclub), and it has to be within a twenty-five mile radius of my home. I have $175,000 on hand to purchase today, as well as a home equity line of credit, for a total budget of $225,000."

This is an actual story from our experiences; only the names have been changed.

> One of the best prepared buyers we have ever dealt with was Jerry Stanley. He signed up on the Web site and looked at three sports bar listings. When we called to talk with him personally, he was very specific and stated that he wanted a sports bar in a certain location and his budget for acquisition included a need for partial owner financing. He had a great background as a general manager for multiple locations. Because he knew exactly what he wanted, we were able to narrow down his choice almost immediately. The best property for him was about $100,000 over his price point, and the seller refused to do any owner financing. We set up discussions anyway. Jerry prepared his biography, his business plan, his marketing plan, and his menu, which we presented to the seller. When the seller saw everything, he was so impressed that he waived his issue over owner financing, and Jerry was able to buy his business with $100,000 financed. That's the value of preparation. Both buyer and seller walked away from this transaction happy.

If you are well prepared with your business needs, both the broker and seller will take you seriously. If you are not, you will significantly lower your chances of getting what you are looking for. Remember that every broker is flooded with e-mail requests from buyers who inquire about five to ten listings at a time ranging in price from $30,000 to $400,000. These buyers do not appear to be serious, and they take time and energy from other buyers looking for businesses. There are much fewer good businesses than good buyers, so you have to be sure you are differentiated as one of the good buyers up front.

Since you have already completed an exercise to determine what you want and are carefully preparing yourself by reading this book, you will stand out as a buyer serious for the best opportunities. Now get ready for the business broker to qualify other elements in your quest as a buyer. A good business broker may request any or all of the following:

Confidentiality Agreement

A signed confidentiality agreement (one per listing) is almost a certainty, and it is not negotiable. While the language of the agreement varies slightly from broker to broker, it essentially acknowledges that you are being provided information on a confidential listing and the information shared with you cannot be provided to anyone else. Here's a brief description of who "anyone else" means:

- Your son home from college
- Your buddy with money that you think might want to partner with you
- Your doctor
- Another business broker
- The franchise
- Your friend in the restaurant business
- Your Sunday school teacher that used to wait tables
- Your brother-in-law
- Anyone else means *anyone else*

Most confidentiality agreements allow for the communication of the business to specific business advisors, but they are also bound by confidentiality. Here's a brief description of specific business advisors:

- Your attorney

- Your certified public accountant, or CPA
- Your banker
- Your equipment inspector

You should tell these parties that you have signed a confidentiality agreement and the listing is not public information, or you may be liable for a breach.

This is an actual story from our experiences; only the names have been changed.

> Rusty signed an online confidentiality agreement and qualified on a sports bar. He met with his business attorney prior to making an offer. The broker, attorney, and Rusty met. His lawyer said, "I had a few beers there the other night. This is what I think." The broker asked whether he made any statements in the bar revealing the business was for sale. He said, "I'm not sure. It's on your Web site; isn't it public?" The answer was no.
>
> It is not public, and the name and address are withheld unless you have signed a confidentiality agreement. Do not assume your accountant and attorney are smart enough to keep their mouths shut. They talk like everyone else, and depending on the agreement, you may be liable for their breach. Tell them you've signed a confidentiality agreement and the transaction is confidential.

The elements of a confidentiality agreement are as varied as the attorneys that draft them, but some items are common to most. We'll cover the basic language you should anticipate. Read every agreement carefully and make sure you understand each provision before you sign or call your broker and ask him to explain whatever section you don't understand. Remember, we are discussing these elements in terms of the business case and are specifically not providing legal advice. If you have questions about the legal nature of any agreement you are considering, please consult your attorney. Here are standard terms that will surface in most agreements:

Use of Confidential Information

The buyer must agree and understand that confidential information or trade secrets provided under the agreement are restricted. That means that the information cannot be used by the buyer either directly or indirectly for any purpose other than evaluating the feasibility of purchasing the business.

The confidential information cannot be distributed, disclosed, or disseminated to any third party, except to professional advisors. Most confidentiality agreements will hold the buyer liable for any breach by his advisors, so it's important to tell your CPA, attorney, or inspector that you are bound by a confidentiality agreement and thus their actions are limited to study of the material and advice to you but they cannot tell other parties about the transaction.

Confidential Information

A general definition of the term confidential information is often included to spell out what information will be treated confidentially. It can include all information disclosed or made available to the buyer regarding the seller and the business, including all financial information, asset and equipment lists, customer and vendor lists, and employee information.

The agreement may also clarify elements that do not fall under the heading of confidential information. Generally speaking, confidential information does not include seller information generally available to the public or obtained independently. For example, employee wage rates supplied by the broker are covered by the agreement. A Web site discovered by the buyer listing all employees is not covered by the agreement.

Survival Clause

Expect to see conditions for a period of time (often a year or two) during which the buyer may not breach viewing conditions, interfere with the broker's contractual right to collect a commission from seller, or wrongfully disclose confidential information. This keeps buyers from shopping the business while it is under a listing agreement, waiting until the listing expires, and then purchasing the business to subvert the commission structure. In general, most agreements will provide for liability for legal damages up to the amount of commission, which is one of the few scenarios by which the buyer would be required to pay commission.

Interference with Business

Usually the confidentiality agreement will also have a section on interference with the business where the buyer must agree not to directly or indirectly disparage or otherwise interfere with the business for a period of time (often two years) from the date of this agreement. That means that a year after looking at the business he or she cannot tell another party something like, "I almost bought that place but backed out because I thought the payroll was too high."

Bound and Liable

The confidentiality agreement will usually state the buyer's actions are bound by his signature and that he is liable for any breach. That means that as a buyer, once you sign the agreement, you are answerable for your actions. A seller can and should attempt to collect damages if he is harmed as a result of the actions of a buyer that signed a confidentiality agreement and then violated its terms. Damages can vary by state or by the severity of the violation. Buyers should carefully read and understand what they are agreeing to before signing the confidentiality agreement, as it is not a document to be taken lightly.

Communication

Virtually all agreements bind the buyer to submitting all communications, correspondence, inquiries, negotiations, and purchase offers relating to the business through the selling and/or listing broker. Most will restrict the ability to directly or indirectly contact the seller, employees, suppliers, landlord, customers, and representatives. It also should normally restrict any visit to the business without the express permission of the broker. This is a critical element of most confidentiality agreements because the main thing a seller is trying to protect is his employees learning of the business being for sale. Confidentiality agreements are in force during the entire due diligence period, and most have survival clauses that continue after the closing.

This is an actual story from our experiences; only the names have been changed.

> A buyer for a sports bar owned a second concept on the south side of town. In the course of his due diligence for the purchase, he discovered they shared a common gas vendor and the sports bar he was buying had a much better rate. He approached the vendor while he was under contract in the due diligence phase to ask for the same rate for his business, telling him, "I know that's what John's Sports Bar is paying, and I want the same deal."
>
> The vendor then went to the John's Sports Bar owner and told him that by disclosing his rate to a third party he had violated the terms of their agreement and his rate was going to be adjusted up. Meanwhile, the buyer backed out of the deal during due diligence.
>
> The sports bar seller contacted his attorney, who advised the buyer that by violating the confidentiality agreement and disclosing confidential information he had harmed the business. He threatened a lawsuit and ultimately reached a settlement requiring the buyer to pay the difference in the previous contracted rate and the new gas rate because the specific harm could be proven by the buyer's breach.

Agency Disclosure

Most confidentiality agreements also address agency or the relationship between the broker and the seller and buyer. The relationship is governed by real estate law in the fourteen states where business brokers are licensed as real estate agents. An agency relationship occurs when the broker is an agent or has the power to act for another person (the buyer). In states governed by real estate law, there is a fiduciary responsibility created between an agent and a principal.

Those are the most common restrictive covenants of the confidentiality agreement, and you may be asking yourself, *This seems highly limiting to me; what does signing this mean I can get?* The answer is quite a bit. By agreeing to hold the seller's information in strict confidence, a broker may now release the most intimate details of the seller's restaurant. His financial earnings, gross sales, and add-backs, even his salary, are now available as you enter the decision-making process. You may now visit the restaurant as a customer, acting normally and within the terms of the agreement, which means no questions of the staff or owner and no obvious conversation with your broker or spouse about the business where others may overhear. You may not grill the waitress about how business is or ask the bartender if the owner is ever there.

Many question why the confidentiality agreement requires that all communications with the owner go through the broker. The broker serves an important role in this transaction to filter dialogue between the buyer and seller. You will usually meet with the owner eventually, but the broker should be present so that someone with an independent interest in the transaction can keep track of discussions and follow up. When we discuss this with buyers, they often say, "Don't worry, I'm not going to try and cut you out of the deal. I just want to speak with the owner." A good broker isn't worried about being cut out of the deal. The confidentiality agreement and listing agreement covers him whether he participates directly or not. The experienced broker knows that the surest path to get a deal off track is with a buyer and seller having side discussions and understandings that are never captured or controlled by the restaurant broker. In particular, thoughts and feelings change before and after the deal is consummated, and the most ridiculous items become sources of friction that can derail a deal or sabotage a smooth transition.

This is an actual story from our experiences; only the names have been changed.

> The Taco West sale was straightforward with a willing buyer and seller. The contract included all the standard exhibits, including a list of equipment that would convey.
>
> Everyone got along well until closing. Then the buyer decided to fire about half the staff while the seller was still training. That started a falling out with the buyer. The buyer and seller had previously agreed (without the broker present or modification to the contract) that the seller could remove an inexpensive piece of furniture (a $300 couch) from the business. Once the bad feelings began to fly between both parties, the buyer changed his mind about allowing the removal.
>
> Both men called the broker and began complaining about the other party. Since the issue came down to whether or not it was on the equipment list of items that transferred (it was), the seller had to return the couch. If the discussions had been in the presence of the broker, he would have modified the schedule of equipment and had both parties sign.

It is in the best interest of the transaction for the buyer and seller to work together before and after the closing. Your broker protects your interests so that can occur. Remember, he has bought and sold more restaurants than either the buyer or seller. Rely on his expertise and do not come to any understandings or make any deals without him present. He will not let a $300 couch begin to derail a deal.

Some buyers decide they don't like portions of the confidentiality agreement and return it to the broker with some areas marked through or redacted. If you choose that route, be prepared for the broker to politely ask you to go away. The language of the confidentiality agreement is written to protect the seller, not the buyer, and edits are not encouraged or generally accepted.

Electronic or Online Confidentiality Agreements

Online confidentiality agreements are becoming more and more common in the industry. Often buyers will click through the process without carefully reading what they are committing to and then say, "I didn't think it mattered; I only clicked a box." Do not think that because you signed a confidentiality agreement online that it has less stature than one that is signed on paper or in person.

In the United States, the definition of what qualifies as an electronic signature is set out in the Uniform Electronic Transactions Act (UETA) released by the National Conference of Commissioners on Uniform State Laws (NCCUSL) in 1999. Under UETA, the term means "an electronic sound, symbol, or process, attached to or logically associated with a record and executed or adopted by a person with the intent to sign the record." In other words, your electronic intent, demonstrated by a signature initiated on your computer, traceable by your IP address, and confirmed by the data you provide about your physical address, name, and phone number is fully enforceable in a court of law.

Many firms, including ours, have transitioned to 100% electronic confidentiality agreements. This makes it much simpler for a buyer versus the old method of faxing, meeting in person, or scanning a signature. It also provides instant access to listing information, which used to require e-mails or faxes back and forth between the broker and buyer. There are incredible benefits for buyers that can electronically sign and get instant access to photographs, the full listing presentation, the address, and even directions. It is just as binding as your physical signature.

Make sure you read and understand every word of a confidentiality agreement, especially the section that pertains to agency relationship. A confidentiality agreement usually provides for the agency relationship between a broker and the client, and this should be carefully understood. In a specialized restaurant brokerage practice that focuses on restaurants, it is not unusual for firms to represent both sides of the transaction. This is known as "dual agency" and is legally allowed in certain states under real estate law. For many firms, that does not mean the buyer and seller are represented by the same person, i.e. both sold and listed by the same broker, though this can legally occur. Typically, the listing agent and the selling agent are two different people within the same firm. Because the broker is ultimately responsible for the actions of both parties, dual agency does apply. In some states, dual agency is not permitted. There may be alternate forms of representation whereby the agent does not provide anything beyond specific limited duties. Each state that requires a real estate license is listed in the index along with a link to the state's real estate commission Web site. Interested buyers can look up the form of agency for each state.

Once a form of agency is chosen, it cannot generally be amended. For example, you cannot be made aware of a listing online by a broker, consent to his representation, and then pull your cousin Jim in to work your side of the deal and get the commission. You may bring Jim in to work for you, but any fees for his representation would need to be paid personally and not shared out of the commission fees of the listing agent.

Confidentiality Agreements You Should Not Sign

There are some forms of confidentiality agreements you should not sign. Most of these are not legal on their face, but believe it or not, some brokers issue them, and in these cases, you should stay away.

Blanket confidentiality agreements covering all of a broker's current and future listings are a good example of those to avoid. Some brokers have agreements with language that essentially says in return for providing you with information on this single listing you inquired about, you are forever locked into representation by them for any of their other listings. Do not ever sign an agreement like this.

Business brokers are like everyone else. You're going to love some and hate some. Go on a date for a single listing before you sign a marriage contract for all of a broker's listings. Most reputable firms do not use this type of agreement and would never put one forward for someone to sign. If an agent is procuring cause on a single listing, he should be paid and represent the party. That should not immediately create an ongoing relationship. You may later find a listing you like but want to bring your own broker to the table. This is not the same thing as signing a buyer's agent agreement (sometimes called a buyer brokerage agreement). This agreement says the broker will represent you as a buyer for any purchase. That should only be entered into after you have a relationship and are certain the broker is the one you want representing your efforts.

Most firms simply have an agreement that says we represent you on this single listing and that is the end of the relationship. If you come back and ask about another single specific listing in the future, we represent you on that one. If you inquire on a third with another broker representing you, he is your broker of record for that single transaction.

Another type of confidentiality agreement to avoid is a blanket agreement covering any listing the broker brings to you. This is the same type of arrangement except the broker is saying, "I now represent you in your restaurant search, and if someone else has a listing and I show it to you, I am your representative." If you're inquiring on a lot of restaurant listings at one time, odds are you will find all the listings in the marketplace with or without any one broker's help. You may want him later, but ask for it—do not get locked in. This agreement tends to be overly restrictive against your future efforts in the early stages. We would never recommend you sign this if you are only interested in a single listing from the broker. If you develop a relationship over time and want this broker's expertise no matter which listings you're looking at, then sign a buyer's agreement, which is different from a confidentiality agreement because it means you have contracted with that broker for long-term representation as your buyer's agent no matter who holds the listing.

Here are a few final words on confidentiality agreements. Do not ever misrepresent anything in your confidentiality agreement. Dishonest dealings on confidentiality agreements require that brokers continue to tighten the process to avoid fraud, and it makes the process tougher for everyone. Understand the agency relationship at the point you are signing the agreement and do not attempt to come back after the fact and say, "Well, my cousin, the real estate agent, is representing me in this deal." That is unethical, and if you've learned anything so far from this book, it will ultimately work against your best interest if you go up against an experienced restaurant broker with an inexperienced realtor. Act in good faith.

Confidentiality is the single most important element in a business sale transaction, and the best business brokers treat it as such. Even if you have talked to the same broker several times and completed several different agreements, do not put him in the position of saying no when you ask to "Just let me know where this new listing is without going through all the paperwork." If the shoe was on the other foot and your business was being sold, there is no way you would stand for someone sharing intimate details about your business unless he was bound by a strict confidentiality agreement.

If you are talking to multiple brokers, do not assume that they are aware of another broker's listings and ask their opinion of another firm's listings. There are varying degrees of sharing among brokers, and confidential means confidential. What you should be aware of is that most brokers know one another and do network on a regular basis. If you violate the confidentiality agreement of a broker, the odds of another broker finding out is relatively high. Sellers also talk to other brokers. Brokers talk to other brokers. Buyers talk to other brokers. You can quickly find yourself persona non grata with all the best brokers and forced to deal with the ones that do not have access to the best listings if you violate confidentiality. You only get one chance to make an impression as a serious buyer, and it goes out the window when you violate confidentiality, the sacred element of the business broker's trade.

This is an actual story from our experiences; only the names have been changed.

> A local business broker provided us with a package for Kevin. We responded on the listing. Meanwhile, Kevin called us directly on another listing. We met with him after informing broker one. Kevin went through detailed information, valuation data, and comps and made an offer. It was a lowball offer on an excellent business at $50,000 under the asking price. While the offer was in review by the seller, we got a call from a third broker who said Kevin had contacted him. We thought it was an old contact since we knew he was broker-hopping, but the third broker said that Kevin contacted him that day because he wanted his opinion on his offer. Broker number three said he told the buyer, "You understand you just violated your confidentiality agreement, don't you?" He then wasted no time calling us.
>
> We contacted Kevin, who said, "I thought you guys all talked so it wasn't a big deal." Ultimately the seller rejected his offer. We ended all dealings with this buyer. Broker number three would no longer represent him since he knew he breached confidentiality. Broker number one called us on another listing for this buyer, and when we told him the story and

> wouldn't supply information, he also refused to show him any additional locations. Since these brokers represented the lion's share of all listings in town, Kevin had now—through his actions—effectively locked himself out of the marketplace. One act of bad faith may have far-reaching consequences even though each broker operates independently.

Lastly, do not assume that even if a franchise is marketed under its name that you can contact the franchise and tell them you are looking at a store in a given town. The franchise is not an advisor under the terms of most confidentiality agreements. Most franchise agreements have clauses that say they have first right of refusal and are to be contacted prior to listing the franchise for sale. In reality, most franchisees wait until they have a contract. The last thing the seller wants is a call from their franchise saying, "I heard you're for sale," if they haven't given notice. After you are under contract and in due diligence, you can make appropriate inquiries, but the confidentiality agreement doesn't allow you to do this and, in most cases, specifically prohibits you from franchise contact.

The same holds true for the landlord. While the general terms of the lease are frequently disclosed by the broker, any contact with the landlord is specifically prohibited until a contract is in place. If you attempt to jump the gun and approach a landlord as part of your initial understanding of the business, expect to find yourself hearing from an attorney for interruption of business. This is never handled in the initial stages. Instead, the landlord and franchise are part of an offer contingent upon reaching terms with both that are acceptable to the buyer. As a third party, you have no standing in a contract between either the seller and the franchise or the seller and the landlord and may not approach either of them without placing yourself in a tenuous legal situation.

The business broker that holds the listing owes the duty of loyalty to the seller. He or she has committed to that seller to protect him from the harm of individuals learning that his business is for sale. Imagine a restaurant owner who arrives to work one afternoon to learn that someone was in the bar asking questions or telling someone in the business that it's for sale. His employees are now at risk to quit since they now see their future as uncertain. They may talk about it with food vendors who begin wondering if they should pull his credit terms and put him on C.O.D. (cash on delivery). Vendors visit and talk with competitors. They may talk with friends who have contacts in the media. Once the landlord hears the rumor or is contacted, the seller is at risk for any and all lease negotiations. Breaking the terms of a nondisclosure or confidentiality agreement is an incredibly serious issue that has negative consequences for the seller. Buyers that breach this agreement can be sued for specific harm. Good restaurant brokers vigorously defend and enforce the confidential nature of their work.

Personal Financial Statement

Before you begin shopping for a business, you should prepare a personal financial statement or some method to show you have the ability to purchase a business. You would be surprised by the number of individuals that approach a broker and say, "I have plenty of money, and you should just show me things." Even a residential real estate firm will not let you begin shopping for $300,000 homes without a prequalification letter from the bank. You should expect much tighter standards on the purchase of a business. If you are not comfortable providing the financial statement, figure out what price point you will not exceed in the purchase and have your banker or brokerage account broker put together a statement on his letterhead that says, "John Smith has sufficient liquidity in his accounts to purchase a business up to $400,000," or wherever your maximum purchase price happens to be. Eventually the landlord is going to want your financial statement if you move forward, but this should allow you to start the shopping process with most brokers. A letter from a banker that says "John Smith is prequalified for an SBA-backed business loan up to $300,000," is not worth the paper it's written on in terms of qualification. Many eager lenders will prepare these form letters but will not lend on restaurants. We will cover lending in great detail in a later chapter. Bank lending on restaurants is almost nonexistent.

If you are not prepared to show the ability to purchase, you simply will not get the chance to see a lot of businesses in the marketplace. Unscrupulous or lazy brokers may show you listings, but high quality listings that have verifiable books and records are generally only available for review by a qualified buyer. In the restaurant industry, that usually (though not always) means the cash to purchase combined with some form of owner financing. You are going to have to show you have the ability to purchase. You may also want to pull your credit report and verify your own financial standing before you begin.

Restaurant brokers often encounter those who say, "I don't have the money personally, but I have investors once I find the right business." Do not expect a broker to share the private information on listings in this situation. If you have investors that are willing to put up funds when you locate a business, they need to put the money into an account so it can be represented and verified against a financial statement. If they are not willing to do this, they will not put up the money when it comes time to buy. If you believe little else you read in this book, take this advice to heart. Investors aren't real until the money's in the bank. We've seen countless effort expended by strong individuals who believe their investors will put their name on the lease or the personal guarantee only to be disappointed.

The other point to remember about your financial statement is that if you are shy about providing this information, you may want to reconsider whether you want to buy a restaurant business. A business owner's financials are put forward as frequently as the menu at his restaurant. You have to be qualified with the landlord, qualified for credit with vendors (gas, electric, phone, satellite, and more), and prequalified by the franchise, and that is only the beginning. This is the first of many times the information will be requested, and you should go ahead and be prepared. The minimum a landlord will require is a credit check, financial statement (personal on every party and corporate for the business), and tax returns (both business and personal).

Lastly, some individuals do not want to provide a financial statement because they believe it affects their negotiating position with the seller. You are well within your rights to tell the broker that he may not share information from that financial statement with a third party (like the seller or another broker) beyond telling him you are qualified without your direct permission. You may also show *fewer* assets than you have on hand and provide only one bank balance. While overstating your assets is unethical, understating them does no real harm. This can generally be solved by going to your bank and asking for a letter stating you have a certain dollar amount available—they certainly don't have to state everything you have available. Once negotiations are complete, you can give a landlord the full picture.

Proof of Funds

Do not be surprised if the broker requires that you prove the funds you indicate on your financial statement. Most brokers mask the identity of listings that have very high earnings or are well known. The seller may well require that the broker verify proof of funds in addition to a personal financial statement. That means he may ask you to fax or otherwise provide bank statements that validate whatever assets you list on the financial statement.

Even if the broker does not require an account statement, you should be prepared for portions of your financial statement to be verified at some point in the process. Your financial statement is a snapshot of your financial situation. If you list something on the statement, for example, a bank balance of $100,000, the landlord or seller providing financing usually requires a current bank statement to substantiate the funds. It is a very common business practice for landlords to see bank accounts for cash on hand in the form of a printed statement to make sure the financial statement is accurate. There's a federal law for financial statements prepared for a loan application with a bank, credit union, or for an SBA lender. 18 U.S.C. Section 1014 imposes fines and penalties for fraudulent representation on a personal financial statement form.

With all of that said, treat your financial information carefully. Here are a few tips:

1. Black out (or white out) the account number on any bank account provided to a third party, such as a restaurant broker. As long as your name shows, it should be sufficient to show you are qualified to view the listing.
2. Black out (or white out) any identifiable numbers like your tax ID number or social security number.
3. Always send this information to a secure fax or scan to a private e-mail account so there's no chance any unauthorized person would receive it.
4. Always send the most recent statement. If the statement is more than thirty days old, it is not valid.

This is an actual story from our experiences; only the names have been changed.

> Our buyers have verified their ability to purchase a restaurant any number of ways. The most unusual example occurred early in the formation of our firm. A buyer contacted us for information on a confidential listing. We requested a personal financial statement, but he said he didn't want to provide one. We asked for an account statement. He said he didn't have one. When we asked how he would pay for the business if he

didn't have the money in the bank, he assured us that he could pay cash. We told him that without some proof of the ability to purchase, we would not be able to help, though he was insistent that he had the funds. He asked for our fax number, and shortly after that conversation, our fax machine spit out a picture of the would-be buyer sitting on a couch with the current day's *Atlanta Journal Constitution* held in front of him amidst piles of hundred-dollar bills. Since he was now sufficiently qualified, we released information on the listing.

Preparing the Actual Personal Financial Statement

A standard financial statement form is available from your bank or can be downloaded online from the SBA or from most brokers' Web sites (including www.wesellretaurants.com). You can also use the blank copy provided in the appendix. Following are a few quick items to pay close attention to when preparing your financial statement.

First, your financial statement must balance. Your assets minus your liabilities should equal your net worth. If you cannot complete a balanced financial statement, you will destroy your initial credibility with whoever reviews it. Do not count on your business broker to catch the math or other errors. We receive countless financial statements from other brokers that are incorrect. Secondly, if you list a liability on something, it should show up as an asset as well. Assets without liabilities are fine since it just means they are paid for.

Insurance is often a misunderstood asset listed on a financial statement. Term insurance is not an asset since someone else gets the benefit of this when you are dead. If you have a cash value policy, then only the actual cash value may be included in assets. Lastly, if the majority of your assets are listed under personal effects, you may not have the financial strength for a lease.

Here's a step-by-step preparation guide for your financial statement. This reads from top to bottom of a typical financial statement as well as the sample provided here.

Step 1: List all of the assets, which can consist of everything below, and add everything together to get total assets.

- Cash on hand and in banks: Add up the total of everything you have on hand in cash, savings, or money market accounts.
- U.S. government securities: Provide the total of any government bonds or securities.
- Accounts, loans, and notes receivable: This is the total of everything owed to you. If you previously sold a business and someone owes you $50,000, that would be listed here.
- Cash surrender value life insurance: This is commonly known as cash value insurance. It is not term life insurance amounts. That only goes to a survivor if you die.
- Listed stocks and bonds: Total your 401K, securities account balances, and bonds for stocks bought, sold, and listed on the major exchanges.
- Privately held stocks and bonds: Total your privately held stock (may be in a company or otherwise).
- House (market value): List the market value of your home.
- Automobile: List the blue book or market value of your car.
- Household furnishings and personal effects: Estimate a total value for your home furnishings.
- Real estate (other than house): Market value of lots, commercial property, rentals, or other real estate holdings.
- Other assets: Itemize any other assets not already included in your statement.

Step 2: List your liabilities, which can consist of everything below, and add everything together to get total liabilities.

- Notes payable: This is everything you owe. Example: Balance on your car loan or balance on your home equity line of credit (if not captured in your mortgage loan).
- Loans on house: Balance of mortgage.
- Loans on real estate: Balance of any real estate *except* your home.
- Credit card debt (over thirty days): Self-explanatory.
- Other liabilities: Student loans, business loan, unsecured lines of credit.

Step 3: Calculate your net worth.

Subtract total liabilities from total assets to get net worth. To check this, the total of your assets should equal liabilities plus net worth.

Table 2 shows a sample personal financial statement that is correctly completed and calculated.

Sample Personal Financial Statement

Name(s):	John Smith		
Street Address:	1159 Chedworth Circle		
City:	Atlanta	State: GA	Zip 30005

Assets		
Cash on Hand and in Banks $		215,000
U.S. Government Securities		25,000
Accounts, Loans, and Notes Receivable		n/a
Cash Surrender Value Life Insurance		n/a
Value of Businesses Owned		n/a
Listed Stocks and Bonds		425,000
Privately Held Stocks and Bonds		n/a
House (market value)		895,000
Automobile Number -1		30,000
Household Furnishings and Personal Effects		10,000
Real Estate (other than house)		n/a
Other Assets (itemize)		n/a
	TOTAL ASSETS $	**1,600,000**
Liabilities and Net Worth		
Notes Payable $		n/a
Loan on House		115,000
Liens on Real Estate		n/a
Credit Card Debt (over thirty days)		n/a
Other Liabilities (itemize)		n/a
	TOTAL LIABILITIES $	**115,000**
	NET WORTH $	**1,485,000**
Source of Income		
Salary $		100,000
Dividends and Interest		n/a
Bonus and Commissions		15,000
Real Estate Income		n/a
Other Income		n/a
	TOTAL INCOME $	**115,000.00**

The undersigned certifies that he/she provided this information and it is true and correct.

Date:			
Signature:		Home Phone:	

Credit Report

Go ahead and pull your credit report before you begin shopping for a restaurant. There are several reasons for this. First, you want to determine whether you need to do any cleanup before it is seen. Secondly, you don't want to get yourself in a position where an offer is accepted on a business but the landlord takes one look at your credit and won't approve you for the lease.

Lastly, if you request owner financing of any kind, the seller may want your credit report. If you have it handy, it can easily be submitted from you and avoid multiple credit checks.

If your credit is not perfect, don't panic. A good broker can still find ways to overcome a credit deficiency. Be up front with the broker about your credit so he can structure the deal to overcome this issue. We've had clients approved with bankruptcies, bad credit, no credit, and more. Credit is a measurement of risk. The landlord wants to minimize the risk that you will not pay the rent. The tenant wants to minimize the assets you can attach if he or she doesn't pay the rent. There are many creative alternatives to minimize risk to the landlord including but not limited to: additional months of deposit, irrevocable letters of credit, guarantee against other assets, alternate parties on the lease, and more. We'll discuss these strategies in detail in the chapter on leasing titled "The landlord is not your friend."

Criminal History Check

With few exceptions, those entering the restaurant business will be applying for a liquor license. Before you and any partners enter into an agreement, do everyone a favor and pull your criminal history. This is a simple process that costs from $5 to $15 at your local police department and is also generally available through online resources. If you have any kind of felony or drunk driving conviction in your background, most states will automatically disqualify you for a liquor license. If you believe that youthful DUI from college was expunged by Uncle Joe the attorney, it's better to be safe than sorry and pull this up front to make sure nothing's on your records, even mistakenly. Do the same thing for any spouses or partners. If there's a spouse with an issue, don't put them on your corporation or your liquor license application. They will only have to be dropped when the issue comes to light. Here's an example:

Buyer A and Spouse A 50% owners, no felonies

Buyer B and Spouse B 50% owners, Spouse B has a felony

Spouse B can't be listed on the corporate paperwork as an officer or on the liquor license application in most states. The individual state licensing boards for alcohol are listed as an appendix to this book. The easiest way to understand their requirement is to visit their Web site online and download the application.

This is an actual story from our experiences; only the names have been changed.

> A club went on the market at a rock bottom price for a super fast deal. Several parties competed for the business with one partnership offering the fastest closing and highest price for the seller. Everything moved forward without a hitch until the day before closing when one partner learned the other had a felony conviction from twenty-two years ago for assault and battery. The charges stemmed from a fraternity fight in a college bar. The record was supposed to be expunged, but it showed on the background check submitted to the Alcohol Licensing Board. The two parties scrambled, and the secondary partner was cut loose. The remaining partner without a record had to borrow additional money, amend his corporate officers, and struggle to meet the closing schedule. Go ahead and get a background check up front to avoid these issues.

Chapter Summary-Key Points

* Preparing yourself for the business search includes understanding a confidentiality agreement, preparing your personal financial statement, pulling together your proof of funds, and doing a background check and credit check on yourself.

* A properly completed personal financial statement sets the tone for your credibility. Your total assets minus your total liabilities equates to your net worth.
* A criminal history that includes any felonies will keep you from getting a liquor license in most states. Run a background check on any partners before you submit paperwork for your license.

The Restaurant Search is On

So far, we have focused on preparing you for the search. Now we are going to review the actual process of finding the restaurant: what you should be looking for and how to perform your initial diligence in order to make an offer. Begin your search online with the national Web sites. Although there are many Web sites available, the well-known and well-searched sites are easily found by entering the search term "restaurants for sale," "buy a restaurant," or "restaurant for sale," along with your city or state.

Most Web sites break out their offerings by geographic area and by business type. You will find restaurants listed under restaurants, food-related businesses, bars, and liquor-related businesses. There are both specialized restaurant-only Web sites as well as general Web sites, and most brokers advertise on several of these simultaneously. Here's a brief list of the most popular sites:

- WeSellRestaurants.com
- BizBuySell.com
- SellingRestaurants.com
- Bizilla.com
- Businessforsale.com
- RestaurantsforSale.com
- Businessbroker.net
- Bizquest.com

The advantage of the national sites is that you will begin to see the listings and the brokers for restaurant listings surface over and over. You can easily find the ones that are restaurant specialists. Contact those brokers with e-mails and phone calls first to see how they respond. Here are a few critical things you should ask yourself:

1. What's the quality of the data posted online for the listing? Does the ad state that earnings are verifiable by profit and loss statements or excellent books and records?
2. How long does it take for the broker to respond either by e-mail or phone? Does a live person return your call promptly or is the phone answered? If a broker doesn't respond when I contact them, how can I count on them to respond going forward?
3. What does the broker's Web site share about the listing? Are there multiple photos online? What about listing details, square footage, rent, equipment?
4. Is the process for signing a confidentiality agreement streamlined? Does the broker's Web site have a way to sign the confidentiality agreement online and do initial research?
5. Does the broker's site include actual listing information, or is it just an advertisement for the broker?
6. Does the broker truly specialize in restaurants, or does he handle everything from grocery stores to manufacturing facilities?

Almost all sites list the same basic information about a listing. The key items include: gross sales, net income or owner benefit, lease terms, lease cost, number of employees, amount of training to be provided, and designation as franchise or non-franchise. Remember the example of the business broker who listed nothing but a name, a headline, and call for details from the earlier chapter. Don't bother to call on his or her listings.

Once you contact the business broker to see the listing, here is what you should expect:

1. Expect to sign the confidentiality agreement for the business. Some brokers accept these by fax. Others will accept an electronic signature, and still others require that you meet with them personally. Carefully read and understand the confidentiality agreement and execute this.
2. Expect to be prequalified financially to view the business. The lending environment in the United States for the years of 2008 and 2009 virtually wiped out the prospect of any bank loan financing. Prepare to be able to finance the business from your own resources and/or from some level of owner financing. Refer back to the earlier chapter to see why you should have already pulled your credit, put together an experience worksheet, and more if you're going to ask for owner financing. Typically the broker will want to see a personal financial statement form and proof of funds.
3. Expect to ask that you visit the business as a customer first before seeing the kitchen and setting up a meeting with the owner. 80% of the restaurant can be seen while dining, visiting the bar, and the bathrooms. Go first as a customer and check out the business, and then if you like what you see, request a meeting to see the kitchen.
4. If you like the restaurant from the initial visit, the next step is a viewing of the kitchen. Since most listings are confidential, you may be asked to view the space early in the morning before the restaurant staff arrives or late at night after the kitchen closes. It is not uncommon for showings to occur after midnight in this industry. If you go during the day, you may be asked to mask your real

identity and see the kitchen with the owner as an insurance adjuster, marketing person, or potential franchisee. Remember, confidentiality is paramount. Save your questions for outside the restaurant and never ask them in front of the staff unless the owner tells you this is a partner and it is appropriate ahead of time.

Restaurant Site Visit

The site visit is one of the most important steps in looking at the business. Visit as a customer and, most importantly, view through the customer's eyes. Go at different days for different meal services (breakfast, lunch, dinner, happy hour, or events). Don't rush too quickly to conclusions but formulate your ideas from your visit. Remember, a bad staff often equals the greatest opportunity. Here are some of the questions you should be asking yourself:

1. What does the environment of the restaurant feel like? Is it advertised as a sports bar but seems more like a family restaurant with no one at the bar?
2. How's the service? Slow to respond or eager to show interest in the customer? Bad service is one of the most fixable things for a restaurant, so this means there is opportunity.
3. Are they out of anything on the menu? This could be a sign that they are either busy (a good thing) or trying to squeeze costs in food ordering (a bad thing).
4. Order a drink from the bar, even if you would not normally drink, to gauge the bartender's actions. Is your $10 drink payment rung through the POS system or pocketed by the bartender?
5. Go to the bathroom. Is it clean? Expect the condition of the bathroom to reflect the condition of the kitchen.

6. What's their health inspection score? It should be posted right by the entrance under the law of most states. It can also be found online in most states, but it may be out of date.
7. How's the traffic? How many people are seated, and are any waiting for a table?
8. Who looks to be in charge, and what are they doing? Mingling with customers is a good thing. Ignoring the customers is a bad thing. An owner or operator should not be hiding in the back of the store.
9. How do you like the neighborhood as you approach? Are there other restaurants nearby? Multiple restaurants nearby is actually a very good thing, though most people have trouble wrapping their head around this concept. People go to shopping centers out of habit, and if their usual restaurant is busy and they have already parked, they'll give you a try.
10. Is the restaurant promoting events? Is the server promoting specials? Are they selling gift cards? Are they gathering your information (e-mail or text message campaigns)? If not, you're looking at opportunity to capitalize on existing traffic in ways the current owner is not taking advantage of. That means extra sales for you that are not calculated into the current pricing model.
11. What is the condition of the signage and the exterior? If the restaurant is poorly lit or maintained, this is another easy fix and points to opportunity for a buyer.
12. Can you see yourself in charge of this place?
13. Look at the items being ordered and take a guess at the check average and percentage of liquor sales to total sales.
14. Look around to see if you observe regulars at the bar or tables.

After you leave the business, go home and make notes of all your observations. This becomes a blueprint for changes when you take over. It is not a negotiating tool to reduce the price on the current restaurant. Buyers often make their site visits and then come back with all the things they found wrong with the business, as if they are buying a house. They think that finding a dent in the cooler door will get them a price reduction.

Restaurant pricing is based on key financial fundamentals, not subjective interpretations. Whether or not the service is terrible doesn't matter. That is simply a potential upside to the financials that you are buying and already reflects in their earnings. Here's an example. Suppose the portion size served is three times what you would serve. That means the restaurant food cost is too high, and as a result, net income is lowered. This is already reflected in the profit and loss statement and ultimately the pricing of the business where it is devalued for this poor performance. Whether the bar stools all need to be recovered is irrelevant, as the assets in their current state are generating a return on income (cash flow) that is used to value the business.

If you open negotiations with the seller by pointing out these quite reasonable flaws (or opportunities), the seller could react in one of two ways, neither of them good for a buyer. First, he can become defensive. This restaurant is his baby. Pointing out its flaws does not set you up for success in negotiating since you just called his child ugly. Secondly, he can take your blow-by-blow critique of the business and implement changes, all of which drive his sales up, improve his fundamentals, and make his business more valuable (and thus more expensive) before he comes to terms with you.

So if you observe that he is missing the boat because the sign is on a timer that cuts off an hour early each night and you have personally witnessed the bartender pocketing half the take, smile and keep it to yourself. You are going to be able to buy this business right and get almost immediate financial improvements on the bottom line when you fire the bartender and change the timer.

There are certain things you should *never do* on a site visit. The items listed below are blatant violations of your confidentiality agreement. Prepare to find yourself banned from information on further businesses if you violate this important document or to receive a not-so-nice letter from a seller's attorney. Irreparable harm can be done to a business location if it becomes known on the street that it is for sale. Sellers have clear rights to bring a suit against you in most states for breach of confidentiality under the terms of the agreement you signed.

Never ask questions of the staff or manager that are clearly about the business. Examples like, "So are you guys doing well, or is business off?" No matter how slick you believe you are in phrasing the question, it is a clear giveaway to the staff. In addition to violating the confidentiality agreement, this is not the place to learn whether business is up or down. That can be clearly demonstrated through the financial information.

Do not bring any paperwork to the business or pictures of the restaurant anywhere into the service area. If you bring the broker's package with you for directions, leave it in the car. Since the name of our firm is We Sell Restaurants, we rarely hand out cards or leave a message at a place of business since we don't want any employees to learn the owner is thinking about selling.

If you visit with your business partner, significant other, or broker, do not hold any conversation in the restaurant that can be overheard by a third party. You may think the busboy cleaning the table beside you does not speak anything but Spanish, but he'll go running back to the kitchen if he overhears you say to your wife, "So what do you think? Should we buy this place?" This is especially true for the bar. Bartenders by nature are intuitive and are paid to listen out. Have conversations about the business outside the business.

Listing Package

The listing broker should have a prepared package on each business. This will vary by broker, but the most professional firms provide a well-developed and consistent package that states all the financial elements of the business. Fundamentals include gross sales, cost of goods sold (broken out between alcohol and food), rent, labor costs, other expenses, and net income. It also includes add-backs used to reach seller's discretionary earnings or total owner benefit. A good listing presentation is a full snapshot of the business with key operating elements of the restaurant like the number of employees, status of the liquor license, hours of operation, and photos.

Buyers often enter the search and immediately request tax returns and profit and loss statements. Few firms release profit and loss statements (P&Ls) or tax returns directly to buyers. The practice of e-mailing or faxing this information is increasingly rare amidst business identity theft and personal identify theft. Often P&Ls and tax returns are restricted to release by a confirmed third party source, such as a CPA or lender. This leads to frustration for both buyers and sellers in the process. Buyers always want more information earlier in their discovery, and sellers are reluctant to release anything beyond the bare minimum until they believe the buyer is serious. Without the effort of a strong broker, this could lead to a stalemate situation.

For the buyer seeking information who's thinking, *How can I buy a restaurant if I don't examine every bit of information up front?*, remember that the seller is the one with the larger risk. It is his information being put out there publicly. In order to work around this issue, a due diligence period is established in the contract to perform actual meticulous review on the financial records. This book has an entire chapter devoted to the financial metrics and how to tie out sales, profits, and add-backs in the due diligence phase. In the early review of the business, the buyer may be viewed as no more than a few bytes of data and a faxed confidentiality agreement and account statement. He or she is often working blindly over the phone or Internet.

In contrast, the seller has a bricks and mortar operation. His business is established and earning an income. He has employees that depend on his continued operation for a paycheck. There are plenty of scam artists operating in cyberspace with prolific growth on the business side in recent years.

If the broker's package is thorough enough, it should provide the buyer with everything needed to begin the initial review of the business. Once you are under a letter of intent or contract, you can move into due diligence where materials are exchanged with your CPA or banker that confirm the financial return of the business. Thus the stages of buyer inquiries look like this:

- Initial buyer inquiry.
- Buyer submits confidentiality agreement and proof of funds.
- Buyer receives full listing package from broker.
- Buyer visits business confidentially as a customer.
- Buyer likes what he sees and arranges a meeting with the broker and owner to see the back of house and actual P&L or tax return data (without copies provided).
- Contract is written based on due diligence period.
- Due diligence begins with backup materials sent to CPA or lender and other requested due diligence. Due diligence is a topic we'll cover in detail in another chapter.
- Buyer completes due diligence.
- Business moves to closing, or escrow, depending on the state.

The full steps in the process look like this:

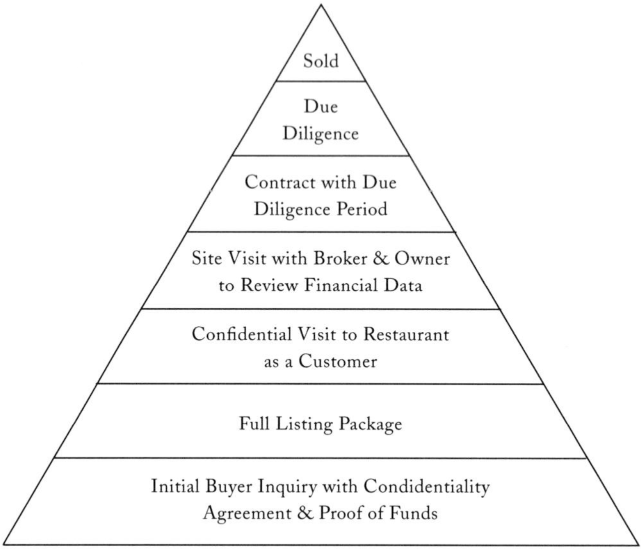

You can easily see how this process affords the buyer everything he or she needs to confirm the details of the business without starting by handing over highly confidential data like P&Ls or tax returns.

Any restaurant listing presentation from an expert restaurant broker should provide you with three key elements:

1. Industry outlook, industry norms, and comparative data
2. Financial performance of the listing, including add-backs
3. Operational statistics (hours, liquor license, employee count)

We issue a report on every listing called the Business Analysis Tool. This financial tool recaps general industry data and financial norms. These standards are then compared to the actual listing data to provide data points for how successfully the restaurant is managing key metrics. The data feeds directly from either a profit and loss statement or the tax return where the financial source is noted. This compromise protects a seller's actual P&Ls from distribution and eliminates the theft of identifying information like social security numbers or federal identification numbers. Once the business is under contract, the source data goes directly to the CPA or lender and can be quickly confirmed. Otherwise, the potential for this incredibly sensitive financial information to be copied or lost by a buyer does not substantiate the risk in releasing information by e-mail or fax.

Restaurant Financial Data

There are a number of questions the buyer should assess for himself when reviewing the financial statements of a restaurant business offered for sale. These questions are based on common United States accounting practices and methods. Some of the focus areas would typically include profits and profit margin, sales, food costs, and labor costs.

Are profitability trends favorable in this restaurant?

The company's net profit margins should be compared to competitors in the industry. No profit statistic is more important than the net profit margin. It is crucial in the short and long run. The other variable to consider is net profit dollars. If sales decrease and expenses remain constant, there is risk to net profit dollars. In particular, restaurants are vulnerable to shifts in sales if they do not control food costs.

Are sales growing and satisfactory?

Sales changes in themselves are typically not vital analytical points. Profit trends are more important. Still, the clear goal over time is to increase sales, since the cost of doing business almost always goes up over the long run. It is difficult to expense yourself out of a bad financial situation, but it is possible to sell yourself into a more profitable one.

Is the company controlling expenses effectively?

Key variables specific to the restaurant industry include both food costs and labor costs, which can dramatically impact the company's profit. Both of these variables should be compared to industry standards to provide a snapshot of any restaurant's operating profitability and opportunity. The good news is that if any restaurant for sale exceeds operating norms for food and labor, you can achieve a bargain based on current performance and almost certainly improve future performance. This is quantifiable and should be considered in your decision making. We will cover this in detail later, but it should not be factored into your offering price or the listing price. It is defined as potential.

Is the company operating at, below, or above industry standards?

Industry-specific comparisons are helpful in understanding the efficiency of a restaurant as well as the opportunity for improvement.

Add-backs

Add-backs occur "below the line" or are added back to net profit to get a figure commonly known as total owner benefit. This is sometimes referred to as the seller's discretionary earnings (SDE) or simply owner benefit. This is the equivalent of all cash and expenses paid to or on behalf of the current owner that will transfer to a new owner assuming the same business performance. The add-backs are expenses that will go away when the current owner leaves the business and thus would appear as net income on the profit and loss statement. Ultimately, what any buyer wants to know is what the total cash benefit to him will be from the business. Usual and customary add-backs are accepted commonly by banks under SBA (Small Business Administration) lending criteria. These can include anything that is fully documented on the profit and loss statement and tax return that are personal expenses paid for by the business. Here are some common categories:

1. *Depreciation.* This non-cash expense is always added back. Your acquisition of the assets and your own tax schedule dictates what your deduction for depreciation will be.
2. *Interest.* Interest is added back as the interest from the current owner, and his debt structure will bear no resemblance to your acquisition and subsequent debt structure.
3. *Owner compensation.* Any owner salary detailed on a 1099, W-2, or K-1 is added back. This is only logical, as that benefit will go directly to the new owner.
4. *Manager compensation.* If the owner operates the restaurant on an absentee basis and the new owner will take over the manager's position, then it is appropriate to also add back a manager's salary. If the new owner will operate absentee, it is not added back, as you will need to continue to pay a manager to run the business.
5. *Owner car expense.* Auto expense, including gas, tires, lease payments, and maintenance, are frequently used as a hedge against taxes. These are legitimate, allowable expenses, as owners use their car for business. You should not add back delivery vehicles that are still necessary for the operation of the business, such as a delivery van. You do add back the owner's Lexus lease, which goes away when he goes away.

6. *Owner's insurance paid by the company.* Health insurance, auto insurance, and life insurance are examples of expenses added back that benefit the current owner directly. Health insurance expense or auto expense for vehicles or employees that remain after the current owner leave are not added back.
7. *One-time expenses.* Extraordinary or nonrecurring expenses that will not be ongoing should be sourced and added back. Examples might include legal expenses incurred for a lawsuit in the prior year or roof replacement due to a hurricane. Reasonable and customary ongoing legal expenses or repair and maintenance are not added back.
8. *Miscellaneous.* Virtually any expense documented with receipts can be considered for add back purposes. If the owner bought two notebook computers and one is his son's school laptop, you may consider it for add back if he has the receipt and it won't transfer in the sale. If he can show you a single food invoice for a $15,000 food purchase where he prepared and catered his daughter's own wedding reception and wrote off the food cost, it can be an add back. His entire family's cell phone bill paid out of the restaurant account is another example.
9. *Travel and entertainment.* Owners frequently book their vacation travel through their businesses, and this is a legitimate add back, as it would not be duplicated under your ownership.
10. *Donations.* The current owner's donation to his son's school would not be duplicated under your ownership and thus would not be added back.

The purpose of an add back calculation is to get a bottom line number for total owner benefit or seller's discretionary earnings in order to establish pricing for the business. That's why there are two very important categories that are not added back in calculating total owner benefit. The first is any operating efficiency yet to be realized. Operational efficiency a new owner or operator could potentially achieve that the current owner has been unable to reach is not added back. Remember, the purpose of the add-backs is to calculate owner benefit and ultimately pricing of the business. If the business could operate more efficiently in the future by something the new owner does, the old owner doesn't get the benefit of that in the pricing of the business. The new owner gets this benefit in their realized returns from their strong operation. That's called opportunity, or "low hanging fruit."

The second category that should not be included in add-backs are cash earnings or money an owner tells you he takes from the business without reporting it. This is sometimes called off-the-books income. Some sellers state they have income generated from their business that is off the books or on another set of books. To buyers for this type of restaurant, we say, "caveat emptor" (buyer beware). This is entirely different than reasonable and customary add-backs, which are documented and can be verified through due diligence. This is a situation where the seller states he takes a certain amount of cash out of the business and it is not reported legally to taxing authorities. Some firms don't list restaurants of this nature or they do list them but state there are no books and records. Here are just a few of the issues with buying a restaurant with off-the-books income:

1. The seller wants more for their business than can be justified. Value can't be established using standard income valuation models since he is underreporting sales and earnings on both his P&Ls and tax return.
2. By including this income the seller is providing a flawed picture to the would-be buyer unless he is willing to operate under the same model. The seller and the restaurant have already received multiple benefits from

these tax-free earnings because of their underreporting over the years. They have not paid sales tax or state or federal income tax. They haven't paid withholding on employees if they paid employees in cash. This can amount to easily 25% to 35% on their earnings. By now, pricing their business with these earnings tabulated but without the tax implications, they are trying to get the benefit coming and going. They got the benefit at the outset because they didn't pay taxes. They are then asking the buyer to pay for it on the back end where it can't be verified.

3. By converting an off-the-books income to one that operates within the law, the entire P&L has to be recast to account for the layers of taxes into the expense categories. On some small margin businesses, the impact of the tax structure may wipe out any potential earnings.
4. By stating to you that a large percentage of his income is off the books, the seller is telling you he has lied to the Internal Revenue Service, the state sales tax authority, the franchise, and his accountant. Despite all that, you're expected to believe that he's telling you—a complete stranger off the street—the absolute truth about his sales.
5. There's no verification. Outside of working in the business for three to four months, there's no way to validate the sales and earnings being put forward in an off-the-books scenario.
6. The owner has stated the business operated illegally. While a buyer should not technically encounter any liability for another's issues, buying and continuing the process places you in the same scenario of illegal operation in order to meet the same stated earnings.

Despite all of this, it is a fact of life that certain owners push the limits of law and certain buyers have dreams of buying an all cash business. If a buyer wishes to obtain a business like this, he will need to work in the business and observe cash contributions for a period of time that would satisfy him regarding the sales and income. Buyers should also carefully examine the seller's food costs. If the owner is not reporting all of his sales, his food costs should be outside the typical norm. He would be capturing expenses for cost of food in order to bring down his income but not capturing the top line sales. If a seller states to you that he's taking money off the books and his food costs are within normal ranges, proceed carefully. If he is truly not ringing up sales but processing the orders, food costs should be too high.

With off the books or opportunity taken out of the equation, all real income is easy enough to trace. Your restaurant broker should be able to detail anything that falls into the add back category in a restaurant for sale. Every line item should be backed up and traceable. We'll cover this completely in the chapter on due diligence, but it's a simple matter to verify add-backs to be certain you're getting a true picture of the earnings.

Any restaurant presentation should present you with the key metrics of the business down to a bottom line net profit line with add-backs after the line to get to total owner benefit. Here are the key elements you should consider:

Financial Terms on a Restaurant Profit and Loss Statement

Gross Margin

Gross Margin = Total Sales–Cost of Goods Sold (COGS)

Compare the gross profit margin or gross margin of the restaurant you plan to purchase with industry standards. The industry standard is 54.9% for restaurants with sales of $1.0 million or less. The industry standard is 56.7% for a restaurant with sales of $1.0 million to $10 million. The higher the gross profit margin, the better, since that allows more dollars to cover operating expenses.

If you are presented with a business opportunity that is far outside these norms, then challenge the broker or seller to explain the difference. There are very legitimate reasons why a gross margin would be higher than normal. These could include an operator who operates incredibly efficiently and keeps meticulous control over food costs. It can also be a reflection that the alcohol percentage is high since alcohol is a higher profit item than food. Lastly, it could be a function of the menu since cost of goods sold includes food costs. A taco stand with 2–3 ounces of meat per taco will operate at a much lower food cost than a steakhouse with large meat portions.

Food Costs

Food Costs = Cost of Food/Sales

A profitable restaurant typically generates a 28% to 35% food cost. Coupled with labor costs, these expenses consume 50–65% of total sales. Because of the impact that the food cost has on an operation, this is one of the first things to examine. Beyond the bottom line, food cost also reflects on operations, food quality, value provided to the customer, and management skill level. High food costs in a restaurant available for sale signals an opportunity for correction and greater profit dollars delivered to a strong operator.

The industry standard shown above for calculation of food costs is based on the Uniform System of Accounts for Restaurants. But while the calculation is the same, food cost is not a one-size-fits-all percentage. The food cost can vary significantly by type of restaurant. A fine dining concept featuring the most expensive cuts of beef will have a higher food cost than an American casual concept. Two fast casual concepts can have varying food costs if one is meat intensive and the other is inexpensive pasta service.

These are typical ranges for restaurant types. In general, food costs should fall between a low of 28% to a high of 35%. Fine dining will be at the high end, or approximately 35%. Expect American casual food to come in around 32%, with pizza or Italian with high emphasis on inexpensive pasta and sauces at the low end of 29% or so.

If food costs are too high in a restaurant you are considering for purchase, it signals opportunity. The business pricing will reflect this poor control over costs, and it is one of the easiest things to fix. High food costs are indicative of poor management and lax inventory control. High costs can be symptoms of too much food ordered from the vendor, too much food going out the back door, or too much food going on plates and ending up in doggie bags or the trash. All are correctable. There is one exception to correcting food costs. If you are considering a franchise that requires the purchase of specific food products packaged and resold through its commissary, you will not be able to modify food costs substantially, as the franchise sets pricing. It is very rare to see food costs too low. Taco restaurants using small meat quantities run at the lowest end of the food cost scale and are sometimes questioned.

Net Profit Margin

Gross Profit–Cost Of Goods Sold–Fixed Expenses–
Variable Expenses = Net Profit Margin

The net profit margin is the money left after everything is paid, or the bottom line earnings. It is sometimes seen on the P&L as EBITDA, or earnings before taxes, interest, depreciation, and amortization, as long as it doesn't include those elements. The industry standard for net profit margin is 10% for a restaurant with sales of $1.0 million or less. The industry standard is 12% for a restaurant with sales of $1 million to $10.0 million. If someone shows you a profit and loss statement showing 30% net income, it is probably not possible without leaving a number of expenses off the books.

Rent

Rent Cost = Total Rent Including CAMS/Total Sales

Physical location is very important to the restaurant owner. The length of the lease and its cost as a percent of total sales is a key factor in a restaurant's success and growth. In large markets, rising rent costs in the past decade have made this variable even more important. Competition to be in the most desirable part of the dining scene can drive rents to unsustainable levels. Evaluation of a property should include some subjective consideration of the lease and location.

Annual rent expense will always include CAMS, or common area maintenance charges. For a triple net lease, it will include all charges, CAMS, insurance, taxes, and all facility costs. We will cover the differences in the types of lease in a subsequent chapter titled "The landlord is not your friend."

In general, restaurants should never exceed 10% rent as a percent-to-sales, though the lower the better. Eight percent as a percent-to-sales is a low industry average. Remember, rent is due no matter whether you've done a single dollar or a million dollars in sales, so this is one expense to fight hard to control.

If you are considering a restaurant where the rent is too high, one of two things has to happen. Either top line sales must go up, increasing the denominator and lowering rent as an expense-to-sales, or the rent must come down. Don't automatically rule out a restaurant with high rent, as everything in a purchase is negotiable. You may be able to buy the restaurant contingent on a rent reduction. There's almost no such thing as rent too low unless the restaurant owner owns the building and isn't paying himself any rent. In this case, if you add back rent as an expense, you can see a formerly highly profitable restaurant become a losing proposition.

Labor Costs

Labor Costs = Cost of Labor/Total Sales

A profitable restaurant typically generates a 25% or lower labor cost. Coupled with food costs, these expenses consume 50–60% of total sales. Because of the impact labor costs make on an operation, they are also important to examine. Beyond the bottom line, labor costs also reflect an operator's management skill level. High labor costs in a restaurant available for sale can be an opportunity for greater profit dollars delivered to a strong operator. Owner compensation is added back if he or she is an owner/operator. This includes all owner compensation, including bonus income.

The industry average for restaurants is 25.0%. A low labor cost can signal an owner paying some individuals off the books. A high labor cost is a good thing since it signals opportunity for a new buyer to bring staffing costs into line and make significantly more money.

A small amount of knowledge can be dangerous, and you now possess just that. After reviewing all the financial information during your site visit, sit down and have a conversation with the broker to ask any questions you may have about the business. Remember, businesses that fall outside the industry standards actually demonstrate strong potential that can be calculated using the ratios in this chapter. Don't get so tied down by the numbers that you rule out opportunities that could have tremendous potential under good leadership. The typical problem with most restaurants is poor management or absentee ownership.

Continue to base your restaurant search on key fundamentals and stay true to your requirements. By reaching the end of this chapter, you should be clear on what you want to search for and able to identify several target restaurants. You now understand what your confidentiality agreement requires and how you should conduct a site visit. Now that you know the key metrics, you can analyze their profit performance against key industry variables to narrow down some subject properties. You are getting close to being able to buy a restaurant. The next chapter teaches you what the restaurant's worth and why.

Chapter Summary-Key Points

* The steps in the restaurant search are:
    - Initial buyer inquiry, confidentiality agreement, and proof of funds
    - Full listing package from the broker
    - Confidential site visit to the restaurant
    - Owner meeting
    - Contract with due diligence period
    - Due diligence
    - Sold
* *Add-backs* is the term for expenses paid on behalf of the owner for which he derives direct benefit. Net income plus add-backs equates to seller's discretionary earnings (SDE) or owner benefit. Examples of typical add-backs include owner salary, auto expense, owner health expense, or travel and entertainment.
* The most important elements of the restaurant financial statement are gross margin, food costs, labor costs, net profit margin, and rent.
* Two items that are never included in restaurant valuation are opportunity and off-the-books income. Neither can be substantiated.

The Fundamentals of Restaurant Valuation

The last chapter took you through the key variables in operation and provided industry comparative indices. We also covered add-backs, a discussion focused on getting the answer to "What is the owner benefit derived from this business?" The reason for all that effort is to use that result to answer the ultimate question, "What is this restaurant worth and why?"

There are three methods of restaurant valuation used in the industry. We will take you through all three methods while spending the most time on the income valuation method. This is the most commonly relied upon approach for valuation.

Income Valuation Method

This is the most favorable and trusted method used to value a restaurant by nearly all buyers. In the days of restaurant lending that existed prior to the collapse of lending by the market, it was the method used to secure financing on a business. If the restaurant had solid profits, and under normal economic conditions, it was likely a buyer could purchase the restaurant with 20% down and obtain an SBA secured or other type business loan. At some point those lending scenarios will return. Until then, the income valuation method still provides the most acceptable method of valuation for banks, lenders, and individuals in assessing the business. In a situation where a buyer is paying cash, this helps to reduce fear of the transaction, as the business has a proven track record.

A business with strong books and records assessed under the income valuation method has the highest number of potential buyers for a restaurant and hence commands the highest possible price.

Your restaurant broker should go through the profit and loss statement along with tax returns to find the seller's discretionary earnings (SDE) or owner benefit that is customarily accepted by lenders to value the business. As stated in the earlier chapter, this includes net income plus reasonable and customary add-backs such as:

- Owner's compensation (1099, W-2, or K-1 income)
- Owner's health insurance
- Owner's auto expense
- Owner's cell phone expense
- One-time expense that is extraordinary or nonrecurring (roof replacement or major repair for example)
- Receipts that document owner purchases (i.e. personal computers purchased for wife and two college kids included in the expense that won't transfer in the sale)
- Noncash items such as depreciation and amortization
- Travel and entertainment
- Donations

Remember that what is not allowable for add back purposes are efficiencies a new owner could potentially achieve that the current operator hasn't. It should factor in your decision to buy but should not be calculated in the pricing. The entire purpose of the add-backs is to calculate owner benefit and ultimately pricing of the business. If you can identify strategies to be more successful in the future than the current owner, that benefit belongs to you as a buyer, not to the seller in the pricing of the business.

This is an actual story from our experiences; only the names have been changed.

> Greg was selling a chicken finger concept. Greg started the business from scratch but was an absentee owner without family members running the business. His seller's discretionary cash flow with add-backs was barely $30,000. His food cost was exorbitant at 42% for fast casual food, and his sales were $500,000 a year. Based on getting food costs to a normalized 30% food cost basis, the new owner can expect to benefit from an additional 12% if nothing else changes. This goes directly to the bottom line for an additional $60,000 in earnings. Greg understood these factors and wanted to include it in the pricing. We told him no. Opportunity cannot be priced into a valuation model. He was priced at assets at only $49,000. A smart buyer recognized the opportunity and got a bargain.

Once the seller's discretionary earnings is appropriately determined, then it becomes the basis for a multiple for pricing purposes. Every buyer wants the answer to the question, "What's the multiple for restaurant pricing?" and the response rarely satisfies anyone. In general, restaurants can be offered and sold somewhere between 1.70 and 3.0 times earnings, with market factors adjusting this up or down. For purposes of this book, we are limiting our discussion to single restaurant units. Multi-unit sales (anything above two, especially franchise) changes the multiple significantly and requires a whole different analysis and pricing model. "What's the multiple?" can be affected by any of the following variables.

Strength of Books and Records

The better the books and records and more provable the add-backs and earnings stated on the P&L are, the higher the multiple applied. In the case of a strong business with perfectly documented numbers, expect to pay closer to the higher end of the pricing multiple (2.5 to 3 times earnings or owner's benefit or seller's discretionary earnings.

Saturation of Concepts in the Marketplace

Pizza concepts are prime examples of restaurant types that experience ebb and flow. A recent saturation in the market drove the multiple down. Therefore, even a pizza restaurant with strong earnings and good books could be seen on a devalued basis down to as low as 1.85 to 2.25 times earnings.

Seasonality

Sports bars are always hotter in the fall when football season starts, and you can expect to pay at the higher end of the multiple when you're buying in August along with everyone else rather than in April or July. All restaurants suffer in the summer months unless they are in a high tourist area, so pricing is better then.

Location

Restaurants with premium locations in desirable places with an assumable lease are at the higher end of multiple. The same earnings would bring the lower end of the multiple in an average or below average location.

Comparable Sales Information, or Comps

Despite the confidentiality of listings, strong restaurant sales firms are up-to-date on all pricing and sales data in the marketplace. A good restaurant broker should have access to comparable sales data for similar restaurants, bars, or nightclubs selling in the marketplace that may also be influencing the multiple used.

Franchise or Independent Offering

Franchises can impact the multiple positively or negatively depending on the franchise. A hot concept in the marketplace will bring a premium totally unrelated to actual earnings, while those on the downside of a growth curve can be undervalued for the same reason.

Number of Units

The number of units involved in the sales changes the multiple dramatically. Multiple franchise unit transactions can go up to eight or nine times the earnings, depending on the strength of the business, and require a much more in-depth analysis.

Geography

Wine bars flourish in the Pacific Northwest while diners thrive in the Northeast. Put either concept in the Midwest and you have a different result. Geography can influence the pricing multiple.

Competition in the Marketplace

If several sports bars come onto the market at the same time, the best priced one will sell first.

Strong brokers that know their markets and restaurant comps should be able to share exactly where a restaurant is priced based on the multiple and why. Here are some questions to ask your broker to be certain they fully understand restaurant pricing. If you're not satisfied with the response, find another restaurant broker:

1. What is your experience and understanding of restaurant valuation?
2. Do you have a financial services or banking background?
3. Do you have an MBA, finance, or accounting degree?
4. How do you define seller's discretionary earnings?
5. What are reasonable and customary add-backs you use in determining owner's discretionary earnings?
6. How long have you been doing restaurant valuation?

7. What is the multiple you are using and why?
8. How many restaurants have you sold?
9. Do you have a statistical resource for sold comps as a multiple of cash flow?

This is an actual story from our experiences; only the names have been changed.

> A new restaurant broker entered one of our markets a few years ago and experienced some quick success in securing listings. I called on one of my former clients who told me they just listed with the new competitor. Surprised, I asked why. The seller said, "I never like what you tell me my business is worth. These guys came in, asked me what I wanted for the business, and listed it for that. It's twice what you told me."
>
> We smiled and told the seller, "Look, the name of our company is We Sell Restaurants, not We List Restaurants, right? Call us in a few months and let me know what's happening."
>
> Sure enough, three months later the seller called back and said he'd had no activity and no offers. The buyer's feedback on the pricing was "Are you crazy?" He cancelled his listing with the other broker and listed with We Sell Restaurants at an appropriate valuation where we secured a buyer for him in short order.
>
> Buyers are smart and do their homework. If the broker doesn't set the right pricing, the marketplace will tell the seller and the lazy broker where the price needs to be. Deal with experience and compare based on the numbers. Valuation is a math problem with a right and wrong answer. If a broker has a lot of listings at crazy pricing, that's probably not the only thing they are doing wrong.

Annual Gross Sales Valuation Technique

Though not relied upon by most, unsophisticated brokers may sometimes use a percentage of annual gross sales to determine a restaurant's value. The percentage used depends on the lease, location, condition of the equipment, and validity of the annual revenue number. The better these traits, the higher the percentage commanded. Restaurants without records and in poor condition will command about 15% to 20% of gross sales. One with a good lease, location, and sales records could command up to 30% of gross sales.

We do not recommend or rely on the annual gross sales valuation technique. Some brokers, however, will quote this method. It is the most unsophisticated form of pricing and is sometimes used by real estate agents that don't sell businesses for a living or do not understand restaurant valuation.

Replacement Value Method

The replacement value technique assumes a buyer pays the seller some amount based on the opportunity to benefit from the existing investment in the restaurant facility, leasehold improvements, equipment, lease, and location of the restaurant. In other words, the buyer will pay for the right to avoid spending time and money to build and comply with city regulations, impact fees, and delays in building a new restaurant. There are very rare cases, depending on market conditions whereby someone gets a premium for a location. One example is the lease for the Inn on the Tavern restaurant in New York City. This closed restaurant space was essentially auctioned at a multimillion-dollar premium based solely on the Times Square location. This is a rare example, and generally the replacement value method is used for a seriously devalued asset sale. This is when second-generation restaurant space goes on the market after a concept fails. The seller ends up getting pennies on the dollar based on the cost of his or her original build-out. The replacement value method is only used when only assets are available for sale without earnings. The advertising on this type listing should state it is an asset sale only and that no books and records are available.

Using a standard valuation worksheet, here is a comparison of how the three valuation methods work. This clearly demonstrates why the income valuation method has the most validity in pricing. Using all three methods, the same sales and earnings result in widely different valuation estimates. The worksheet below shows the P&L data in Column B. Column C is adjusted for items that would be added back to net income on a P&L or decreased under new ownership. Column D states the reason for the adjustment, and Column E shows the new expense line.

Based on sales and expenses from the P&L, the restaurant shows a net loss of $53,716 before add-backs of owner salary, depreciation, travel, donations, et cetera. Total owner add-backs are $72,180. Depreciation and interest of $27,355 are further added back. All add-backs are totaled against the loss on the P&L to get to total owner benefit or seller's discretionary earnings of $45,819.

Taking the revised owner benefit amount of $45,819 times a multiple of two results in a sale price of $91,637, the low end of the income valuation method. The same owner benefit of $45,818 times a multiple of 2.5 results in a sales price of $111,548. Most frequently, restaurants sell somewhere in between the high and the low, meaning a valuation for sales pricing purposes places this listing at the midpoint of $103,090. You could expect to see this listing go on the market for approximately $103,000 under the income valuation method.

The table below compares that result to the other two methods—gross sales method and asset valuation method—to estimate the selling price based on the same underlying data for sales and expenses.

	HIGH	MIDPOINT	LOW
Gross Sales Method	$117,000	$78,000	$39,000
Asset Valuation Method	$50,000	$40,000	$25,000
Income Valuation Method	$111,548	$103,090	$91,638

When the three methods are calculated from the same financial data and then aligned, it's easy to see the flaws in the methods. The gross sales method and the income valuation method show similar results on the high side of the estimate. The issue with this is that most restaurants sell for closer to the mid-point rather than the high, and if you relied on the gross sales method to sell, the broker would be undervaluing the business by more than $25,000 ($78,000 versus $107,500). Since the asset valuation method bases the calculation on assets only, the restaurant is again very undervalued.

Here's the worksheet used to calculate the seller's discretionary earnings.

Owner's / Seller's Discretionary Earnings / EBITDA

Business Name: Sample Restaurant Data			
Period Ending		2009	
Data Source (Tax Return or P&L)		P&L	
Cash or Accrual Basis		Cash	
Sales excluding Sales Tax		390000	
Cost of Goods		125000	
Gross Profit		265000	
Selling, General & Administration Expense		306616	
Interest Expense		12100	
Profit Before Tax		-53716	
Add Backs			
Owner Salaries or other Benefit			
	Owner's Salary	31800	1
	Other Salary Add backs (provide Notes)	25000	2
	Medical Insurance	3000	
	Payroll taxes on owner and Management Salary	1988	
	Repairs		
	Travel & Entertainment	1500	
	Auto Expense for non delivery vehicle	7000	3
	Cell Phone Expense	792	4
	Donations	500	
	Auto Insurance	600	
	Other:		
	Other:		
Total Owner Add Backs		72180	
Other Add Backs			
	Depreciation and Amortization	15255	
	Interest Expense	12100	
	Extraordinary Expense		
	Other		
	Other		
	Other		
Total Other Add Backs		27355	
Seller's Discretionary Earnings or Total Owner Benefit		45819	

Notes

1 Owner W-2 Income

2 Owner Wife Salary – non-working

3 Owner Lease on SUV - non delivery vehicle

4 Owner Family Cell Phone Expense

This exercise shows why the income valuation method is the one that should be relied upon by both sellers and buyers in reaching the answer to the ultimate question: "What is the restaurant worth?"

Any qualified restaurant broker with good financial skills should be able to quickly use the income valuation method to arrive at pricing for a restaurant and comfortably explain the thought process he used. Restaurant buyers can use the income valuation worksheet included in the appendix to work through the same exercise for any restaurant they are considering for purchase. Start with the sales and enter the cost of goods sold and gross margin line. Then, using the data provided by the broker, list out the expense lines and pencil in any add-backs. Then divide the total owner benefit into the sales to arrive at the multiple. Ask questions of the broker to understand the pricing multiple being used. Make sure he or she can give you valid reasoning for the pricing strategy used. If it's a pizza restaurant that you understand to be trending negatively, ask why it's priced at three times earnings. If the business isn't making money with add-backs, ask why it's priced at $200,000. Some brokers simply aren't knowledgeable in the marketplace and overprice listings based on pressure from sellers. Ask the broker how he justifies his restaurant pricing.

Off the Books

Sellers often ask about accounting for off the books, or income they failed to report to the appropriate authorities. Our position is that any valuation method should ignore off-the-books income in the restaurant valuation for pricing purposes. The seller has already received the benefit of tax-free income that results in substantial savings on this money earned. It can't be resold for a premium on the back end. For that reason, owner income cannot include cash under the table, tips, or other non-reported revenue. Buyers occasionally argue that this is exactly the kind of business they are looking for. In that instance, remind yourself of the prior chapter's discussion regarding off-the-books income.

First, the seller is admitting by his statement that there is off-the-books income that he has lied on his federal and state taxes, lied to his accountant, and lied to his franchise about sales numbers. Why would he tell you—a complete stranger off the street—the truth?

Secondly, how do you verify what the real numbers are? The only way to validate the sales is to work in the business on the register for a lengthy period of time to confirm the sales are really happening.

Some buyers say that's okay, because if it's really doing that well, they'll just take over and report everything. Consider that if you convert the business to on-the-books income, you may have real issues with earnings. The benefit of not having to pay payroll taxes, sales tax, and more on the top end may recast the financial picture into a losing one on the back end.

You now have a complete picture of the pricing model for a restaurant along with the key operating metrics. There's one more chapter you need to understand before moving on to an offer. Restaurant franchises are a category of their own. The next chapter deals with the special nature of franchise sales and resales.

Chapter Summary-Key Points

* Add-backs are expense items that directly benefit the owner added back to net income to calculate seller's discretionary earnings (SDE) or total owner benefit.
* Restaurants are valued by taking SDE or owner benefit times a multiple of 1.7 to 3 based on market variables.

* There are three methods of valuation. The income valuation method should be relied upon.
* Off-the-books income is not included when calculating a restaurant's value for pricing purposes.

Franchise Restaurants—the Good, the Bad, and the Ugly

Franchise startups have the same inherent issues and risk to failure that nonfranchise restaurant startups face. Franchise resales, however, represent a lucrative opportunity for the restaurant buyer. We'll begin with a history of the franchise process along with the benefits and costs of restaurant franchises.

Franchising as a business model is reported to have begun as early as the mid-1800s when Isaac Singer made improvements to existing sewing machines and wanted to increase the distribution of his product.[3] While unsuccessful in the long run, this is one of the first acknowledged franchising efforts in the United States. Franchising was also adopted by Coca-Cola as a distribution practice, along with the telegraph system, which was operated by the independent railroad companies but controlled by Western Union.[4] The practice spread to automobile dealerships with exclusive agreements for the sale of cars by the manufacturers and ultimately to franchise-based food business.

Modern franchise-based food service was born with A&W Root Beer, which had over 170 franchised outlets operating by 1933.[5] The idea was to let independent operators use the same name, food, supplies, logo, and even building design in exchange for a fee. Restaurant franchises experienced an explosion of growth in the 1950s with the development of the United States interstate highway system. Americans hit the roads in record numbers, and the familiar sight of the McDonald's arches became identified with the road trip experience. McDonald's, with more restaurant units than any other franchise unit in the world, is the most popular example of successful franchising.

Currently, franchising exists in over seventy industries that generate more than $1 trillion in U.S. sales annually.[6] Restaurants make up a large percentage of these franchise offerings. Successful franchises share common traits. Restaurants, while complex in nature, can fit all these characteristics and become very desirable acquisition targets for would-be restaurant owners.

- Good track record of sales and profits
- Unique business proposition—essentially a concept that is identifiable from other offerings
- Broad geographic appeal
- Businesses that are easy to operate
- Businesses that can be easily duplicated

As with any business arrangement, however, there are both winning and losing sides of the equation in the relationship. Advantages for the franchisor (the seller) are often disadvantages for the franchisee (the buyer).

Advantages for the Franchisor (Seller)

Other People's Money

Franchise owners are able to expand the reach of their brand using OPM, or other's people's money (like yours). They have no investment in the expansion but will reap the benefits of royalty income from sales, an expanded distribution network, and limited risk for loss.

Get Out of Jail Free Card

The franchisor is protected from most of the effort in starting a new franchise, such as obtaining licenses, permitting, insurance, and most importantly, liability. Essentially, the franchisor is protected from virtually all of the legal downside. Franchisors are strictly prohibited by federal law from making any representations as to the expected financial results of the units. They are also generally protected from lawsuits because of the nonnegotiable contracts they require franchisees to sign acknowledging that they are buying knowing the inherent risk and that they have not been promised profits.

Someone Else Does the Work and Pays Them for the Privilege

Franchisors have no operational requirements. They are paid whether any earnings are achieved based on the first and last dollar of sales that come in the door.

Advantages for the Franchisee (Buyer)

Quick to Market

A franchise is an expedited route to business ownership. Most franchises have well-developed timelines, as their most important goal is to get you open for business and paying franchise fees. Remember, the franchise makes money when you start making the first dollar of sales, long before you see the first dollar of profit. It is in the franchise's best interest for you to be up and running. Expect any franchise to demonstrate its strength in operations and contribute heavily to getting your doors open for business. After that, it is probably best not to hold them accountable for many results.

Training

New operators to the restaurant business will be trained by the franchise in virtually all tasks. This generally takes place at a training store location and includes front of house, back of house, point of sale or POS training, food, beverage, and bar training. They also cover accounting and reporting requirements in detail since they rely on your sales volume for income.

Systems

The established franchise has systems in place and a tried and true method for everything from order, preparation, and delivery of the product (in this case, food). This is the most valuable purchase you're making in the acquisition. There is no experimentation about what method works best.

Brand Recognition

Building your restaurant brand as a startup is a long and complicated process. An established franchise is familiar and known to the marketplace, which gives you an instant boost in startup sales.

Marketing and Advertising Support

Restaurant owners are often novices at building complete marketing and advertising campaigns that can drive sales and increase traffic to their stores. Virtually all franchises require participation in advertising funds that are then spent on complete campaigns that range from electronic media (radio and television) to e-mail marketing or social media campaigns. This has the effect of establishing your location and top line sales quicker than messaging on your own.

Disadvantages for the Franchisor (Seller)

Loss of Control

The franchise operator is required to operate the restaurant within the franchise parameters. There are varying degrees of success in doing this at the individual level. The franchise can guide, instruct, inspect, and assess, but ultimately they cannot control the actual operation performance. The most important element to the franchise is to protect their brand and provide a *consistent* experience to every person that comes in the door. They are placing the responsibility for that delivery in the hands of the franchise owner.

No Guarantee of Success

Franchises perform due diligence on operators to insure they have the financial assets to establish a store, but that is generally where the process ends. There is no process to predict who will be a successful operator versus who will fail. Some, if not all, franchises conduct a meet and greet with a would-be operator. They will also perform testing or ask you to do an online psychological profile to see if you're a fit for the concept. Each time they open a store, they are placing faith in the operator to succeed.

Disadvantages for the Franchisee (Buyer)

Intensive Capital Requirements

While a franchise cannot legally provide estimates of earnings, they do have estimates of build-out costs. Virtually every franchise will have language on their Web site that states minimum capital requirements for building a new store. Would-be franchise owners should spend careful time considering how quickly—if ever—you can earn back the capital invested of several hundred thousand dollars serving ice cream at $7 a serving. Restaurant for sale listings are littered with language like, "seller invested over $375,000 in build-out and will take pennies on the dollar for a qualified buyer." Cost of capital is an exercise you should carefully consider with your banker, your financial advisor, your broker, or someone else before you invest several hundred thousand dollars into the latest ice cream fad. The resale value of assets is generally around twenty cents on the dollar. Later we'll discuss how that figures into the Rule of Three for savvy buyers that want a franchise resale.

Conflicts

Part of what drives the entrepreneur to start a new business is the opportunity to control his or her own destiny. The franchise system inherently leads to conflict between the operator and the franchisor because the two parties have distinctly different goals. The franchise wants sales at any cost since franchise income is based purely on top line revenue. The franchise owner wants net earnings. Recent court cases over value pricing options are testing the franchise's limits to set pricing and affect earnings. In a recent court case still pending, franchisees sued because the pricing for the franchise value hamburger offering at $1 meant they lost money on every single sale.

Control

There is very little deviation from the franchise model. Inspections from corporate staff are in place to ensure that no operator is changing the menu, the décor, the hours, the service method, or any other facet of the brand unless the entire franchise undergoes a change. The hallmark of a franchise is consistency. That system discourages out-of-the-box thinking and takes control from the operator.

Fees and Costs

Fees for franchises vary by restaurant, but it's pretty common to see an initial franchise fee on the low end of $25,000 and up to $100,000 for certain concepts. That is the initial fee for a franchise term of ten years. At the expiration of the first ten years, franchises often charge a fee to renew that's a smaller amount.

Recurring fees break down into royalties and advertising expense. For certain hot franchises, it is not uncommon to see fees as high as 12% combined for royalties and ad expense while a more typical approach is about 8% all-in (4% royalties, 4% ad funds). Royalties and ad funds are calculated on gross sales dollars and begin with the first dollar of sales long before you make a single dollar in net profit or earnings. As we learned in earlier chapters, typical restaurants average 10–15% net earnings without any franchise fees, so in order to calculate the difference in what a franchise does to your cost structure, simply back the fees off the net earnings. You can see that a franchise operator's earnings diminish as much as 50–75% in this scenario. You risk 100% of the capital, and the franchise takes 50% of the profits. Before entering into a franchise agreement, understand exactly what this does to your bottom line.

This is an actual story from our experiences; only the names have been changed.

> Eddie bought an existing franchise resale. The restaurant was netting owner benefit of $75,000 on $1.8 million in sales. The franchise earned $90,000 in fees. Eddie came from outside the restaurant industry but had strong financial skills. The franchise trained him in their model, and for six months he operated exactly according to the plan. After that, he started down a new path.
>
> He examined every sale and expense line on the P&L and decided to eliminate delivery. The franchise strongly recommended delivery but did not require it. When he told them he was eliminating the $50,000 in sales from delivery, a war ensued. The franchise was adamant that giving up any sales line was never in the best interest of a restaurant since revenue was too difficult to build. Eddie demonstrated the losing nature of the delivery sales through the following exercise. He went to his insurance agent and asked for a calculation on

the insurance policy without liability for delivery. Without delivery, his insurance would decrease by $19,218 a year. Since his net income on delivery sales was only $7,150, he would improve his earnings by $12,068, a 59% improvement. Here are full calculations.

Delivery Sales:	$50,000
Gross Margin 55%	$27,500
Franchise Fees: 5%	$2,500
Net Income: 14.3%	$7,150

Eddie then thoughtfully decreased his sales line another $150,000 (elimination of entertainment that didn't generate an increase in sales but carried high costs for additional insurance, employees, security, and ID check services). By the following year, his P&L reflected $1.6 million in sales, a decrease of $200,000. Meanwhile, franchise fees reduced to $80,000, but net earnings increased to $220,000. The franchise wasn't happy, but Eddie was singing all the way to the bank.

No Guarantees

Many franchise buyers invest in a franchise because they believe it is safer than buying a non-franchised brand. While it true that a non-franchise startup business will fail at a slightly higher rate, the difference is negligible, and both fail at a rate of six out of ten. That distinction does not hold true when looking at resale businesses that have established track records. A franchise has zero history in the location you are looking at because it doesn't exist. A restaurant that has been established for several years does have a history you can review.

Remember the study conducted we discussed in the first chapter by H.G. Parsa, an Ohio State University hospitality management professor?[5] He studied the restaurant industry, analyzing health department records for around 2,400 independent and chain restaurants in Columbus, Ohio, between 1996 and 1999. Fifty-seven percent of the franchise restaurants failed compared to 61% of the non-franchise startups. That's not a ringing endorsement for the security of a franchise when nearly six out of ten startups fail after three years.

What does this mean for the would-be restaurant owner? Buy restaurant history, experience, and the business books and records. A restaurant with a three-year history in the same location with profitable books and records is a far safer bet than a franchise startup. That brings us to the Rule of Three. If a franchise is your game, it is our experience that you should use the We Sell Restaurants Rule of Three to make the purchase. The Rule of Three ensures you get the maximum benefit from buying a franchise without overpaying for it.

We resell plenty of restaurant franchises. We see the original owner invest $375,000–$400,000 in build-out with stars in his eyes about how great this is going to be. Forget the fact that he's invested $400,000 in a unit that sells premium ice cream with an average ticket of $8.50 and is only busy in the summer months. He is convinced after the franchise boot camp that he has the next McDonald's on his hands. He calls us after a disappointing year of red ink and wants to know who will give him what he has invested in his business. The answer, sadly, is no one. If the franchise is a hot concept in a pristine location, the next buyer may be willing to pay as much as $99,000 to $149,000. That is overpaying based on seller's discretionary earnings since at this point the restaurant is still losing money. There's often a huge transfer fee (these range from $15,000 to 10% of sales depending on the franchise).

The second owner more often than not ends up with a restaurant losing money for which he paid around $150,000. Because his cost structure is lower (lower cost of capital to attain) and the sales line has matured, he may be able to get it out of red ink and into the black with franchise fees due and payable on every transaction. He usually makes it through year one or two before he says, "Enough is enough. I'm earning minimum wage here and working fifty hours a week in the store. I have to get a job to feed my family." That's when the bargains kick in. The franchise goes on the market as a mature concept for a multiple of earnings. The third owner is the one who buys it right.

The price has now decreased a third time. It's listed and sold for no more than three times earnings on the books. The expense is minimal, and the sales line has had time to mature and catch up with fixed costs. The buyer for a third-generation franchise ultimately gets the best deal in the marketplace. He gets a good brand, top line sales, limited earnings, and a low (or fair) cost of entry. The first guy is the one that takes the bath. The second guy is a close second, but number three is the winner. That's why we developed the We Sell Restaurants Rule of Three for buying a franchise.

We Sell Restaurants Rule of Three for Buying a Franchise:

1. Make sure you're the third owner of the franchise at that location if you want the best possible deal.
2. Buy early in the third year of operation to maximize the long-term earnings. The business is still immature enough to see long-term growth in sales but priced based on low current earnings.
3. Never pay more than three times earnings no matter how glamorous the franchise wants to paint the potential to be. Remember all the other factors of valuation you've already learned and apply them to this listing.

Owner number three buys a bargain and ultimately continues to manage expenses and develop top line sales in order to remain relatively profitable. Remember that as the buyer of a franchise, you are still held to the same approval process as the original owner. You will have to submit a personal financial statement and be approved. You will have to sign the receipt for the FDD and wait the mandatory federal cooling off period before you can close. You will also have to attend training.

An important thing for you to know is that the franchise doesn't make money on a transfer. The fee they charge to roll over the business to a new owner does not net the franchise new top line sales numbers or a new unit—important metrics for their operation. Essentially you are a lot of work without much benefit to them. They want franchise sales, and they have a savvy and sophisticated sales operation. Read the next paragraph to understand the importance of that before you go and meet with the franchise for "Discovery Day" or whatever their term is for meeting potential franchisees.

A typical day at the franchise, or "Discovery Day," will begin with welcoming signs at the door. You'll meet lots of people with very impressive titles. Often the franchise president or CEO and multiple vice-presidents (sales, training, et cetera) will want to see the new potential franchisees in person. You'll spend a day being told that the franchise is very special. You'll watch videos of franchise owners saying, "This is the best thing I ever did." They will tell you that in order to join this special group you must be thoroughly interviewed and vetted. They may give you a test. They will make you simultaneously nervous about whether you're a good candidate for them and drop hints that the last guy (you're buying from) left lots of money on the table. Then the happy news is delivered. Not only are you approved, but based on your skills and financial statement, they are willing to approve you for additional locations! We are not kidding. This happens to every person we send for franchise approval. Do not learn the Rule of Three so you pick up a great bargain on a franchise and then go in for your franchise meeting and get stars in your eyes and buy two more. That's what at least one of our clients did before we started counseling them up front about the sales pitch they would encounter.

This is an actual story from our experiences; only the names have been changed.

> We had a barbeque franchise fast casual restaurant for sale for nearly eight months and finally got a contract. The buyers operated multiple unit pizza franchises but weren't able to get more territory. The seller had invested $395,000 in build-out and contributed another $100,000 in operating capital in the first two years. He took a huge loss on the business. The buyers got it for $119,000 with top line sales of $550,000 and about $35,000 in earnings. The franchise requested a meeting to approve the transfer. We followed up after the meeting and were shocked to learn that not only was our buyer approved by the franchise but they were thrilled to report the franchise was selling them three more locations at the discounted price of only $30,000 per unit. We tried to talk the buyers out of signing the agreement, but they were now thrilled with the potential for the franchise. They wrote a check for $119,000 for the existing location and coughed up $90,000 for their new stores to be determined.
>
> A year went by, and the buyers called. They were granted the territory where they wanted to extend their pizza franchise. They wanted to dump the barbeque place fast; could we sell it for $99,000 and throw in the extra franchises for $45,000? Ultimately, we couldn't get a bite on the franchise for more than $49,000, which is where it sold. The extra franchise's rights for three more stores were money burned.

Potential is an intriguing word in the restaurant industry, and it is one we stay away from. The greatest potential known to man is the lottery ticket, but the odds of it paying off are slim to none. After the experience with our barbeque clients, we never let anyone meet with franchises until we've warned them that the franchise will do their best to sell them additional units. Sure enough, the ones with nice, fat financial statements leave their franchise meeting saying, "You were right. They offered me two more units." Stick to the one you bought at the right price. Additional units are always available at We Sell Restaurants Franchise Rule of Three pricing, or the franchise will sell you additional territory if you are successful.

Many buyers mistakenly believe that since the sale of franchises is governed by the Federal Trade Commission that it affords them widespread protections. They also think a franchise is much less risky than a startup, another myth we've already dispelled. A franchise is not a life jacket. If you're buying a franchise, even a resale, it is subject to the same laws as new franchises, so here is what you will need to understand.

Franchise Regulation by the Federal Trade Commission

Franchise transactions are regulated by the Federal Trade Commission, or FTC. If you're considering a franchise, there's a mandatory federal cooling off or "dark" period to consider whether to go forward. Carefully read the franchise agreement and use this time wisely if you're considering a franchise. Do not count on the FTC regulation and oversight of the industry to substitute for your own due diligence and business instincts. In 2007 the Federal Trade Commission updated the FTC Franchise Rule for the first time since 1979. Prior to 2007, franchisors would be provided with a UFOC, or Uniform Franchise Offering Circular. They are now provided with the FTC Franchise Disclosure Document, or FDD. The new format is sometimes called a UFOC-Plus because it has additional disclosures over the old requirements.

FDD, or Franchise Disclosure Document

The FDD, previously known as the UFOC, has twenty-three individual items (called chapters) that are consistent to all franchise agreements. These twenty-three chapters of disclosure are intended to give prospective franchise buyers enough presale information so an intelligent franchise investment decision can be made before long-term contracts are signed, money changes hands, and sizeable financial commitments are made.

Attached as exhibits to the FDD are the franchise company's audited financial statements, franchise agreement, operations manual table of contents, and a list of operating and departed franchise owners. If the company elects to make franchise earnings information available (now called Financial Performance Representations in the new FDD Item 19), it will be set forth in Item 19 or attached as an exhibit to Item 19. The entire FDD document is quite lengthy and can exceed several hundred pages.

In certain states (known as FDD franchise registration states like California, New York, Illinois, et cetera), the FDD makes reference to being registered with the state. This simply means the state requires registration and should not imply any review by the state regulatory boards.

FTC Franchise Rule Changes

The new FDD rules changed one item significantly, and that relates to how long you must have the franchise disclosure document in hand before contracts can be signed or money can be paid. The former rule said the UFOC had to be delivered at the "first personal meeting" and in-hand for at least ten business days. A separate, completed franchise agreement (with all negotiated areas and blanks completed) also had to be delivered to the prospective franchise buyer for at least five business days to comply with the old FTC rule.

Under the new FTC franchise rule, the first personal meeting requirement is eliminated entirely. Instead, a fourteen calendar day minimum review period is supposed to simplify the complexity of completing franchise transactions. Upon a "reasonable request" (which is a defined term), franchise companies must give a complete FDD to a prospective franchise buyer earlier in the sales process than fourteen calendar days before the franchise buyer signs or pays. Failure to comply with a reasonable request for an FDD is an independent violation of the FTC Franchise Rule.

If changes are made to the franchise contract or other agreement attached to the FDD, an additional seven calendar day review period is required.

Electronic Delivery of FDD

The new FTC rule permits delivery of the Franchise Disclosure Document by electronic means, such as e-mail or download from a company Web site. The cover page of the FDD now contains the franchise company's Web site and e-mail address, if the company has one. Finally, the new rule allows a prospective franchise buyer to sign a FDD receipt electronically.

There are some electronic prohibitions: disclosures must not include electronic features such as pop-up windows, audio, video, and links to external documents. However, features that enable a prospective franchise buyer to review the FDD efficiently are allowed—things like scroll bars, search features, and internal links (for example, links between the table of contents and the specific FDD items).

FDD Record Keeping Requirements

Under the new FTC rule, for every completed franchise sale, franchise companies must keep a copy of the signed receipt page (Item 23) of the FDD for at least three years. Franchise companies are also required to retain a sample copy of each materially different version of their FDD for at least three years after the close of the fiscal year when the FDD was last used.

Franchise Registration

Registration of a company's Franchise Disclosure Document means they've paid an initial franchise registration fee to a governmental agency, hired an attorney to prepare the documents, and submitted their FDD. This does not mean that the franchise company has to demonstrate any level of success before it sells franchises. You don't have to prove business experience, length of operations, operating stores for an amount of time, or any other element before filing. In fact, there are plenty of documented cases of franchises filed without a single operating profitable store.

What is not disclosed in the Franchise Disclosure Document?

In addition to what is required for disclosure, there are plenty of areas that are not required by law to be shared with a prospective franchisee.

Operating Capital

Item 7 of the Franchise Disclosure Document requires an estimate of what is known as additional funds. By definition, this is a ninety-day estimate of working capital needs. When you consider that many new franchises can take eighteen to twenty-four months to get to a break even point—the point where total revenue equals total costs associated with selling the product—this seriously underestimates the capital required to maintain the business until it operates out of the red. Unsuspecting franchise buyers without strong financial skills look at their initial build-out and the additional funds requirement and fail to consider the additional eighteen to twenty-one months of operating in the red that will need to be funded by their checkbook before they make their first penny of earnings.

Item 19 Financial Performance Representations, or FPR's Financial Performance of Franchise Owners

Franchise Disclosure Documents do not require the seller to tell you how much money the franchises are making. Franchise disclosure laws make this optional for the company. If the franchise does provide financial information, it will be found in Item 19 of the FDD titled "Financial Performance Representations." Fewer than 15% of all franchises provide this information, which begs the question—why would you invest your money without having a reasonable understanding of your expected return? Franchise resales have books and records, and buyers will have them available for review in making a buying decision.

Current Franchise Owner Performance

Current franchise owners are named in the document in Item 20 of the Franchise Disclosure Document. Often you will read online articles telling you that the best way to learn about a franchise is to contact existing owners. There are definite drawbacks to this approach since you are dealing with a subjective interpretation. They are giving you opinion, not facts. If you could get them to release their financial statements to you, that would be different, but in our experience, it doesn't happen. Many franchise owners do not have a strong financial background. Why would they have invested $350,000 if they did? First, the franchise owner may not want to admit his mistake (who does?). Secondly, he might be looking to sell. It's not uncommon for the buyer calling for information to be asked by the franchise owner if they want to buy his store.

They may unknowingly exaggerate their financial performance because, despite the fact that they are working in the store forty-five hours a week without taking a salary, they see a bottom line income of $30,000 on the income statement. They don't break that down to realize they are earning about $13 an hour.

Franchise Resales

The last thing missing from the FDD are the franchise resales. The document will tell you how many units are operating and how many are closed, but they don't calculate the turnover in ownership. That means the people we've taught the Rule of Three to that bought a franchise flipped twice already will still count as one unit with no data on the corresponding decrease in value of the unit.

Despite all the downside to putting a new franchise up, the lure of the next big one is still a call that many can't refuse. The franchise market remains incredibly strong and growing.

You have now learned the key metrics in restaurant evaluation as well as the key principles of restaurant valuation. You have learned how to figure out which restaurant is right for you and conduct your initial review. Finally, you now understand the We Sell Restaurants Franchise Rule of Three and how you can use this to your advantage in a purchase. You might be ready to make an offer. The next chapter covers the art of the deal from negotiating to writing the contract.

Chapter Summary-Key Points

* Advantages for franchisors include:
    - Other people's money
    - Limited liability
    - No operational requirements
* Advantages for the franchisee include:
    - Expedited route to ownership
    - Training
    - Established systems
    - Brand recognition

* Disadvantages for the franchisors include:
  - Loss of control
  - No guarantee of success
* Disadvantages for the franchisee include:
  - Intensive capital requirement
  - Conflicting goals
  - Loss of control
  - Fees and costs
  - No guarantee of success
* The We Sell Restaurants Franchise Rule of Three says you can get the best deal on a franchise when three items are met:
  1. You're the third owner.
  2. It's in its third year of operation.
  3. You never pay more than three times earning.
* The FTC does not protect the consumer in the purchase of a franchise. Read and understand the Franchise Disclosure Document before signing.

The Art of the Deal-Negotiating the Offer and Writing the Contract

Once you have found the right restaurant, you are ready to make the offer. Now is the time for all your hard work to pay off. There are multiple forms that an offer can take, and we have a strong point of view about this step, but we'll present all the alternatives along with the pros and cons. Before we launch into the discussion of making the offer, here are some general points on negotiations.

Everyone Needs to Feel some "Win" in a Negotiation

Hitting the seller on every front is a strategy used by some buyers in an attempt to drive pricing down. They want the lowest possible price and the longest time to deliberate. This leads to the longest possible time frame between offer and closing and, inevitably, the lowest chance of acceptance. There are several key elements to a contract, but generally speaking, the key negotiating points are price, terms, and time.

View these as an axis of variables that require flexing on one of two dimensions in order to keep the deal moving forward. When writing offers for clients, we frequently advise them that the two key variables for the seller are time and money. If you're going to offer less than the asking price, then expedite the time schedule for closing. If you're going to ask for seller financing, then meet the offer price. Don't be greedy and ask for everything at once or you set up a tug-of-war in the negotiations.

If you aren't willing to compromise on those elements, find a throwaway item you can use in the negotiations. Training is a good example of this. Most sellers don't want to hang around after the sale and are interested in a short training time since they usually aren't paid. Buyers often request two weeks of training and then send the seller away after four days. Make this throwaway item appealing in your offer. Agree to pay for training at a rate of $500 per week for up to four weeks with the ability to cancel at any time. The seller will see dollar signs without considering that you might not need him after three days. You just offered the seller a win even though it's of no real significance to you. This tactic will get more initial cooperation on your offer than trying to lowball every element. Stubborn sellers will just say no and refuse to counter if they feel you are being overly aggressive on all fronts. You end up negotiating against yourself.

Time is Your Enemy–Move Quickly

In any negotiation, the element of time is the greatest enemy to the transaction. This is particularly true in the negotiations for a restaurant between the time of an expected offer and acceptance. A seller knows you're looking. He builds up anticipation for the offer, and the more time between the expected offer and the showing, the more time he has to consider and the lower the chance of acceptance. Certainty of the closing is a second element related to timing. If you make an offer that closes three months into the future, he'll take a lower offer than if you agree to consummate the transaction in two weeks.

We have buyers that have worked with us for months that finally determine an offer and then say, "I have to get my attorney to review the contract." They chase their attorney for fourteen days to get an answer only to have them respond that everything looks okay. In the meantime, someone else enters the negotiations and puts an offer on the table. No matter how strong your intent, unless the offer is signed and accepted by countersignature, you will not get the restaurant. Request a copy of your broker's contract for review early in the process and pay your attorney to give you comments before the offer is written.

On the other side of the equation, we have sellers that drag their feet when we request materials. We get an offer pending owner financing of some portion, and they cannot find the time to respond with an e-mail requesting a credit check or provide updated financials or an equipment list. Do not assume that since the broker has brought an offer that it is secure and will go to closing without work on both sides. The more delays encountered by the deal, the greater the chance that the buyer will get cold feet. Once the buyer makes up his mind, any delay introduces doubts. Is the seller hiding something? Why doesn't he just call his CPA and get this or that thing? Is he making it up? These are only a few of the questions going through the mind of the buyer when it takes two weeks to get a copy of sales tax receipts.

This is an actual story from our experiences; only the names have been changed.

> Bill listed his burrito store with strong earnings verified by three years of tax returns. A strong marketing message got an offer from another broker's client quickly. The buyer wanted to meet the seller before he signed the contract. It took four phone calls, two messages, and three e-mails to get him to respond with a time to meet a week later. The buyer then said, "I'm good to go, but I need to see a year-to-date look at the numbers." Bill took three weeks to prepare the documents, and by this time the buyer walked because he had cold feet.
>
> Four months later we had another offer and went through the same thing. It was now September, and his current year was ending and the tax return filing was due. The buyer wanted the current year. Since it was at cutoff, Bill couldn't get it for him. The buyer said, "That's okay; get me copies of sales tax filings for this year and we'll move forward." It took another

two weeks and dozens of calls and messages to shake information loose from Bill that was readily available online with a keystroke from the Secretary of State Web site. Bill had a great business and nothing to hide since the sales tax filings matched the P&L, but it wasn't his priority. This buyer walked too. At that point, we advised the buyers that what we had on the business was all that was forthcoming since Bill was so nonresponsive.

Two more months went by, and Bill wanted to know what happened with all his offers and why we hadn't sold his business. Time is your enemy. Think hours and days in response time if you're selling to keep deals on track.

You're Not Buying a House; Bad Mouthing the Restaurant Doesn't Improve Your Offer

Buyer callouts about things that may be wrong with the business will not win you friends in the transaction or make negotiations any easier. As long as the restaurant is priced appropriately based on the earning multiple, small fixes and cosmetic changes or even process changes shouldn't enter into the negotiations.

If you determine that his food costs are skyrocketing because the kitchen manager is offloading food into his own SUV at closing time, smile, make your offer based on current performance, and fire the kitchen manager the day you take over. You're not in this to critique his restaurant, solve his problems, or point out his deficiencies.

Seesaw Negotiations Have a Limited Life

Some buyers love the thrill of the hunt while others live for the art of deal making. Be aware that there's a finite timeline in the negotiations for a restaurant if you're in the latter camp. Restaurant owners selling a profitable business earning a healthy return have typically been in the business for a while. If it's not a distressed sale situation, the back and forth in offer and counter will typically end at round three. There's no science to that statement, only years of experience in seeing deals unfold. If you cannot get to terms by offer, counter, offer, counter, offer, it is unlikely to happen. The seller is in a business he likes that is making money. He has beaten all the odds to both survive and thrive. Unless he has a pressing issue like sickness or death, it is very likely he'll just hold out for the right offer. Factor that into your negotiating process.

Making the Offer

Now that you know how to position your offer, let's look at the forms it can take and how that also affects negotiations. We'll cover the pros and cons of each type of offer as well as its impact on negotiations and the chances of closing.

Verbal Offer

A verbal offer takes place when the buyer's broker contacts the seller's broker and says, "We have a verbal offer for you. The buyer is willing to pay this amount with closing by this date."

> Pro: You get almost instant feedback on the offer since the broker only has to call his seller and get an answer.
>
> Cons: No one really takes this offer seriously. Why would you, the seller's broker, or the seller feel bound to something that isn't even as formalized as a single sheet of paper?

Without escrow and the weight of a signed contract, it is nonbinding and comes down to "he said, she said" in the matter of a dispute. If a second, better offer comes in, even if the two parties verbally agree, the second offer in writing instantly holds the upper hand. Brokers are required by law to present all offers to sellers if they hold a real estate license (review the appendix for a list of these states), but for your own protection, you want a paper trail that shows the seriousness of your own intent and to confirm that someone reviewed and then either accepted or rejected the offer.

Letter of Intent

A letter of intent, even a fairly detailed letter of intent, is still only that. It represents a goal for a sale between two parties without the binding weight of a contract. Every letter of intent we've seen states that the letter is nonbinding upon the parties until a contract is signed. Someone presenting a letter of intent is often not serious. They want all the protections of a contract so they can shop without committing to anything. There are both pros and cons to the buyer for writing a letter of intent. On the pro side, you can preview the details of the contract in a letter of intent, so the more meaty issues can all be worked out later once there's agreement on the substantial issues of price and financing terms. On the con side, there are three issues. The letter of intent is not binding to either party. No matter how tied into the purchase you believe the seller may be, if another offer surfaces that is better than yours, he can walk away from the transaction. Most letters of intent say the business will not continue to be marketed while it's under a letter of intent. That does not preclude those already aware of the business from surfacing with offers where you lose the deal. Unscrupulous buyers also use this tactic to shop all the details of the business before making up their mind. If you're not sure you're ready to buy, admit that to yourself and don't waste everyone's time with this ploy.

Issue two with the letter of intent is that it highlights the issues without settling the terms, leaving every item open to negotiation for the final contract. The greatest point of leverage you will ever have in an offer is when it is first presented. The seller is flush with that successful feeling of having an offer on the business. It might not be what he wants, but he feels powerful and assured that his business has value. After that first blush, everything goes downhill when the seller starts figuring out who has to get paid out of the proceeds and how much he's really walking away with. You avoid that by spelling everything out in a contract that, if he accepts, gives you what you want in the deal.

The third issue with a letter of intent is that at some point it has to move to a contract, later driving up costs and increasing the number of parties involved. The old adage of "too many cooks in the kitchen" is certainly true when it comes to contract negotiation. Time is your enemy. The potential for failure increases exponentially as time goes by, and the number of parties to the transaction increases. The seller's broker and seller's attorney, along with the seller's partners and the seller's family, will now all have an opinion on every item in the letter of intent that has to be solved. Add in your broker, attorney, family, and any friends and you can see why items like training, inventory, alcohol license transfer, and more go from business as usual to a fight on every point. Keep the parties to a minimum and work to get this under contract, not under letter of intent.

Contract

A contract is written and accompanied by escrow funds (usually) before presentation to the seller. It states an up-front understanding between all parties on every key element of the deal, and most importantly, it is binding. This is the tricky part for some buyers because they aren't really ready to make the offer. Here's our advice: don't make the offer. Continue your due diligence and don't move forward if you're not ready. Some buyers simply aren't ready to pull the trigger, and if that's the case, don't put everyone through the motions of a deal and then walk away. If, however, you're serious about the acquisition but want to be sure the due diligence is firm and the lease is what you want, those are items that can be handled easily in the stipulations of the contract. All the contract elements will be covered in this chapter, including the ways a buyer is protected against moving to closing if the terms you seek can't be met.

> Pros: A contract is binding to all parties. No other offers can be accepted, even if someone offers twice as much for the restaurant tomorrow. Agreement is reached on all issues related to the transaction while the seller is still excited about the money and hasn't had a chance to get cold feet about selling. Every item of the contract is measurable and has an end date so there are no surprises in the transaction. It is the final road map to ownership,making the road clear and easy to follow.
>
> Cons: If the contingencies of the contract are met, then all parties do move to closing or there is typically a penalty to the defaulting party, usually the forfeiture of the escrow or damages equivalent to the escrow.

Here are some of the most frequently asked questions about the restaurant contract:

1. Do I need my attorney to draft the contract?

   No. A good restaurant broker will have access to a contract that he can complete on your behalf and then provide to your attorney for review. Your attorney may have minor changes,but the cost will be substantially reduced from having him execute the full document.

2. Do I need to hire a certain type of attorney?

   Yes. Hire someone that has executed asset purchase agreements in business transactions. Do not use your sister-in-law. Don't use the guy that did your will. Don't use a real estate attorney. You're not dealing with real property. If you don't know a good resource, ask your broker to give you three recommendations and interview all three before making a decision.

3. How much will the closing cost?

   It depends on the attorney. We advise you to get a total price on the closing, including the setup of your corporation if needed. Don't pay by the hour.

4. Who pays closing costs?

   Generally speaking, the buyer pays the closing costs because the benefit is to him in the transaction. He's the one that needs to be sure there's a lien search and the title passes free and clear. However, everything's negotiable, and your contract terms can state that the buyer and seller split these costs. Make sure any stipulations are clear and measurable. A contingency that says, "Buyer and seller to split all closing costs," is likely to be rejected since it can't be defined. Restate the same contingency to read, "Buyer and seller to each pay 50% of closing costs not to exceed a total of $2000." This may meet with the seller's approval since his costs are now defined.

5. Can my sister, the real estate agent, use standard forms and write this contract to me?

   No. Standard real estate contracts are written for real property. In 99% of the cases, restaurants are transferring assets, not real property. The contracts are not interchangeable.

This is an actual story from our experiences; only the names have been changed.

> Barbara Deal called for help. She owned a restaurant and was a real estate agent. She sold it herself six months earlier with owner financing. The buyer hadn't paid, and she needed to take it back.
>
> She sold the business using a standard state real estate contract. There was no mechanism in the agreement to repossess the business. The form she used was for real property and didn't cover the restaurant assets she thought she sold. We

gave her the name of an attorney since she really needed legal advice. We later learned that she never could repossess the business and recover any of the assets. The landlord ended up taking over the equipment since the buyer hadn't paid the rent and his lease agreement did allow for that. She was never paid. Anyone with a real estate license can write a contract. Don't let them.

6. Do I need a corporation to buy a business?

   Ask your attorney and your accountant for advice on this, but most businesses are sold to corporations, partnerships, or LLCs rather than to an individual personally due to tax and liability reasons.

7. Who gets the escrow?

   Escrow is held by an independent third party to the transaction and is governed by state real estate law. Each contract should include an escrow agreement that specifies disposition of the escrow. It may be held by the brokerage firm, but actions regarding escrow monies are strictly governed by law in most states.

8. Do I need to put money down on the transaction, or isn't the contract enough?

   Escrow is what is known as consideration to a contract and gives weight to your offer. We recommend a minimum escrow of $10,000 on the businesses we transfer, and the more the escrow, the more seriously your offer will be taken.

This is an actual story from our experiences; only the names have been changed.

A couple approached us to buy a site for their new restaurant. We located a building priced at more than $1.5 million. It was perfect for their concept, fully equipped, and could open with minimal renovations. The seller was offering owner financing with 20% down. We wrote the contract, but when it came time for the escrow, they balked at submitting a large amount. They wanted to put an escrow check of $5000 with the contract since they weren't sure it would be accepted.

We had multiple conversations but could not change their mind on the matter. We submitted the contract for $1,490,000 with the $5,000 escrow they wanted. The seller's broker called us back the next day and said the offer was declined. It turned out two offers came in at roughly the same time. The other offer was for less, they were only paying $1,450,000, but their offer was accompanied by an escrow check of $100,000. The seller viewed them as more serious about the transaction, especially since he was financing the building. Don't be cheap on escrow. If you have the means, make your escrow as large as possible since it validates your intent to the seller.

9. What if I change my mind?

   Changing your mind is not a reason to get out of the contract, but a thoughtfully written contract with the appropriate contingencies gives a buyer plenty of wiggle room to exit the contract. Typical contingencies that allow for the buyer to exit without default include a contingency for a lease acceptable to the buyer and the due diligence time period.

10. What are the assets? How do I know what I'm buying?

   Every contract should have a list of the included furniture, fixtures, and assets that transfer in the sale. This should be initialed by both the buyer and the seller. Since, in almost all cases, you are only buying assets, these must be clearly defined.

This is an actual story from our experiences; only the names have been changed.

A gentleman called our firm to sell his business. His little soul food place served up plenty of volume, but he and his partner had acquired it only six months earlier and it was proving to be more work than they wanted. We went on a listing appointment and asked for the books and records along with their lease. They stated that since they were only in business six months they didn't really have any books, so they would take a loss to get out and just sell the equipment as assets and move on.

We asked the owners how much they paid for the business. They paid $120,000 (their life savings) to a friend. Unfortunately, they didn't use a broker, a contract, or an attorney familiar with restaurant transactions. A quick read of the lease showed that the assets (all furniture, fixtures, and equipment) actually belonged to the landlord. There was nothing for them to sell. Their only option was to continue running until they had built records to sell on earnings or shut down. The gentlemen were crushed to learn this.

Every contract must include the assets that transfer in the sale so that at the worst case scenario, assets can be sold for something even if you're not making money.

Backup Offers

We often find that a listing will sit on the market for a period of time with little to no interest, but when the listing heats up, it goes from lukewarm to red-hot quickly. Multiple buyers descend on the listing at one time, and it is very common to have several offers submitted within hours. When this happens and a buyer loses out on a property to a higher bidder or someone with better terms, we are often asked about the strategy of a backup offer. That's an offer submitted in the event that the first accepted offer should fail. This is a strategy that buyers all too often overlook or reject out of hand without considering the benefit.

Once a seller has committed to sell and has accepted an offer, he or she undergoes a profound psychological shift from a restaurant owner or operator to someone that sees the finish line fast approaching. Deals can fall apart for any number of reasons during the initial time period of the contract. Due diligence may reveal something unexpected. Buyers simply change their minds and exercise a due diligence clause to get out. Attorneys can't come to terms on language to protect both sets of clients, or the financing for the acquisition can fall through.

As a general rule, our firm has a very high percentage of closings for businesses placed under contract, with nearly 90% reaching the closing table. That is unusual in the business brokerage industry for several reasons. First, many buyers do not execute full asset purchase agreements but work with their broker to do letters of intent. For the reasons already discussed, a letter of intent is nonbinding for almost everything, but the intention to try to make a deal happen that is tenuous at best. Secondly, brokers have to be very talented to keep all parties engaged in the process and keep deals from being sidelined for any number of reasons. Lastly, deals fail because buyers never had honest intent in the first place to buy and simply don't mind putting up escrow to get a full and complete look at the business.

This brings us back to the discussion of backup offers. Buyers should always consider extending a backup offer with a specific end date to ensure they are in line for the opportunity if the first prospect falls through. From the buyer's perspective, we are often asked to call a buyer if the deal falls through. Conscientious brokers will do so, but others may lose track of who was most interested, and the opportunity you wanted may not end up under contract to you. Buyers with a backup in place can seal the deal quickly if the original offer fails. It eliminates the risk that yet another party will enter into the mix and begin to alter pricing through their negotiations and locks you into place to close on the business. Also, once the deal falls through, the seller who was already in the mind-set to sell who may have rejected your original offer because it was not the right price or terms is now psychologically committed to leaving the business. Rather than drive results through marketing and wait for someone new to surface, you're sitting there ready to go. For these reasons, we encourage buyers to consider putting a backup offer on the table even if you lose out on the original contract.

This is an actual story from our experiences; only the names have been changed.

> David's Pizza went on the market at a rock bottom price. Multiple offers came in almost immediately, and the seller accepted the highest offer with the shortest closing period. It was almost identical to a second offer except the offer price was $500 more. We asked buyer two if he wanted to submit a backup offer. He said, "I really want this place, but I don't need to formalize it. Just call me if the deal falls through." Meanwhile, a week went by, and the original buyer walked out because of personal reasons. During the week that the first offer was pending, a new buyer surfaced. We told him the business was under contract but he could put a backup offer on the table. Buyer three put in a backup offer for full price. The minute the other contract failed, his contract was presented. We advised the seller that we had another client interested, but in his mind a "bird in the hand was worth two in the bush." He had already committed to the sale psychologically and wanted out. He immediately accepted buyer three's offer.
>
> About a week later, buyer two called. He asked if the original contract had closed, and we said no. He asked why we didn't call, and we told him that we didn't have an offer from him but had received a valid contract from buyer three, which took the second position for presentation. His failure to put in a backup then moved him behind buyer three, who had formalized his offer even though the seller knew there were other interested parties. Without an offer in writing, the seller didn't want to risk another failed closing. If you really want a business, go ahead and put a backup offer in place. There's always a chance you will get the restaurant you want that way.

Business Terms of an Asset Purchase Agreement

This section deals with typical language and protections in a contract. Nothing in this language should be construed as legal advice, and you should consult an attorney before proceeding with any contract. This is meant to guide you on typical business terms that should be considered as part of the contract between two parties and is business advice, not legal advice.

A typical agreement between a buyer and a seller is referred to as an asset purchase agreement because the buyer is acquiring the assets of the seller's business but not the corporation itself. Anyone considering acquiring the assets of a corporation should discuss the legal ramifications of such an action with his attorney. By purchasing the assets of a business, it is generally understood that you are not liable for any of the corporation's outstanding liabilities or obligations. A stock purchase is an arrangement whereby you actually purchase an operator's corporation, leaving you with all their liabilities as well as assets. These are the key elements of each contract and what you should pay close attention to on the contract.

Legal Name of Purchaser

Make sure that any contract written on your behalf identifies your name as well as "your assigns" as the purchaser on the contract. If you form a corporation or other entity, you can assign the agreement to the newly formed company with this language. If your corporation is already set up and you're purchasing in that name, ignore this.

Address for Notice

This is a very important element of the contract and serves as the address for all communication under the contract. Make sure the address is correct and it's one that you frequently check. Fax communication is an accepted form of notice in most states, so verify that the fax number you use is correct. E-mail is not an accepted form of notice under most contracts. This is very important in the event you want to make a change to a contract or modify it.

This is an actual story from our experiences; only the names have been changed.

> A group of young men wrote a contract for a restaurant for closing in a short period of time—roughly fourteen days. They had five days under the contract for due diligence, which would expire at 5 p.m. on a given date. They waited until 4:55 p.m. on the final due diligence date and sent an e-mail saying, "We changed our minds and don't want to go forward." Because there was no notice as defined under the contract (fax or mail), the buyers lost their escrow money. Make sure you understand the terms of notice under the contract.

Broker's Information

Brokers for both the buyer and seller are included in the contract. There should be no direct contact between the buyer and the seller's broker or the seller and the buyer's broker. The brokers have representation obligations defined by law to their client, i.e. the buyer's broker for the buyer and the seller's broker for the seller.

Business Information

The business name and address, along with a brief description of the business, should be included in the contract. If it is a franchise business, the description should include this information.

List of Assets

A list of the assets of the business should be attached to the contract. This includes the furniture, fixtures, and equipment that conveys in the sale. Compare this list to what you've observed in the business. If the massive painting over the fireplace is not on the list, it's not included, and you have to decide whether things left off are worth fighting for. Assets attached to the premises that can't be removed may not be on the list because they become the property of the landlord once they are affixed (known as *chattel* in real estate language). Examples might include the walk-in coolers, hood vent system, or grease trap.

Escrow Agent

The escrow agent should be identified in the contract. The escrow agent is an independent third party to the transaction that simply holds money until closing. His duties are typically clearly defined by state law, and there should be an escrow agreement between the buyer and the escrow agent detailing the escrow function and escrow return. The broker may serve as the escrow agent.

Date of Closing and Binding Agreement Date

The date of closing is always listed. When putting forth an offer, remember that two things are important to the seller: time and money. If you're offering below his asking price, make sure you're also not extending closing out three or four months. If you want to increase your likelihood of acceptance, keep the time short. After the contract is signed, an extension can always be written to push it out. Every contract has a binding agreement date, which is the date by which both parties have signed and accepted with no more changes. All clocks on the contract start ticking on that date. Here's an example:

Buyer extends a contract with ten days of due diligence. What is the binding agreement date, and when does due diligence end?

June 1: Buyer signs and offers a contract with acceptance valid until June 3 at noon.

June 3: Seller signs but makes two changes to the contract—one on price and the other on training.

June 4: Buyer signs and initials accepting change on price but marks through training change.

June 7: Seller initials training change.

Every change wipes out the preceding agreement on the terms until the document is countersigned and accepted by both parties. The binding agreement date (by which both parties have ultimately signed, initialed, and accepted all changes) is June 7. Due diligence ends ten days later.

Due Diligence

Due diligence is a critical element of the contract and needs to be a very robust clause that gives the buyer the right to inspect and walk away for any reason he uncovers during that time period. Due diligence can include any and all of the following items:

- Review of the books
- Physical inspection
- Equipment inspection
- Availability of capital, financing, and any other financial matters
- Any other item of interest for review prior to moving to closing

Buyers should be certain they clearly understand the time period for the due diligence and either send a notice to extend the due diligence (which the seller does not have to agree to) or be completed on time.

Seller Financing

Any terms related to seller financing should be clearly spelled out in the contract, including the term of the note, the interest rate of the note, period of payment (monthly, quarterly, annual balloon, et cetera), periodic amount, and means of security for the debt. In the seller's case, he wants the maximum security he can get for the loan of capital, so he may request any of the following:

- Personal guarantee
- Security interest in the assets (lien on equipment)
- Other, which could be anything. Notes can be secured by a 401K account, other real estate holdings, or virtually anything of value the seller is willing to hold as security.

Inventory

The food and drink inventory on hand is typically not included in the purchase price of the business unless specifically stated. Make sure that if you want inventory included that this is confirmed in the contract. The most common method of handling inventory is that an estimated amount of the inventory is put into the contract as a placeholder. An inventory is scheduled within the last twelve hours before closing, and the final purchase price is usually adjusted up or down based on the inventory on hand at cost. If you want your offer price to be all-in, this should specify that on hand inventory of a stated amount will be included in the purchase price. The agreement should specifically state that this must be at the cost of inventory and cannot be marked up in any way to the buyer.

Assumption of Liabilities and Accounts Receivable

The contract should specifically state that the buyer is not assuming any liabilities of the seller, including all accounts payable prior to closing regardless of when payment is due. Anything purchased by the seller prior to closing is his expense. Some restaurant operators have large catering operations and bill their clients. All accounts receivable, unless specified, should remain the property of the seller.

Closing

A date for closing shall be clearly spelled out in the contract along with the responsibility for fees. The benefit of the closing belongs to the buyer, who needs the attorney to ensure that a lien search is undertaken and that clear title on the assets passes to the buyer. For that reason, the buyer typically hires and pays the fees for the closing. However, everything is negotiable, and it is certainly within the buyer's prerogative to request that closing costs be split or even paid by the seller.

Proration

Prorated amounts will be captured at closing for anything billed and paid in advance. Since all billing for utilities and vendors will switch into the buyer's name at the point of closing, this typically only refers to the lease if you close on a day other than when the rent is due. This is calculated just like a home closing. The day of closing belongs to the buyer. That means cash sales and credit card sales for the day of closing belong to the buyer, and he pays employees and rent beginning with the day of closing.

Allocation of Purchase Price at Closing

The Internal Revenue Service requires that the parties allocate the purchase price among the classes of assets involved, goodwill versus cost of assets. There are tax implications for both parties depending on how this is allocated. Make sure you consult a certified public accountant, or CPA, to understand the best strategy for your tax situation.

Familiarization and Training

The contract should clearly state the number of days and number of hours of days that the seller will remain on board to train the new owners. This is in addition to any training offered by the franchise if this is a franchise transfer. Most buyers tend to overestimate the amount of time they want. We are called countless times by buyers after the sale asking, "Can I tell him not to come back?" The training wheels come off pretty quickly once it's yours to run. The training period should be specified as free of charge to the buyer or with an agreed upon compensation amount spelled out in the contract.

Restrictive Covenants

The buyer and seller need to agree up front how the actions of the seller will be restricted going forward to ensure that he does not unfairly compete with you once the business is sold. This is to keep him from going two doors down and operating another restaurant of a similar nature. We typically address four separate areas of restrictive covenants.

1. *Covenant not to compete.* This sets a specific time frame and specific geographic scope during which the seller may not operate a competitive business. Generally speaking, this is approximately three years or three miles but can be any number the buyer and seller agree to.
2. *Covenant not to solicit customers.* This sets a specific time frame during which the seller cannot contact customers with marketing offers and is generally about one year but can be any number of years the buyer and seller agree to.

3. *Covenant not to solicit employees.* This defines the specific time during which the seller may not solicit any of the existing employees to work for him. Many states are known as employment at will states, meaning that there are no contracts and you can't force someone to stay, like a manager or key employee. What you can do, however, is restrict the seller from soliciting them to work for him by contract. This subject surfaces a lot with buyers who believe the existing employees are key to the business. In our experience, employees almost never leave when the new owner takes over. Their loyalty is to their paycheck and their job, not the owner.
4. *Covenant not to divulge proprietary information.* Both parties should be restricted under the terms of the contract from sharing information about each other to outside parties indefinitely.

Termination and Default

The contract should include some language stating that either party breaching the contract has a specific and measurable remedy under the contract. Our contract states that the breaching party has the right to liquidated damages up to the amount of escrow. That means if you decide to walk without purchase, you would forfeit your escrow money. It also means that if the seller changes his mind for no reason, you can bring civil damages against him for the amount of the escrow.

Agency and Brokerage

The contract should itemize the agency relationship between the brokers and the parties to the contract. An entire chapter could be written on agency relationships, but the main thing is to understand who is working for you in the transaction.

Indemnification

There should be some language indemnifying the parties to the contract against third party claims.

Loss or Damage and Operation of the Business

The contract should include language that if anything happens to the restaurant prior to closing that the risk for loss or damage is the responsibility of the seller. Anything that happens after the closing is the risk or damage of the buyer. It is critical that the buyer has all insurance in place with a binder coinciding with closing for this reason. This will be covered in the "Buyer's Checklist for Closing" to be covered later. There should be specific language that the seller will operate normally during the period between contract and closing. He or she should also commit not to undertake campaigns or costs that have a life beyond the closing date. For example, he or she can't take out a $1000 a month yellow page advertisement.

Trade Name

For individually owned businesses, you want rights to the name, their phone number (especially for delivery), and their Web site. All of this should be covered in the contract. A seller can't give you rights to something they don't own, such as a trademark name for a franchise.

Confidentiality of Transaction

The seller, buyer, and all parties to the transaction should be bound to keep all details confidential even after the closing. You don't want someone after closing revealing the purchase price. We post purchase prices of our sales for comparable sales data, but we are bound by the contract to never disclose the actual name of a business with the selling price.

Time is of the Essence

Make sure the contract contains a provision that time is of the essence. This is a phrase in the contract that means performance by one party at or within the period specified in the contract is necessary to enable that party to require performance by the other party. This is important, for example, when it comes to due diligence. If you require certain materials in order to do your due diligence on the transaction and have fifteen days of due diligence but the seller doesn't give you P&L data until the fourteenth day, your due diligence can be extended on the basis that his failure to act impacts your ability to complete your requirements under the contract.

Typewritten or Handwritten Provisions

Laws may vary by state, but most contracts that have typewritten provisions (such as contingencies typed on the contract) take precedence over any text within the contract when there's a conflict. Handwritten provisions outweigh any text within the contract plus anything typed if there's a conflict. To be certain that there is no misunderstanding about intent, every contract change should be initialed with a date and the time.

Representations and Warranties

The seller and buyer represent and warrant certain conditions at the time of contract and for some period of time after the transaction closes. The seller's list of representations and warranties can include everything from disclosure on pending lawsuits to any known roadwork affecting egress. The buyer generally has to represent and warrant that he or she has the authority to enter into the contract. Survival of the representations can vary depending on the state, the parties, or the attorney advice. There generally is a survival clause, which just means that everything represented will remain true for a period of time (thus "survive") the closing. An example of this would be a leaking grease trap that becomes an environmental hazard. If the buyer finds outs six months after he buys but can prove the seller was cited by the health department and knew of this before selling, he would have standing under a one-year survival clause to bring action against the seller to recover any damages.

Special Stipulations or Contingencies

Special stipulations or contingencies in the contract are some of the most valuable protections for the buyer and should always be carefully worded. Contingencies are your get out of jail free cards. These are typewritten additions to the contract overrule the contract language.

Contingencies or Stipulations to the Contract

There are key business terms that should be stipulated or entered as contingencies to a contract. These contingencies address business terms so that a buyer does not inadvertently end up with a business but no way to run it. An example of this would be a franchise restaurant without a franchise agreement or a sports bar without a lease. Another example combines both elements, a ten-year franchise that refuses to transfer without a lease term corresponding to the franchise term. By placing protective language in the contract, you'll be able to ensure that all moving parts come together or you will not be required to close. Examples of key contingencies to include in your contract follow in the section below.

Lease

The purchase of the business should always be contingent upon the buyer obtaining a lease from the seller's landlord with terms that are either a) acceptable to the buyer or b) substantially the same as the terms of the seller's existing lease or c) with a rate not to exceed a specified amount. It is better for the buyer if this language is purposely vague since it is then open to whatever negotiations he or she wants. It is better from the seller's viewpoint that the language be specific. If you have a strong point of view about the lease, i.e. the current lease amount is $13,000 a month and your offer is contingent upon getting rent to what you view as a reasonable level, i.e. $9000 a month, then write that into the contingency. The seller knows the landlord's limits, and he should have the opportunity to just reject the offer when it's a given the deal will fail on the lease terms. The next chapter, titled "The landlord is not your friend," goes into detail demonstrating why it is critical that a valid lease with required options be included in the contingencies.

Alcohol License

The purchase of the business should always be contingent upon the buyer being assured that no liabilities exist that would block the ability of the purchaser to serve alcohol at this location and that there's a method in place for the smooth transfer of the license so alcohol can flow before, during, and after the closing. This varies widely by state and should be understood carefully at the local level. The appendix of this book lists the alcohol licensing authorities for each state. You must contact them to understand your responsibilities for application and understand your ability to obtain a license. There are parties and attorneys that specialize in liquor licenses, known as liquor license facilitators, who assist you in this process for a fee.

Franchise Agreement

The purchase of the business should always be contingent upon reaching an acceptable agreement with the franchise whereby the franchise accepts the new franchisor and the franchisee accepts the terms of the franchise. You don't want to make an offer on a business that's paying 5% royalties and be obligated to purchase if the franchise decides to jack the rate in the new franchise agreement up to 15%.

Franchise Transfer Fees

As the buyer, make sure that the purchase price includes any other fees like franchise transfer fees. It's perfectly clear if you spell it out in the contingencies. For buyers, the purchase of the business should always be contingent upon the seller paying any applicable transfer and training fees required in order to transfer the business. Whether that will be accepted by the seller is subject to negotiation, but it should be requested up front.

Landlord Transfer Fees

The seller has often signed a lease that states he will have some fees if he transfers the lease. His obligation should not be the buyer's cost, so spell this out in the contingencies so there is no confusion. Some landlords will also charge the buyer an application fee. This is the cost associated with doing your credit check and handling the application and should be at the buyer's expense. Again, all these fees are open to interpretation and negotiation, which is why they should be spelled out in the contingencies so there is no confusion.

Other items may surface in the negotiation of the contract, but if these elements are all thoroughly understood and contractually detailed for both parties, you are well on your way to a successful closing. Now that you have the business under contract, it's time to learn what you do next. Continue to the next chapter, "You're Under Contract, Now What?"

Chapter Summary-Key Points

* Key negotiating strategies for buying a restaurant include:
    - Everyone needs to feel some "win"
    - Time is your enemy
    - Bad mouthing the restaurant doesn't improve your offer
    - Negotiations have a limited timeline
* Your offer can take three forms: verbal offer, letter of intent, and contract. The contract is the strongest version and offers the greatest protections for the buyer.
* There are many elements to the restaurant contract, which include:
    - Equipment list
    - Escrow agent and disposition of escrow funds
    - Binding agreement and due diligence dates
    - Inventory handling
    - Familiarization and training
    - Restrictive and non-compete covenants
    - Termination and default
    - Confidentiality of transaction
    - Notice
* Special stipulations should be written so that the contract is contingent upon reaching terms with third parties for:
    - Lease
    - Alcohol license
    - Franchise agreement
    - Transfer fees

You're Under Contract–Now What?

Buyers should understand that negotiating the deal and signing the contract is the easiest part of the transaction. After the contract is signed, the heavy lifting begins. This chapter will give you the tools you need to conduct your due diligence, confirm earnings, and make it to the closing table. Many of the worksheets and checklists from this chapter can be found in the appendix along with a short version of the checklist we'll cover in detail.

Due Diligence

A lot has been written in the industry about due diligence. The key question to ask yourself before you begin the process is "What are you trying to understand or confirm?" It's not uncommon for buyers to ask us for hundreds of pages of documents because they read an online article that says they should request it all. Then they have no clue how to analyze the business or even use the documents. Our firm requires that buyers acknowledge what they are provided with, and again, it's pretty common to find a buyer in a panic two days before closing asking for something that's been in his hands for ninety days. That demonstrates he's not really looking at the data. Buyers tie themselves into knots over this process and overrequest data until they have reams of paper and no idea what they're looking at.

Due diligence, approached from the standpoint of "What are you trying to confirm?" is actually a pretty straightforward and simple process. You essentially have four things to confirm in due diligence. You can do this yourself or have a third party do it. In many cases the attorney handles item four, confirmation of licensing and permits, as part of the closing.

1. Confirm sales
2. Confirm expenses, including add-backs
3. Inspect and confirm equipment condition that transfers
4. Confirm licensing and permits

That's it. Here are only some of the items buyers get caught up in requesting that they don't need to confirm anything relative to buying a restaurant. View these in terms of the question "What am I trying to confirm?" and it's easily apparent most don't make sense.

Receipts or Checks that Show Equipment is Owned Free and Clear

You don't need to confirm this since the closing attorney does a lien search before closings and ensures that everything transfers free and clear.

Wage Records and 941 Filings

Buyers that request 941 filings are trying to confirm whether employment taxes are paid, which is irrelevant to you and your new corporation. He may not have paid, but that's not your problem. You're buying assets only and not the seller's corporation, so you should have no liability for his unpaid taxes (consult your attorney and CPA). You will have a new tax identification number to file employment taxes against. If he owes unpaid taxes, there will generally be a lien filed on the business. The Internal Revenue Service tends to be pretty quick about those for employment taxes. If there's a lien, the closing attorney should uncover it and pay it out of the closing proceeds.

Statement of Cash Flows

You're trying to confirm the cash requirements of the business when you request a statement of cash flows. This is meaningless in a restaurant with add-backs unless you're going to go through and adjust every month of the statement of cash flows to add back the cash diverted for owner's benefit. The entire concept of add-backs means the benefit exists outside the cash flow to the business, as the owner derives benefits from increasing expenses and lowering cash. Most restaurants don't have these anyway.

Balance Sheet

Buyers that request balance sheets for businesses they are buying on cash flow don't understand what they are buying. They are trying to confirm that they aren't overpaying for assets when the assets have nothing to do with the purchase. The valuation is based on the return generated by the assets even if they are fully depreciated. If you're buying based on assets only, the balance sheet still doesn't come into play. You're trying to confirm the value of the assets, but you're buying them on a supremely discounted level from the amount carried on the balance sheet. If the seller opened a franchise and has $125,000 on the books in equipment and $200,000 in leasehold improvements, what meaning does that have to you if you're only paying $129,000 based on $35,000 cash flow?

Bank Statements and Check Copies

What you're trying to confirm with bank statements is sales matching. This is forensic accounting level effort that doesn't provide any more value than confirming sales through the method we're going to teach you. Since the sales don't neatly match by day and go into the bank as one nice number that matches the POS, or point of sale, report (credit card sales are often deposited in batches and may lag by twenty-four hours), you'll make yourself crazy trying to add up all the deposits and reconcile them back to a month.

Four-Step Method to Confirm Sales through Due Diligence

Due Diligence Step One—Confirming Sales

Sales are a critical item you do need to validate, and here's everything you need to confirm them. Start by requesting the following items for the prior twelve-month period. If you are buying a restaurant based on cash flow and you're comfortable with the multiple, there is no reason to do this for longer than twelve months. The last twelve are the ones used in pricing and reflect current trending. Request the following items:

- Profit and loss statement or P&L (monthly or, more commonly, annual for restaurants with sales under $1 million)
- Tax returns for the same period
- Copies of monthly sales tax filings for the same period
- POS (point of sale) system reports (monthly printout)

For most restaurants, the starting point to confirm sales is the POS (point of sale) system. This is the computerized system that will simultaneously handle the orders (input by the waitstaff), handle the form of payment (credit card processing always goes through the POS), and total the hour and day part (breakfast, lunch, and dinner) to compile results. It is a rare restaurant operation that does not operate with a point of sale system in this electronic age. For one thing, restaurants must meet compliance standards for transmitting credit card data. Gone are the old years of printing out all digits of a credit card on a receipt and required are government-mandated credit card controls.

The POS system is linked into telephone lines for credit card processing and is then almost always simply a straight feed to either the franchise or the accountant for upload to a P&L. Here's a sample of what the POS system captures and compiles for eventual breakdown on the P&L:

1. Sales
2. Food
3. Liquor
4. Beer
5. Wine
6. Other beverages
7. Cigarettes
8. Retail
9. Door
10. Game exchange
11. Comps
12. Food comps
13. Liquor comps
14. Total comps
15. Promotions/discounts
16. Voids
17. Over/short
18. Catering

Confirming the sales is a simple matter. All the POS transactions net to the total sales for the month. Here are the four steps to confirm sales:

> Step One:
> Compare total sales on the POS system for a monthly time period to the P&L for the monthly time period. If there is no monthly P&L available, use the annual numbers.
>
> Step Two:
> Compare the POS sales for the month to the monthly sales tax filing with the state. Do it for twelve months.
>
> Step Three:
> Add up the monthly sales tax filings and make sure the total is a match to the annual P&L.
>
> Step Four:
> Compare the annual P&L sales number to the income tax return sales line.

If sales match (within 1% to 3% or so for rounding, lagging of booking credit card receipts and nontaxable sales), congratulations, you're done! If they do not match or are off by substantial amounts, call a meeting with the seller and his CPA to understand why. Despite the multitude of advice you'll get about making sure the sales are real, this very simple method can easily confirm sales. Anyone good in Microsoft Excel or on a calculator can be done in about two hours. Legitimate reasons for why the sales tax and P&L will be out of balance (small amounts such as 1% to 3% or so) include:

1. Credit card sales lag in deposit and can create timing errors.
2. Sales tax filings are generally on the fifteenth for the month following the sales, so there will be a slight timing difference for the periods you review.

3. State sales tax is often not charged to certain nonprofit or tax-free entities, so if the restaurant does large catering orders for a government office or university, sales tax is not charged and collected.
4. Restaurants typically don't report and pay sales tax on cash shortages.

Here's a sample of a confirmed set of records; the blank form for this exercise is included in the appendix.

	POS SALES	SALES TAX FILING	P&L SALES	ANNUAL INCOME TAX	P&L ANNUAL
January	$49,215	$49,015	$49,015		
February	$51,712	$51,690	$51,690		
March	$61,911	$61,900	$61,900		
April	$55,110	$55,002	$55,001		
May	$57,212	$57,015	$57,015		
June	$59,425	$59,400	$59,400		
July	$61,110	$61,015	$61,015		
August	$56,510	$56,015	$56,015		
September	$59,725	$59,715	$59,715		
October	$61,400	$61,395	$61,395		
November	$61,212	$61,195	$61,195		
December	$63,015	$62,295	$62,295		
TOTAL	$697,557	$695,652	$695,652	$695,650	$695,652

In this example, POS sales are $1,905 higher than sales tax filings. That's pretty normal if you review the reasons listed above for why these would be slightly out of sync. Also, make sure you're looking at net sales in the POS system. If you compare gross sales (which include the sales tax amount) to net sales (net of sales tax paid), they will be higher every month.

In our example, the P&L sales by month vary only slightly from the sales tax filing and annual income tax, a function of rounding. This restaurant has annual sales of $695,652 proven beyond any reasonable doubt. Now, some readers are already saying to themselves that it can't be that easy. The answer is yes it can, as long as you are buying a business with verifiable books and records. If they don't have verifiable books and records, you are not buying a restaurant with cash flow; you're buying a fairy tale. Here are some other common questions:

What if they don't have a POS system?

Substitute the "Z" tape from their daily cash register reading and perform the same actions, checking it against the sales tax filings, P&Ls, and tax returns.

What if they don't have monthly P&Ls?

Use the annual P&L and make sure it matches annual sales tax filings and annual income tax filings.

What if they haven't filed monthly sales tax filings?

Don't buy the restaurant. You will not be able to get a liquor license in most states if they aren't filing and paying their sales tax. Walk away.

What if they haven't filed their income tax yet this year?

Use last year's for the same confirmation process so you can validate a full year. Then repeat the process for this year using only the P&Ls, monthly sales tax filings, and the POS system. If both years correlate roughly the same between the available data, you should be fine.

What if they can't locate their sales tax filings but say they have made them?

Go to the Department of Revenue Web site for almost any state and download a form they need to sign and notarize giving you permission to get these from the state. Go in person and expect to pay about fifteen cents a page for copies.

We have restaurant buyers that work themselves into a state of turmoil with statements like, "I need to be sure the numbers are real." Certain buyers sit in the parking lot of the restaurant and count cars or people going in and out and assign an average price. Then they say, "They can't be doing that volume; I only saw thirty people go in last night." Never mind that they were doing their count for a sports bar on a Tuesday night in the middle of the summer; they have now estimated in their mind what they believe to be a baseline of sales. If that is your method to confirm sales, you might want to consider another business because you are destined to never have enough proof in the numbers.

Consider the effort and cost a restaurant owner would have to go through to fake sales data and trick the confirmation process and you'll see it doesn't make financial sense. In order to increase sales $100,000 to outsmart the confirmation method you just learned, an operator would have to:

1. Enter fake sales tickets into a POS system that has a time stamp on every transaction.
2. Do this for twelve months.
3. Then he would have to pay sales tax (no small change at 6% to 9%) for the same period of time—monthly. Thus, faking $100,000 in sales (a pretty small sales number) would cost him in cold, hard cash $6000 to $9000 in sales tax.
4. He would then have to file an income tax return and again pay taxes on money he hasn't earned. Since every fake dollar of top line sales has no corresponding expense, he's creating an automatic dollar of profit. He is then paying either a corporate tax rate (15%) on the sales or a personal tax rate (30% or more). Again, this extra $100,000 in sales will then cost him another $15,000 to $30,000 in real, hard cash outlay dollars with no guarantee that he's going to get a penny more in the sale.

5. All this would net him an additional top line number of $100,000 and net income of $15,000 for which he would get 2.25 times earnings in the sales price (or $33,750) at a cost of $21,000 to $39,000 in additional taxes paid. Do the math yourself and see if it makes any sense.

Use the method described above to confirm sales and you'll have the real picture of sales at the restaurant. It's the most important variable to understand and, fortunately for you, the easiest to audit.

Due Diligence Step Two—Confirm Expenses and Add-backs

The next step is to confirm expenses and any add-backs. This is a very important step since it's not unusual to see a tax return or P&L with minimal income that is selling for a multiple comprised primarily of add-backs. The reason for this is the tax code of the United States. Owners use legal methods to shield income from taxes. That system puts a seller at odds with a buyer who's looking for nice, clean bottom line income. Total owner benefit or seller's discretionary earnings has to be recalculated or recast outside of those legal and allowable adjustments to get a clear picture of owner benefit. We're providing you with a simple worksheet that easily recalculates this using some key documents. Here's what you need:

- Profit and loss statement. You already have this from Due Diligence Step One.
- Tax return. You already have this from Due Diligence Step One.
- Receipts and checks for any itemized add-backs not readily apparent on the tax return—cell phone, owner's auto expense, extraordinary or one-time expenses.
- Copy of owner's salary W-2, K-1, or 1099 income statement reported to the IRS for the prior year.

This method recasts the P&L quickly and captures every owner add back to get to bottom line seller's discretionary earnings. We call this our Valuation Analysis Tool. A blank copy is included in the index. We'll walk through an example using the Valuation Analysis Tool to confirm the financial information and seller's discretionary earnings. Here are the key elements of the sample data:

1. Seller's discretionary earnings according to the selling broker are in excess of $118,000 and you have the restaurant under contract for $265,000.
2. Sales confirmed through Due Diligence Step One are $695,652.
3. The restaurant P&L does not include depreciation or amortization and shows net earnings for twelve months of $22,497.
4. Depreciation shown on the restaurant tax return is $14,055.
5. Amortization shown on the restaurant tax return is $6,000.
6. Interest on the restaurant tax return is $9,100, and interest reported on the P&L is $9,250.
7. Owner add-backs provided by the selling broker total $78,576 exclusive of depreciation, amortization, or interest. They include the owner's salary and payroll taxes, cell phone expense, travel, donations, auto expense, auto insurance, health insurance, and office supplies.
8. The owner states he hosted his youngest daughter's wedding reception in June and paid for the food and alcohol in a single invoice for $11,000.

Using the Valuation Analysis Tool, enter the amounts from the P&L or tax return into Column B. If there is no adjustment to the number, then Columns C and D remain blank and the number carries without change to Column E. If there is an adjustment, the amount of the adjustment is entered into Column C as a negative with a note in Column D stating the reason. Using the example data above, the sample Business Valuation Tool would be adjusted for the following items:

1. Cost of goods (COGS) would be reduced $11,000 for reception. Verify the receipt and payment against the date of the wedding and accept adjusting entry of -$11,000 to COGS.
2. Depreciation and amortization are adjusted to the numbers on the tax return, and Column E reflects adjusted expense amounts of zero.
3. Interest is adjusted to $9,100, the number reflected on the tax return, since in our example there's a discrepancy between the tax return and P&L. That means only $9,100 is adjusted out of the valuation, leaving $150 in Column E as an adjusted expense amount.
4. Auto expense is adjusted by $12,000 and confirmed by a copy of the checks and detail ledger for auto lease payments. The lease is for the owner's Lexus SUV that is not used for delivery and will not remain with the business.
5. Donations are adjusted down by $1500 and documented by a cancelled check made payable to the son's school.
6. Auto insurance is adjusted down by $1200 and documented by a copy of the auto policy showing the owner's Lexus SUV as the only vehicle.
7. Health insurance is adjusted down by $3000 and documented by a copy of the monthly billing at $250 a month that shows the owner as the only person covered.
8. Office expense is adjusted down by $1500 based on a receipt and check provided by the seller showing the purchase of a laptop. He states this was for his son's use at college, and you check to ensure it's not listed on the equipment list transferring in the assets.

9. Owner's salary confirmed by a W-2 is adjusted down by $31,200. A second W-2 showing income to his wife of $20,000 is also adjusted. The wife does not show up on the schedule or work in the business.
10. Payroll tax withholding in the amount of $4,580 is adjusted down based on the W-2 for $51,200 for the owner and his wife.
11. Telephone expense for $1496 is adjusted down based on a copy of the monthly cell phone bill showing that the restaurant pays for a family plan including the owner, his wife, daughter, and son's phone.
12. Travel and entertainment is adjusted down $1,500 based on receipts provided showing this is the owner's annual vacation to Vegas with his wife and no company business is conducted on the trip.
13. The total adjustments to COGS are $11,000, resulting in a revised gross profit of $419,262. The expense adjustments total to $107,731. The total seller's discretionary earnings or owner benefit is now proved out at $121,173, slightly higher than the broker's estimate. You have the business under contract for $265,000, meaning you are purchasing for 2.19 times earnings, a respectable multiple.

Valuation Analysis Tool – Sample Restaurant Data

A	B	C	D	E
Line Item	**Amount**	**Adjust +/-**	**Adjustment Reason**	**Adjust Expense Amount**
Gross Sales	$ 695,652			$ 695,652
Cost of Goods	$ 287,390	$ (11,000)	Daughter Wedding	$ 276,390
Gross Profit	$ 408,262			$ 419,262

Expenses

Accounting	$ 1,650			$ 1,650
Advertising	$ 17,900			$ 17,900
Amortization	$ 6,000	$ (6,000)	Usual/Customary	$ -
Auto Expense	$ 12,000	$ (12,000)	Personal Use	$ -
Bank Charges	$ 11,500	$ -		$ 11,500
Depreciation	$ 14,055	$ (14,055)	Usual/Customary	$ -
Donations	$ 1,500	$ (1,500)	Usual/Customary	$ -
Insurance	$ 6,825			$ 6,825
Insurance Auto	$ 1,200	$ (1,200)	Personal Use	$ 2,400
Ins. Health	$ 3,000	$ (3,000)	Personal Use	$ -
Interest	$ 9,250	$ (9,100)	Usual/Customary	$ 150
Maintenance	$ 6,700			$ 6,700
Office Supplies	$ 2,350	$ (1,500)	Owner Personal	$ 850
Owner's Salary	$ 31,800	$ (31,800)	Owner W-2	$ -
Rent Facility	$ 55,600			$ 55,600
Repairs	$ 8,165			$ 8,165
Salaries	$ 133,629	$ (20,000)	Wife W-2 Income	$ 113,629
Supplies	$ 6,000			$ 6,000
Tax	$ 6,500			$ 6,500
Tax Payroll	$ 22,000	$ (4,580)	Owner % PR Tax	$ 17,420
Telephone	$ 3,496	$ (1,496)	Owner Cell	$ 2,000
Travel/Entertainment	$ 1,500	$ (1,500)	Owner Vacation	$ -
Utilities	$ 42,000			$ 42,000
Water	$ 1,200			$ 1,200
Total Expense	**$ 405,820**	**$ (107,731)**	**Total Adjusted**	**$ 298,089**

NET INCOME	**$ 2,442**		**Owner Benefit**	**$ 121,173**

That's it. You're now done with expense and add back due diligence. Once again, some readers are already saying to themselves, *It can't be that easy.* The answer is yes it can, as long as you are buying a business with verifiable books and records. If they don't have verifiable books and records, you are not buying a restaurant with cash flow; you're attempting to buy something unknown that can't be proven. Here are some other common questions:

What if they don't have receipts for an add back?

Then the expense doesn't count. Every item with an add back should be substantiated.

What if the P&L doesn't show any sales or income for lottery sales but they claim income of $6000 a year?

Lottery sales in most states don't book directly into a P&L. These are sales outside of food and alcohol that don't ever hit the POS system. The lottery account is generally a sweep account where the state leaves behind commissions to the seller and sweeps the lottery earnings out. Request the bank statements for this account, and it's a simple twelve-month view to confirm.

What if the P&L doesn't show the cigarette sales and game income but every other line ties out?

If it doesn't factor into the pricing, it doesn't matter what the sales and earnings are. If these sales are calculated into the earnings, you should be able to get sales receipts to prove the data, or it doesn't count.

What if both the owner and his wife work in the business every day but I'm buying on my own?

Don't add back both salaries. If there's only one of you, that salary will need to be paid out to someone to help you do the work she was doing.

What if I'm not going to work in the business? I'm going to be absentee.

Don't buy the restaurant. You're probably setting yourself up for failure. If you know that but want to do it anyway, then don't add back any owner salary. You'll have to pay someone to do the work you won't be doing.

What if they haven't filed their income tax yet this year?

Use last year's tax return and P&L to this year's P&L to be sure expenses are trending the same way. Make sure you have receipts or checks for all items being added back. If both years correlate roughly the same between the available data and the business appears stable, base your offer on the P&L data.

What if they haven't paid certain expenses like franchise fees?

Make sure every expense you anticipate is listed on the P&L. You must increase expenses to reflect anything that was unpaid in order to get a true picture of the expenses. If their royalties should have been $18,000 but they only expensed $9,000, then increase expense by $9,000 and decrease owner benefit by $9,000.

What if there's no rent on the P&L?

If someone doesn't pay rent, you have to adjust this to be increasing expenses and decreasing earnings. Occasionally restaurant operators will own their building outright and not pay themselves rent. This is a problem since it dramatically changes the value of the restaurant when you layer on 8% to 10% expense for the rent to be carried by the new owner.

This is an actual story from our experiences; only the names have been changed.

The owners of Beachside Bar bought their oceanfront bar and grill in 1972. Nearly forty years went by, and they were ready to sell the restaurant but wanted to keep the real estate since it was paid off and now quite valuable. We requested P&L data, and the earnings on the books were well over $150,000, which meant they were looking at a sales price of $375,000 or so. The only catch was that they didn't pay themselves any rent on the business. We called and said, "Where's the rent?" The answer was, "We don't pay any." Meanwhile, they wanted a new owner to pay $6000 a month rent, comparable for their location. It took a while to explain to them that this would increase costs to a new owner by $72,000, which then took the buyer's potential earnings down to $78,000. At $78,000 in earnings, the bar was worth less than $200,000. Their choice was to sell with the real estate or pay themselves rent on the books for a year so they could prove six-figure earnings with a rent payment. Ultimately, they decided to sell the property along with the business.

What about comps as an add back item?

Comps (short for compensations) occur on every restaurant owner's P&L at an average level of approximately 2% of sales. These show up on the POS system when they are rung through for goods and services provided without payment. They usually don't show up when a cash register is used since they are never rung or get voided.

These transactions occur for several reasons. Someone will have a bad experience, and the owner will comp the table. The owner's son will entertain his baseball team, and the owner will comp the event. Some bars give the bartenders a set comp amount per night ($25 or so) for their discretionary use. Some restaurants feed coupons and discounts into this line as well, so make sure you understand what's being rung this way in the POS system.

When comps are excessive, i.e. 7% of sales, and there are multiple owners taking a payout on the business by eating and drinking for free, then some level (we estimate 50%) should be added back. It is not uncommon to see sports bars operating in the red with lots of small partners who all come in each weekend to eat and drink. While that can seem like a small number per night, it adds up and can often mean the difference between operating in the red versus operating in the black.

In excessive instances, we reasonably and necessarily add back approximately 50% of comps. The important thing to remember here is that some level of comps is to be expected. Never add back 100% of comps.

The other way to think of it is to apply the same thought process as all other add-backs. If the expense for comps goes away when the owner goes away, some level should be added back to establish owner benefit. Confirm the comps through the POS system reports during due diligence to validate the add back.

This is an actual story from our experiences; only the names have been changed.

> Taco Loco was a sports bar with a mix of partners that owned small pieces along with the sons of some partners that worked in the business. They were not making much money, and they asked us to place a value on the business. We got their P&L, POS reports, tax returns, and lease and went to work. It was pretty easy to see the issue right off the bat. Two partners were getting paychecks but not working in the store, driving labor costs up. Every partner—and there were eight of them—was eating and drinking at the place to a rate of 7.4% comps as a percent-to-sales.
>
> The good news is that they were tracked on the POS system by partner name. The bad news was that only 2% were legitimate customer comps for service. The remaining 5.4% were food and drink being eaten by the partners without paying. Since top line sales were $1.5 million, this equated to an incredible $81,000 in comps.
>
> In recasting the P&L to perform the valuation, we added back one half the comps in the interest of being very conservative. When we presented to the partner, they were shocked to see how much they were costing each other in earnings. Since all owners would be eliminated by a sale, we added back half the number. Remember, if the expense goes away when the owners go away, add it back. As a rule of thumb, we add back half to be very conservative.

What if the expenses are out of control on this P&L? They are overpaying for everything.

If you validate P&L expenses through the preceding method and match it to the tax return only to find they are dramatically overspending on every line item, then the only thing to do is move up closing. Remember, the point of due diligence is only to confirm the current earnings. If the restaurant is appropriately valued based on cash flow from the current operation, then how poorly they manage hasn't factored into the pricing. You can buy it, fix expenses, and enjoy your bargain.

The last step is to run the common ratios against the P&L data and make sure it looks in line with expected parameters. Going back to the original example, we find the following results: Labor costs are 26.94%. Combine all salaries, including owner's salaries plus payroll taxes, into a labor cost ratio. These fall within expected ranges. Gross margin is 60.27%, slightly on the high side of normal. Food costs are 39.73%, slightly high, which indicates some work to be done in this area.

That's it. Your second phase of due diligence is complete. If your estimate varies significantly from the original stated earnings, start finding out why, but if it reveals opportunity, you're done. You can ask for forty other documents, but the financial proof of owner benefit is accomplished with the ones above.

Due Diligence Step Three—Conduct Your Equipment Inspection

If you don't know someone in the restaurant business focused on restaurant equipment service, ask your broker to recommend someone. If the inspector doesn't handle HVAC, bring a separate party in to handle this inspection. Make sure he pays particular attention to the expensive items for repair, like the hot water heaters, refrigeration units, HVAC, hood system, and grease trap. Ideally an inspector should be able to provide you with a complete report of the repairs needed as well as the cost to repair. This is necessary to negotiate with the seller on repairs. Most contracts state the equipment will be operating at the time of closing. If your inspector wants every item steam cleaned and made pretty before closing, it's not unusual for the seller to have you take a hike. It's only on reality TV shows like *Top Chef* that most kitchen equipment looks beautiful and shiny on every visit. Most commercial kitchens feature heavy duty machinery that will last for years of service but might look slightly worse for the wear. Making sure everything listed on the assets that transfer list is in working order is the key issue.

Due Diligence Step Four–Confirm Licensing

Check online for liquor licensing and look at the business license and health inspection hanging inside the business to confirm the license status.

That's it. With those four steps, your due diligence is complete. Despite the advice you receive on how to perform due diligence from your attorney, your wife, what you read online, and your friends, these four steps will confirm sales and earnings on the restaurant you are buying as long as it has books and records available for review.

Closing Checklist

With due diligence out of the way, here's a checklist of everything else you're going to need to do to keep moving down the path to closing. These are in order of priority, with the most time sensitive items listed first.

Contact a Closing Attorney

You will need an attorney to perform the closing, review the lease, conduct the lien search, and make sure that the title passes into your hands. If you haven't already identified that resource, do it quickly. Remember, this should be someone well versed in business asset sale closings, not your aunt Mary, the wills and estate attorney who will do it for free. The protections afforded at closing (lien search, bill of sale, et cetera) are primarily for the benefit of the buyer. Generally, attorney fees for closing are at the buyer's expense unless negotiated otherwise within the terms of the contract since he is the one that benefits. We have had buyers require the closing costs to be paid by the seller and then allow the seller to pick the attorney. This is a very bad idea. You want to choose your own attorney and have it clear that he works in your interest. Closing costs in general are very little compared to the risk for not having an appropriate transfer.

Expect to pay between $1500 and $2500 for a basic closing, depending on where you're buying a restaurant. Closing costs can vary widely by region. The most important issue is to get an all-in, or bundled, cost for closing rather than paying by the hour. Restaurant closings can end up with all sorts of unexpected issues that are worked on by the attorney. You don't want to be shocked by an attorney bill at closing for several thousand more than you budgeted.

If you need help finding an attorney, ask for three referrals from your broker. You can also check the affiliates online at the state business brokerage organizations (see list in the appendix) or ask friends that have experienced business closings. Interview the attorney, ask questions, confirm fees, and make a decision quickly.

Prepare the Landlord Package

This is the most important item after selecting your attorney. The specifics of this step are laid out in the chapter titled "The landlord is not your friend." The landlord can be a major holdup in getting the deal to closing on time. Your broker should be able to give you guidance on the landlord package, but expect for a large firm to require most of the following.

- Personal financial statement or corporate financial statement if secured corporately
- Two years of personal and corporate tax returns

- Complete lease application and/ or consent to credit check
- Background and experience on the principals (if not included in the business plan)
- Business plan that details your concept
- Menu

Decide on Company Structure

You'll need to form your corporation, LLC, or partnership in advance of closing. Consult your attorney and your accountant for advice on this step to understand the benefits of each structure.

Process Your Financing Package

If you are obtaining financing for any portion of the purchase, stay on top of the loan officer to keep the deal moving forward. You'll need to provide a loan commitment letter to your broker. You'll also need to funnel the list of requested items from the bank to your broker or put him directly in touch with the bank. This is probably a better solution, as the delay of two days between the time you hear from the bank that they need last year's 1099s and the time you communicate it to the broker (two days later) and he gets it from the seller (two days later) can result in numerous delays. Expect several months before you can close on the loan no matter what you are led to believe by the bank.

Transfer Funds to the Closing Attorney

All attorneys request wire transfers in lieu of checks for most closings. Your broker should provide you with the closing attorney's wiring information or you need to request it from the attorney so funds are in place to close the deal.

Schedule Inventory

Virtually all restaurants are sold with either a set amount of inventory on hand or with the provision for the sale to be plus inventory at the lower of cost or book value, meaning the seller cannot mark up his product but must sell it to you at his original cost. An inventory has to be conducted, and for obvious purposes, this generally takes place within twelve hours of closing. Since the inventory amount is in addition to the sales price, make sure you have a rough estimate so you can wire the additional funds to the closing attorney to cover inventory or pick up a certified check for this amount; it's usually small relative to the purchase price.

Transfer Utilities

The broker should make sure that the seller provides the buyer with a list of utilities and the account number. The buyer needs to contact them and arrange for service to transfer into his name. There's only one problem with this. The utility companies will not transfer service out of the seller's name until they have been contacted, so this has to be coordinated between the buyer and seller. We typically tell the seller to make a list of all utilities and account numbers and call to disconnect service for the day after closing. Then he or she gives the list to the buyer, who calls to transfer service into his name the day of closing. This important step keeps someone at the power company from ever terminating service to the building because the last thing you want is to try to cook your first meals without electricity or lose the phone number for a pizza place that does 50% deliveries.

Set up Credit Card Processing

Find out the current credit card provider and understand their rates. Then begin shopping for a company to handle your credit card processing. You need to arrange for this to begin as soon as closing is over. Generally speaking, the day of closing belongs to the buyer. That means your credit card receipts need to feed into your account on the day of closing. Remember, a large percentage of sales are always settled through credit card. No matter how many times we warn people about this, we still field calls from buyers saying the money is still going into the seller's account after closing. Usually the seller and buyer can work this out, but it's the buyer's responsibility to be sure he's taking possession of the credit card receipts on the day of closing. It may be simple enough to keep the existing credit card processor for the short term and just change the bank account so it's going into your account and not to the seller's account. Talk to your bank or ask your broker for recommendations for this service. You can also call the POS provider, as he or she typically bundles this service.

Set up your Bank Account

You're going to need to cash a check for petty cash to make change for the POS or register system. The sellers own the funds in the drawer, and you need to be able to operate. Buyers often forget this, and it can be a surprise to pull together several hundred dollars in change. You can also simply count the seller's till and add it to the closing so you don't have to physically go to the bank. You're also going to have suppliers who will need payment when they make deliveries. Get the bank account set up.

Get an Insurance Binder in Place

Contact your insurance agent and make sure you have a binder securing coverage before closing. If you don't have someone for commercial coverage, once again, ask your broker; he'll have some recommendations for you.

Set up a Training Schedule

The sales contract should specify training in a general way. Make sure the there's a definitive schedule in place post-closing.

Coordinate with the Seller to Advise the Staff

If everyone's done their job, the closing should be a complete surprise to the staff. Coordinate who will say what and whether you're pulling people in to advise them about the change in ownership.

Liquor License Filing

If you are getting a liquor license, work with your attorney or facilitator on all the paperwork, including fingerprinting, attending the alcohol training class, and background check, so the process is moving forward.

Review the Lease

Both the lease and lease assignment should be carefully read so there are no surprises. The lease is never executed until closing. The last thing a buyer wants is to have a lease in full force and effect and not own a business or own the title to a business but have no legal right to operate under a lease. The execution of the lease document as part of closing makes sure this doesn't happen.

Franchise Only Items

A franchise will have its own set of checklist documents to handle prior to closing. This will include the initial meeting, receipt of FDD, franchise transfer, and training. The broker is typically not a part of this process. You'll need to work with the franchise personally to undergo their approval process. Here are some key elements that must be completed:

Sign Receipt of the Franchise Disclosure Document

Federal law dictates the cooling off period on this, which is a minimum number of business days after signature when you cannot have any contact with the franchise.

Review the Franchise Agreement

Make sure you're comfortable with the language. It's not uncommon for the agreement to span more than 150 pages. You're signing up for a big commitment. Sit down and read it carefully before accepting the terms. It is now legal for the franchise to provide this electronically, but if you can't carefully read a large electronic document, send it to an office supply store and get it printed out. You're going to live with this document for ten years. Make sure you understand your rights.

Schedule Franchise Training

Every franchise has different requirements. We've encountered some that refuse to allow the franchise to transfer until you've trained and others that won't let you train until the closing has occurred. The franchise will tell you their process and provide you with dates. Most franchises hold training classes one week of the month, and if you miss that window, you'll end up pushing off a closing, so secure this timing early.

Sign a New Franchise Agreement

The new franchise agreement or franchise transfer of an existing franchise agreement occurs at closing. Your attorney should be sure you have this as a condition of closing. Just like the lease, you don't want to own a business with no legal claim to continue operating as Mary's Burger Franchise. That's the situation you'll find yourself in if you don't insist on the document at the closing table.

Closing

The closing is the point at which your attorney becomes worth his weight in gold. He will be making sure all documents are in hand that allow you to operate and protect your interests. He will make sure that everything's executed so that you simultaneously get the authority to operate a franchise, transfer a business, and sign a lease. He will produce the closing documents, secure the seller's signature on the representations and warranty, and make sure you don't miss an alcohol pour. He will handle the escrow and transfer of money. Don't sign anything outside the knowledge of your attorney before the closing occurs. The closing is the finite place in time when ownership transfers and dollars change hands.

This is an actual story from our experiences; only the names have been changed.

> We wrote a contract with a franchise contingency for franchise approval and a contingency that the seller paid the franchise transfer fee to the new owner. The transfer fee was $17,500. The buyer met with the franchise and received approval, along with a list of requirements before training. The franchise requirements stated that no training would occur until the franchise transfer fee was paid. The franchise copied us on notice to both the buyer and seller.
>
> Weeks went by, and the franchise scheduled the buyer training. While at training, he signed the franchise agreement but didn't advise his attorney. At closing, we asked where the franchise agreement was but were assured by the buyer that it was already handled. The attorney said he would get the fully executed copy and moved on. The franchise transfer was not part of the closing statement.
>
> A week later, the buyer called in a panic. The franchise just realized they never received money for the franchise transfer fee and were demanding it from the buyer. He had assumed the seller paid it since the franchise scheduled the training. We told the buyer that since the contract and franchise com-

munications stated it was the responsibility of the seller, he should have no issue. After all, he had a valid franchise agreement and documentation that the fee was owed by the seller. That's when he said, "I signed the franchise agreement, but I never got a copy back signed by the franchise." At that point we told him to get to his attorney because without a franchise agreement in place, the franchise might hold him up to get the money from the most ready source—him.

The preceding items covered what the buyer should do in preparation for closing. You're excited and have a whole list of things that you're dying to get started on, but they must wait until the closing takes place. Here are a few tips on what not to do:

Do not tell friends, family, suppliers, vendors, or anyone that you're buying the business. You are still bound by the terms of the confidentiality agreement, and many things can go wrong before closing. Do not make a fixture of yourself at the seller's restaurant so that it becomes obvious to the staff or employees that you're more than a loyal customer. Lastly, do not approach vendors. Food and alcohol vendors know everyone in the business. You cannot negotiate pricing or start working on menus until you own the restaurant.

Chapter Summary-Key Points

* Much has been written about due diligence, but it all comes down to four key elements: 1) confirm sales, 2) confirm expenses, including add-backs, 3) inspect equipment, 4) confirm licensing and permits.
* The information you need to confirm sales is straightforward: 1) profit and loss statements, 2) tax returns, 3) monthly sales tax filings, 4) POS (point of sale) system reports.
* The information you need to confirm expenses is straightforward: 1) receipts and checks for itemized add-backs, 2) copy of owner's W-2, K-1, or 1099, and the items you already have (P&L and tax returns).

The Landlord is Not Your Friend

If there's one lesson every would-be restaurant owner should take away from this book, it's this one: *the landlord is not your friend.* He's not even your casual acquaintance. He is, in fact, the opposite, someone that most directly works against your interest.

One of the first steps after the contract is accepted is to contact the landlord. This never happens until after the contract is signed and the seller has given notice the landlord. Buyers that circumvent the process and get to the landlord early in the game can find themselves on the receiving end of an attorney's letter advising that they have breached the terms of the confidentiality agreement and interfered in the seller's business. The seller and the landlord have a contract with one another. Until the business is under contract and notice has been given to the landlord, you are not a party to that lease contract and have no standing to enter into discussions about the lease.

Once you're under contract, however, the sale requires landlord approval and either an assignment of the current lease or a new lease. That's why every broker should include a lease contingency to the asset purchase agreement. Lease negotiations typically begin in the due diligence phase but may continue well beyond due diligence. It's not uncommon for every element of the contract to be met (due diligence, franchise approval, inspections, and more) with the final lease approval still pending until just before closing.

There are multiple forms that the new lease understanding between the landlord and the buyer can take. It's important to understand the difference.

Lease Assignment without Change

Some leases—generally older ones written by small landlords that control only a few units versus national landlords with hundreds of properties—will have simple lease assignment language. This language allows the lease to be assigned in its current state to a new restaurant operator in the same location. The new buyer must still be credit qualified, but this language is a huge benefit for the buyer if the lease terms are favorable. It eliminates uncertainty about what the rent and lease terms will be. It also retains any favorable language in the lease for any kind of term that already exists. It's often quickly provided and keeps a closing on schedule. On the flip side, if there are unfavorable terms or language that binds a buyer in a way he's not comfortable with, it's best to request a new lease rather than accepting the existing terms. In general, leases with simple assignment language are used by smaller local landlords, and the lease and terms tend to be simpler, less binding, and thus more valuable for the buyer.

Lease Assignment with Changes

This is the most common form of lease assignment with a seller and buyer. This gives the landlord the opportunity to assign the lease to the buyer but also renegotiate any terms and insert new language. In a down real estate market with high commercial vacancies, this can be a benefit. Buyers can maintain that business conditions have changed since the initial lease and rent should be reduced. In an up-trending real estate market with low commercial vacancies, landlords can take the opportunity to renegotiate the lease terms unless the original language precludes this.

Landlord Requirements

The landlord has specific requirements before he will consider the transfer, assignment, or issue of a new lease. Careful preparation of this package up front will eliminate surprises and move you more quickly into negotiations on the space. It's important to remember that the landlord will generally not meet with a prospective tenant and enter into negotiations until he has performed initial credit checks and received a full information package on the tenant.

A piecemeal submission or something lacking from the package signals a lack of experience on either the broker or the buyer's part, and landlords will not negotiate until they have everything. Generally speaking, the more properties a landlord controls, the more demanding he can be in the qualification process for a new tenant. You can generally look online on the landlord's Web site and find pdf versions of his requirements, or your broker should be providing this within hours of a contract. It's sometimes possible with local, smaller landlords to simply submit a personal financial statement and a menu. However, most are sophisticated enough in their tenant prequalification to require a complete package. Here's a full list of what is commonly requested, in order of importance:

1. *Personal financial statement.* Brush off the financial statement you prepared in an earlier chapter and make sure the information is current. It is not uncommon for landlords to ask for account statements to verify any cash or cash equivalent holdings (brokerage accounts, certificates of deposit, et cetera) on the financial statement. Do not attempt to fudge this information.
2. *Consent to credit check.* The landlord will pull credit, and he will need your social security number and consent to pull this.

3. *Credit application.* Some landlords require a full application in addition to the two items above, but it repeats most of the information on your personal financial statement or the consent to credit check.
4. *Two years of tax returns.* This is not negotiable for most national landlords (smaller, local ones are always exceptions). Thcy want to see sufficient income and liquidity between the tax returns and financial statement to give them assets to attach if you don't pay the rent.
5. *Menu.* Every landlord wants a menu. This is especially important if you're doing a concept change. It's the starting point for the business. It also allows the landlord to be sure the concept does not invalidate any lease agreements already in place for their center. It's common for a large grocery store anchor to have language in the lease that blocks the lease of other space to a bakery. Though it's becoming less common, many leases have restrictive covenants that protect other types of existing businesses; that is, no second Italian restaurant or no other sports bar can be leased.
6. *Background and experience.* Our process always includes a brief background and experience worksheet on the buyer (sample in the appendix). This reassures the landlord that he's looking at someone that knows the industry and typically just recaps the buyer's experience and the restaurants where he or she worked.
7. *Business plan.* Some of the national landlords do require a business plan. Since a business plan is a topic that expands into full books on its own and can range from five to five hundred pages, we'll cover the complete basics of a business plan in a separate chapter.

Some buyers find the landlord qualification process to be incredibly intrusive and don't want to provide this much information. Unfortunately, there is no way around it. The lease is a financial commitment that the landlord is seeking to secure. One of the few alternatives is to submit the information for a corporation instead of personally. That requires that you have an operating corporation with established credit. For most, this isn't a viable alternative since buyers are setting up new corporations for the purchase that don't have any corporate financial history like financial statements, two years of tax returns, or lines of credit. Even if you do, the landlord still wants personal financial information since, in most cases, he'll require that you secure the lease personally or sign a personal guarantee.

Once the package is in hand, the landlord will begin lease negotiations. Generally speaking, the stronger your financial picture, the more leverage you have in the deal. If your net worth doesn't exceed $50,000, you'll have little room to negotiate, as the landlord sees his risk as greater. He won't want to give you three months of rent since he's not sure you'll last more than four. In the event that your financial picture is weak, don't worry. Landlords are securing against risk. There are multiple ways to overcome either a credit deficiency or lack of liquidity. These can include any or all of the following:

1. *Extra months of deposit.* A well-secured buyer may need only one month of deposit. One that has less credit can offer up as many as five months of deposit with the lease stating that one month is returned each year or credited against rent for every year the tenant is current on the lease.
2. *Second guarantor on the lease.* It's not uncommon to see someone outside the buyer come on to the lease as a guarantor. This can be anyone ranging from a family member to a silent business partner with sufficient assets. You should understand that any guarantor is essentially cosigning a loan on your behalf. If you go down, the landlord will attempt to recover rent and the lease guarantee from this individual. It's not something to pledge or ask for lightly.

3. *Secure an irrevocable letter of credit.* Sometimes buyers have assets that can be provided to the bank as collateral for what's called a secure line of credit. This is like a loan with the item in question held as collateral drawn on in the event of a default by the tenant. An example might be the fifty acres of land your grandfather left you. You don't intend to sell it, so you pledge it to the bank as collateral on the letter of credit. The letter of credit is, in turn, pledged to the landlord in the event of default. The downside here is that if you default on rent and the landlord draws on the letter of credit, any asset attached to it then becomes subject to foreclosure. Be careful before you bet the farm. Our recommendation is to position this as a diminishing letter of credit with a certain percentage pulled back each year for every year of payment on time, such as 20% a year until after year five the instrument is withdrawn. After five years of on-time payments, the landlord's risk is minimal.

Strategies to overcome credit deficiencies are as varied as the individuals seeking leases. If there's a willingness between a buyer and a landlord to get to terms, the credit issues can be resolved. A good broker should be able to suggest strategies to overcome most issues.

Lease Terms and Options

For most landlords, a usual lease is a five-year term (the *initial* term) with negotiated options that must be exercised prior to the end of the first term (often six months in advance). The number of five-year options can vary, but it's pretty typical to see an initial lease with a five-year term plus two five-year options. That's a total of fifteen years. At the option exercise date, the tenant typically has the right to walk with no further obligation, but every lease is different and you should carefully review your own language. The important thing to remember is that the option to renew or not renew generally requires that you give notice up to six months before the option date.

It is rare that the landlord will transfer or assign the existing restaurant lease, meaning you may get the exact same terms. In some cases you don't want this, since the initial term may be expiring in only two years and you want additional options. That's why the contingency language in an asset purchase agreement must spell out your expectation for the lease.

If the new terms vary significantly from the existing operator, the metrics for the deal will also change. If you are looking at a restaurant with a $9,000 monthly lease payment and the new rent will be $11,500, you just lost $30,000 in earnings, and the business is now devalued by whatever multiple you're paying for it (2.25 times earnings now reduced by $30,000 results in a value reduction of -$67,500).

If the business is appropriately priced and you make an offer contingent on a rent reduction of $3,000 a month or you walk, this isn't fair to the seller. The business is already priced with the rent factored into the multiple for pricing purposes. If your offer is contingent on rent being reduced by $18,000 a month (again, based on a 2.25 multiple), then what you're saying is "I'll buy this business if I can steal it for $40,500 under market value" (rent reduction of $18,000 times 2.25 is an increase in value of $40,500 for the drop in expense).

Buyers often request rent abatement or half rent for a period of time when they are buying a restaurant. This strategy only works if you can demonstrate to the landlord that you will be making improvements to his center that will provide benefit to him. If you plan to make improvements, it's best to outline those; bring them to the negotiations and show the landlord you're investing in his property and you need some time to make the changes before paying full rent. Where possible, include estimates of your investment that are larger than the rent concession you're requesting. Getting the hood steam cleaned is basic maintenance, and the landlord doesn't care. Enclosing the patio adds value to his property. Remember, simply buying the restaurant isn't a good enough reason for him to give you rent concessions. From his perspective, if he doesn't approve the transfer, he's in the same position. The guy paying the rent is on the hook to keep paying the rent or he has recourse against him. Why would he disadvantage himself by giving half rent or free rent? If he does nothing, he gets full rent. You're going to have to demonstrate two things: an investment that makes his property more valuable and a time frame for renovations to sell him on a rent reduction strategy.

There are some exceptions for when you can expect to command and receive rent concessions. A landlord amortizes any free rent over the life of a lease. In the case of a new lease, he has room to offer concessions to a buyer. There are three examples of this. The first is new space that's currently unoccupied. The landlord isn't receiving rent now. He's writing a new lease term and can amortize concessions over the life of a new lease. The second is closed restaurant space that is currently unoccupied for the same reason. He's writing a new lease. The last opportunity is when you're buying from restaurant tenants at the end of their lease. If you are acquiring a restaurant that has only a few months left on the lease, then rent concessions are open for negotiation even without investment in the property. The landlord would be offering concession to write a new lease for a tenant anyway.

Once you've qualified financially, met with the landlord, and come to terms on the rent, it's time to begin negotiating the details of the lease. Here's what you need to think about whether you're working through an assignment with changes or a new lease.

Important Business Strategies That Should Be Part of Your Lease Negotiations

Exit Strategies

The most common error in the business terms of a lease is failure to plan for an exit strategy. No one enters business expecting to fail, but it happens. Partners get sick or walk out of partnerships. Couples divorce, or liquor licenses get pulled. On the flip side, businesses sell. You get an offer you can't refuse. There are countless reasons why a business owner will need to get out of the lease. That's why we want you to have an exit strategy going in. Often, exit clause language isn't inserted unless you have a broker on your side making recommendations for business terms. In fact, the landlord (who is not your friend) is putting language in that would countermand most of these recommendations. Here are the key elements to focus on for when you get in—before you sign—so you can get out.

LEASE TRANSFERABILITY

Most leases contain language that says "the transfer of this lease shall not be unreasonably withheld." This standard language is far too broad. The more specific the language, the more you benefit in the exchange. The broader the language, the more loopholes a landlord has to block the next tenant.

Get your attorney to work specific language into the lease that compels transfer if they are presented with a financially qualified tenant or a tenant with a net worth that exceeds that of the current tenant, you.

Lease transfer is the single most contentious issue in the sale of a business and kills more deals than anything else. Even though you're on the buying side now, you may want to sell in the future. You don't want to get your business sold at some point down the road only to find the transfer stopped by the landlord. Your only power in this negotiation is at the outset of the lease.

EXPERIENCE CLAUSES

You may enter into a lease with a landlord as a multi-unit operator with lots of experience, but always think in terms of selling the store at a later date. Plenty of successful individuals enter the restaurant industry without experience, but that doesn't preclude their eventual success. Landlords often will try to sneak language into the lease that requires restaurant experience, even for franchise operators. Even if the language doesn't apply to you, strike it early, or it will cause problems when you're ready to sell. If you can't get rid of it altogether, get some language that excludes franchises since they have standard practices and training built to buttress lack of experience.

This is an actual story from our experiences; only the names have been changed.

> This sports bar franchise was a business that needed to sell. The owner was working with his father in the family business, and absentee leadership was driving the business into the ground. A very well financially qualified buyer made an offer that was accepted. The franchise approved the buyer, and everything proceeded smoothly until the landlord became involved. The language of the lease signed by the seller required that the buyer have restaurant experience.
>
> The buyer had a much stronger personal net worth than the seller. He had operated a multi-unit car operation for the past two decades, so he had more management experience, more cash, and was purchasing a franchise operation that required a month's training. The landlord didn't care and fully used the language of the lease to blackmail the seller and his father into leaving a $100,000 irrevocable letter of credit with the landlord for a period of one year in order to transfer the business. This was after months of negotiations that almost killed the deal and discussions with attorneys who all agreed that the definition of experience was broad but legal under the lease signed by the seller originally.

It was legal—but reprehensible—that the landlord would do this to both the buyer and seller. Remember, the landlord is not your friend. A year later, the irrevocable letter of credit was refunded to the seller when the "inexperienced" operator that was on-site turned out to be a huge performer that grew sales and profits by double digits in the first year. He was never late a single day on a lease payment, but the seller's father had $100,000 in equity tied to his success for a year.

TRANSFER CHARGE CLAUSE

Determine up front what the amount of the transfer charge will be and do not agree to "reasonable attorney fees" or any other such loose language. If at any point in the future you sell the business and the lease is transferred, this is your expense. Cap it, identify it, know what it is, and make sure it's minimal, such as "$1000 fee to transfer a lease shall be the maximum allowable charge." Remember, the advice in the previous chapter recommended this amount be included in the contingency language as the seller's expense.

TRANSFER TIME

Try to force a time period on the transfer, such as "transfer shall occur within thirty days of submission of a formal request." Landlords are famous for dragging out deals. When you're negotiating the original lease, you're in the driver's seat. When you want to transfer it later on, they're losing you as a tenant, and you're not a priority anymore. If this is required in the lease or there's a penalty involved for the landlord, you can ensure that we can get a lease transfer happening. Push your attorney hard for this one.

CONFIDENTIALITY

Have your attorney insert language that says any future sale of the business is a confidential transaction between you and any would-be buyer and that the landlord is not entitled to a copy of the purchase contract. In recent deals, we've had multiple landlords insert themselves into the deal by asking for a copy of the purchase contract. It is none of their business. There are multiple reasons you don't want them to have the information. Their duty of confidentiality under the transaction is negligible to none. We have had landlords freely disclose to us what a restaurant sold for when it changed hands in their shopping center.

SALE COMMISSION CLAUSES

One despicable landlord in a major city just attempted to sneak language into a lease transfer stating, "If this business is sold, the landlord is entitled to 10% of the purchase price." Essentially, he wanted a commission on any future sale. He is not an investor in your business. He's taking zero risk on your plan. He is not your broker. Remember, the landlord is not your friend.

PERCENTAGE RENT

Landlords often want percentage rent for lease. Before you begin saying no, consider that this can be a useful tool for negotiating the lease. The easiest way to solve this is to make sure the percentage rent kicks in at such a high sales dollar amount (and then adjusts upward by 3% each year) that you never have to pay any percentage rent. It can actually be a good strategy to get a low base.

VACANCY RATES AND ANCHOR ABANDONMENT

If possible, write language into the lease stating that if a major anchor tenant vacates, then your rent reduces by a certain percentage. The same may also be attempted for shopping centers that become more than a certain percentage vacant (say 50% or more) on a square footage basis. That automatically does it in most cases since, if a grocery store moves out, they are usually about 30% of the space and a couple more vacancies would reduce your rent.

CAPPED AMOUNTS

Wherever possible, cap the amounts in the lease for any items you pay the landlord. This includes CAMS, or common area maintenance fees. These are charges shared by the tenants in the center for items like security lighting, trash pickup (sometimes), landscaping, and exterior maintenance. It also includes the charge for real estate taxes on a pro-rata basis, which is where your share is based on the amount of space you occupy. Landlords will often put an estimated CAM amount in the lease, and it's reconciled at year end. Restaurant owners can be surprised to see a CAM adjustment from an estimate of $7,200 for the year, or $600 a month, to $15,000 due and payable within thirty days with no real explanation. Put language in the lease that your increases are capped at no more than 5% increases per year. We often see landlords jack up fees for expensive landscape revisions or other things that blow your costs out of the water. Cap the CAMS, especially in newer centers (less than three years old), since taxes may not be reflective of the landlord's improvements. You could be looking at CAMS based on unimproved property versus a fully constructed shopping center.

ADMINISTRATIVE CHARGES

Do not agree to administrative charge percentage add-on to CAMS, taxes, and insurance. You shouldn't have to pay the landlord's agent a fee to bill you for fees. You can see from most of the language and examples in this chapter why we suggest that you have tenant representation on all deals. Landlords negotiate terms that benefit them for a living. For the average buyer with limited experience, it's easy to agree to language that demonstrates why the landlord is not your friend.

Letter of Intent

An existing lease or lease assignment document is the starting point for negotiations when the existing business is being sold to a new buyer. When there is no existing tenant in the case of closed or new restaurant space, the starting point is a letter of intent.

Below is an example letter of intent that would be submitted in initial discussions with a landlord. The key elements are addressed to establish business terms. This is prior to subsequent iterations of a lease that is negotiated between the parties with the assistance of a broker and attorney. Below the sample letter of intent is an explanation of each element and why it is important to include them early in the negotiations.

Letter of Intent for ______________________________

1. Furniture, Fixtures, and Equipment: Furniture, fixtures, and equipment included in building (and equipment list attached herein) shall be available for tenant use upon commencement of lease term.
2. Tenant Name: John Smith, DBA Delicious Bites
3. Premises: Approximately 1,631 sq. ft. former "Atlanta Deli" sandwich shop space at 500 Peachtree Road, Atlanta, GA 30305. Patio space to be provided at no cost.
4. Terms: 5 years plus one 5-year option
5. Base Rent: (based on 1,631 sq. ft.) $18.50 per sq. ft. fixed for three years with .50 cents per square foot increase thereafter for each year of the lease.
6. Common Area Maintenance: Tenant shall reimburse Landlord for Tenant's pro-rata share of all common area maintenance costs relative to the shopping center. 2009 amount estimated to be: $8.49 per sq. ft. Tenant will pay no increase for the first 24 months. Pass-through increases thereafter will apply at rate not to exceed 5% per year.
7. Tenant Improvement Money: Tenant requests that Landlord bring operation into compliance for food service code by installing a 1,500 gallon grease trap, Ansul hood system, and increase of HVAC to 1 ton per 200 sq. ft. In lieu of Landlord's commitment to handle these improvements, Tenant requests $35,000 in tenant improvement money to execute these same improvements.
8. Rent Abatement: Landlord agrees to abate the first 3 months in order to allow for permitting and construction. Landlord further agrees to abate half (50%) of the rent for the next three (3) months. Full rent would begin thereafter. Tenants would still pay CAM at agreed rate (pro-rata share) for this period.
9. Signage: Tenant shall have the right to put signage on the exterior fascia of the demised premises utilizing maximum width of storefront area. Tenant shall further be provided Peachtree Road signage for the pylon sign already located here for his exclusive use. All signage must conform to local codes and shall be mutually agreed upon with Landlord.
10. Lease commencement: October 1, 2010, with possession on this date.
11. Security Deposit: One month base rent.
12. Personal Guarantee: Diminishing personal guarantee of $250,000 decreasing by 1/24th for each month of the first two years paid on time and eliminated as of month 25 provided Tenant has been current on all remittals to that point.

1. Always spell out that any existing furniture, fixtures, and equipment will convey for your use at the beginning of the lease. Include a complete list. You don't want to rent a space only to find the previous tenant has stripped it of equipment between the initial showing and the time the lease is signed. Landlords often take possession of prior equipment when someone defaults but sometimes show a space and don't explain that the assets will be removed prior to rental.
2. Use the name of the business that will be signing the lease.
3. Describe the square footage as advertised but add the term *approximately*. It's important to note that patio space is not included in the cost estimates for footage estimates for calculating rent unless it's a fully enclosed patio with walls, ceiling, heating, and cooling.
4. Terms. Indicate the terms. It is usual and customary to request and receive a five-year initial term with an option to renew. If you request a shorter term, expect to be countered. If you are requesting free rent months, realize that the landlord is amortizing that over the initial term, so fewer months in the initial term will result in fewer months of discounted or free rent.
5. Rent is always quoted and calculated as base rent plus CAMS on an annualized basis. That's a confusing concept for most. Here's an example based on the LOI sample: base rent (based on 1,631 square feet) $18.50 per square foot fixed for three years with .50 cents per square foot increase thereafter for each year of the lease. In this example, the rent would be as follows:

   1631 square feet times 18.50 = $30,173.50 annually

   Divide this by 12 months to get the payment monthly

   $30,173.50 divided by 12 = 2514.46 per month base rent

No matter how many times we go through this exercise, there is a tendency to misunderstand the calculation. In this example, the rent would increase by .50 cents per foot in years four and five of the initial term, so the calculation would look like this.

> Years One–Three: $2514.46 per month (shown above)
>
> Year Four: 1631 square feet times $19.00 = $30,989.00
>
> Divide this by 12 months to get the payment monthly = $2582.42 per month base rent

6. Common area maintenance is always distributed among those who benefit. In a freestanding building, you are often given a net, net, net lease, sometimes called a triple net lease, which means you pay the building's property taxes, building insurance, and the cost of any maintenance or repairs to the building. In a traditional shopping center, everyone's money is pooled on a square footage basis, and they pay for things that can include anything from garbage pickup to landscape work. In our sample LOI, note a few key elements. First, we agree to pro-rata share. Pro-rata is defined as "in proportion" to a factor that can be exactly calculated. That factor in a lease is square footage. If the shopping center has ten businesses and a total of 10,000 square feet, the pro-rata share of the common area maintenance would never exceed 16.31% (1,631 square feet divided by 10,000 square feet total). If the entire shopping center empties out, you're not on the hook for any more than 16.31% of the common area expenses, including taxes and insurance. Continuing with our example LOI, note that we are stating the known CAM rate for some period of time ($8.49 per square foot for 2009). We state that we won't pay any increase in this amount for the first twenty-four months and that increases after that time will apply at a rate not to exceed 5% per year.

Sometime landlords will sign up for this language or some variation, which is important for controlling costs. Part of the expense the landlord can pass through are taxes and insurance. If they are lazy about fighting the city for outrageous increases or working for the best price on insurance, the 5% cap keeps a lid on what you might be expected to cover in terms of escalations.

7. In the LOI example in the table, we request specific tenant improvements. Bringing a restaurant space into compliance to local codes for food service is a reasonable request. Asking the landlord to handle this is also reasonable, as he has more resources for construction than the average restaurant owner. We're attempting to hedge our bet in this instance by saying either do it or give us the money to do it, but we know what it costs.
8. Requests for rent abatement like the language in Item 8 asks for full rent abatement for a period of time. Three months is reasonable when you consider the time to permit, make décor changes, and order signage. We further request half rent for six months. This is aggressive but, depending on the landlord, could happen. Note that CAMS are rarely, if ever, abated. The landlord has to pay the taxes and keep the property operating. Rent abatements refer to base rent, not the full load for CAMS.
9. Signage covered in item nine is a very important element of lease negotiations. You want the maximum exposure you can get for your business. Do not assume the existing signage will convey to you; ask for it in black and white.
10. Include the commencement date and indicate possession.
11. Security deposits are a function of the financial picture the landlord put together from your package. If you submit a letter of intent before you've been credit checked, always try to get away with a single month.

12. Personal guarantees are such a weighty topic that they deserve an entire section. Read the next section before deciding how to approach the personal guarantee.

Sign and submit the LOI and you have a letter of intent that covers the key points. The balance will be negotiated in the legal language of the lease. Use an attorney and make sure you understand what you are agreeing to in the final lease.

Personal Guarantees

Almost every landlord expects a personal guarantee on the lease. That means that you are personally guaranteeing or pledging your personal assets on behalf of your company. If the business fails and you bankrupt the company, you can still be personally liable for the remaining term of the lease. Before you or your attorney consent to the personal guarantee, remember that there are many forms a personal guarantee can take to minimize your risk. You should attempt each of these strategies before you blindly sign the personal guarantee that your landlord (who is not your friend) wants. Think carefully before you ask a family member to sign up for this as well, as it can bankrupt him to answer a judgment or lien from a landlord if you go under. Here are just a few strategies to lower that risk.

Diminishing Personal Guarantee

We've done countless leases where we structure a diminishing personal guarantee. Instead of guaranteeing the lease over the entire term, the tenant guarantees a fixed amount that diminishes with each month that the rent is paid on time until the personal guarantee rolls down to nothing. We've had very good success with this strategy in negotiating a twenty-four month diminishing personal guarantee so that if your business is going south after twenty months, the most you're on the hook for is four more months.

Fixed Personal Guarantee

Some landlords will consent to a fixed amount for the guarantee, and at least you know what that number is so you can contain the maximum amount of your personal wealth you are putting at risk.

Removal of Personal Guarantee at the End of the Initial Term

Most leases are for an initial term plus options for additional terms. If at all possible, negotiate to remove the personal guarantee at the end of the initial term since you've already proven your credit worthiness if you make it the first five years. Another reason is for the benefit of the future tenant. What landlords fail to consider in writing this language that keeps every future tenant on the hook is the nightmare it creates when trying to transfer the lease to a new party.

Removal of Personal Guarantee at Any Point in the Term that the Lease is Transferred with Landlord Consent

Dozens of leases we work with every day in second-generation spaces require that the original tenant stay on the lease. The landlord has no interest in letting any securing party (that means you) off the hook when the lease transfers. The best and only time to negotiate this point is before you sign the lease. Make sure your attorney inserts language for this contingency in the lease. If the landlord transfers the lease to a new tenant that is credit qualified, there is no reason for you to stay on that lease as his additional guarantor. Close to 100% of all leases we see have this nasty language in it, and we have transferred businesses that have personal guarantors on the hook from more than ten years earlier. Be prepared to fight on this one.

This is an actual story from our experiences; only the names have been changed.

> Our clients operated a quick casual concept in a great location in an Atlanta suburb. They wanted to sell since they weren't very successful, and as luck would have it, we located a buyer within the first thirty days. The new buyer would convert the concept, so he had specific timing he needed to meet in order to launch by his target date.
>
> We contacted the landlord's management company with a full package on the buyer who was financially well qualified and had strong experience with multiple units. Then the fun began. The approval for the new tenant was granted almost immediately, but we needed an actual lease transfer document to go to closing. As weeks went by with no progress, despite phone calls and e-mails and visits to the property manager, we learned that this location had changed hands four times and was originally a McDonald's corporate lease location. Based on the language in the lease—twenty-two years earlier—every prior tenant was still a guarantor and had to sign off on the transfer. Our sellers did not encounter this on their transfer (they owned it four years) since the prior leasing attorney wasn't a stickler for having everyone sign the transfer assignment. This attorney refused to budge and said nothing could move until he got someone at McDonald's corporate with authority (and the three other subsequent tenants/guarantors) to sign. We fought for three months to expedite the transfer, and the buyer walked. Our sellers ended up defaulting on their lease and closing the business because they weren't making money and it was clear they couldn't sell. The space was empty for a number of months, and then, almost a year later, we got an e-mail from the management company's attorney saying all parties were on board and our transfer was ready to proceed. We didn't bother to reply.

Here is one final note on personal guarantees: Landlords, in recent years, have been burned by tenants that form corporations and then bankrupt them. When the landlord tries to recover under the personal guarantee, he finds that the tenant has conveniently moved everything into his wife's name in an attempt to shield his assets. Depending on the state and the original language of the lease, the landlord may or may not be able to go after those assets. For those reasons, we increasingly see leases written with personal guarantees that require the signature of both the wife and the husband. Like all lease elements, everything is negotiable. We point it out so that you are not surprised to find a spousal commitment to a personal guarantee included in the lease language provided to you.

Site Location

Some people wonder, how hard can site location be? They may tell you it's simply calling the number on the sign posted on the property. If that's your position, remember the title of this chapter, the landlord is not your friend. That single lesson will pay for the cost of this book hundreds of times over. There are several myths surrounding the idea of finding a site on your own. The three most common that will get you into trouble will be discussed one at a time.

Myth Number One:

If I do it myself, the landlord won't have to pay commission, and I'll get a better deal.

This is false. The landlord has already predetermined commission on the space. If you aren't represented by a broker, the commission is the same amount except the landlord's leasing agent gets 100%. There's no financial gain if you do not have representation. That doesn't mean the landlord's representative can't provide you with valuable information. He's familiar with the property. He will know a lot about the location and the existing tenants. He will have traffic counts and demographic information, but all that is still available to you if you are represented by a broker. What you have to be more concerned with is what the landlord's representative won't tell you.

The landlord's representative has one goal and one goal only: lease this space for the landlord. He will only show you properties that belong to his developer. He works for the landlord. If a better location for your concept is a quarter mile away and he doesn't represent it, he will not tell you about it. He represents only the property of this landlord, and his duty of loyalty belongs to him.

A restaurant broker represents your interests. He has a duty of loyalty only to you. If another space opens up before the lease is finalized, he will tell you. He will negotiate the lease and give you feedback on the location and share information about other restaurants in the area.

Myth Number Two:

All the broker is going to do is call the number on the sign and get me in to see the space. I can do that.

Remember that once you make a call on the space, you're on your own. The landlord's representative is not going to want to split commission or deal with someone else representing you because he will challenge him and represent your interests first. It's much easier for him to handle it alone. A business broker or tenant representative familiar with the industry provides real value in the transaction. This is another situation where you don't want to have your wife or your cousin that's a real estate agent handling the transaction so you can get the commission for yourself. You may net $10,000 in commission and lose your net worth in bad decisions. Here's what a business broker will do on your behalf.

First and foremost, a restaurant broker can advise you on restaurant-specific infrastructure. Items like the grease trap, HVAC, and hood system are specific to the industry, and only someone familiar with the restaurant business knows this. The landlord's representative is not a restaurant specialist. He would never purposely hide information, but he may not know that the HVAC unit is right-sized for retail but dramatically undersized for a restaurant operation. Once you move in and begin operating your restaurant/sauna and customers are passing out from the heat, added HVAC capacity is up to you. Costs here will more than wipe out any commission gains.

Secondly, a restaurant broker can advise you on competing rents and offers in the market. The leasing agent has only his landlord for comparison. The broker or tenant representative working for you has market-level data from negotiating leases with multiple landlords. He knows what's happening in key areas like rent abatements and concessions, tenant improvement money, current leasing rates, and terms available for comparable centers. Your landlord's leasing agent may have some of this information, but he is not going to negotiate against himself by offering it up.

Finally, remember that restaurant brokers are specialists. They will be able to provide insider knowledge on restaurant space for lease. A good broker has an ear in the industry. He or she knows which restaurants are thriving and which are barely surviving. He can provide you with anecdotal information on restaurants in the location you've chosen. Examples include sales volume for adjacent restaurants, whether there's a lunch or breakfast trade, or whether the county is targeting this area for liquor license abuses. This is valuable insight for would-be tenants. The landlord's representative won't know or, if he does, may be contractually precluded from sharing this information on his own tenants.

Restaurant brokers can often tell you about spaces before they go on the market. They have a good relationship with landlords who come to them with all available restaurant space. In our markets, landlords tell us when they have a restaurant tenant in trouble so we can find a tenant and keep the space from going dark. We find that landlords refer as much business to us as our clients. That's important, since once the sign goes on the space, competition begins, especially for valuable space. Access to these insider postings can save you thousands in build-out if you can take an existing space and just change the sign and décor. If a broker brings this opportunity to you, act to get it quickly or you may miss the chance.

This is an actual story from our experiences; only the names have been changed.

> A noodle concept approached us seeking a prominent location in Atlanta. These spaces are very difficult to find and extremely valuable, so we entered into a buyer's agreement to find the location. The client looked at several restaurants and found issues with each of them. After a six-month search, we were unable to find the perfect space, and his agreement expired. Shortly after that, we were contacted by a seller with a prime location he was about to lose to the landlord. We contacted our former client, though he was no longer under contract with us, to provide him details on the location. We told him we needed to move quickly.
>
> The buyer attempted to negotiate on his own and went straight to the landlord, cutting the firm out of the deal. Negotiations failed pretty quickly since his ability to act in good faith with us was indicative of his ability to negotiate with the landlord. After two weeks of hassling with this client, the landlord called us directly and said he wouldn't work with this guy and to get him another tenant. All this occurred before the existing restaurant ever closed down. Because it was a prime location, we leased it within twelve hours to another restaurant. They did more than $2.4 million in sales the first year.

Myth Number Three:

My attorney will take care of the lease—why do I need both a broker and my lawyer?

A commercial lease is easily the most expensive financial commitment most people will ever make. Consider that the average lease is $8000 or more a month and is a typical lease term of five years. That's a $480,000 commitment subject to a personal guarantee. You need every resource at your disposal working on this to reduce your risk and minimize your costs. Your attorney brings a very strong skill to the transaction, but unless he or she has also done restaurant lease negotiation, you want an experienced restaurant broker looking at this lease. In our experience, attorneys focus on the language of the lease and what it means to you while you're operating.

A restaurant broker will focus on the business terms. When you enter into business, it's like any new relationship. Everyone is certain it is going to work out, and divorce never enters your mind. Remember the title of this chapter. We have seen enough landlords and tenants part ways to make sure that you cover both how to get in and how to get out of the lease. Consider your lease your prenuptial agreement. Remember, one out of two marriages end in divorce.

New Restaurant Space

Though this book focuses on buying existing restaurants instead of a build-out, we'll briefly touch on the types of new space available. New space often comes in the form of either a *vanilla box* or *cold, dark shell* versus second-generation space. That means the space is mostly unfinished and the landlord will provide an allowance or tenant improvement money to help you on the build-out. Here are simple definitions of these commonly used terms for restaurant space:

Vanilla Box or Vanilla Shell

A space is often referred to as a *vanilla box* or *vanilla shell.* This is typically a commercial restaurant building that is minimally finished inside. Typically it will have a finished interior with ceilings, lighting, plumbing, heating and cooling (HVAC), interior walls (painted or unpainted), electrical outlets, restrooms, and a concrete floor. In the case of a restaurant, this generally should also include the grease trap but not the hood. A vanilla shell is considered ready to lease and ready for tenant improvements (TIs). In many cases, the landlord will offer a financial incentive or contribution known as tenant improvement or a tenant improvement allowance to help offset the cost of the remaining improvements needed to occupy the building. These generally do not include furniture, fixtures, equipment, or specific trade fixtures. For example, you could not order kitchen equipment. The landlord will allow for the concession at the signing of the lease but typically reimburses for the expenses after you are open for business.

Cold, Dark Shell or Cold Shell

Another form of restaurant space is called a *cold, dark shell* or *cold shell.* In this case it refers to an unfinished interior that lacks the mechanical, electrical, and plumbing components, such as heating and air conditioning (HVAC), plumbing, and electricity. This unfinished space typically also lacks the interior walls and insulation. In the case of a restaurant, the builder generally plans this as a restaurant space from the design phase. It will typically have an in-ground grease trap stubbed into the space. A cold shell is ready for warm shell or vanilla shell improvements or tenant improvements once the lease is signed.

Second-Generation Space

Second-generation space varies from the two types above because it has already been fully built for restaurant use. This is a commercial building with a fully furnished interior that has previously (in the first generation) been used as a restaurant location. It can have—in addition to everything listed above for a vanilla box or vanilla shell—kitchen equipment, a hood, built-in freezers, and/or refrigeration units and can include everything down to the linens, POS system, small wares, and décor.

Tenant Improvement Money, or TI, is Not Free

This is a word of warning to the would-be tenant. Tenant improvement money, or TI, is not free money. You will be paying this back in the rent amount at some ridiculous rate of interest that's never clearly calculated for you. It's all part of the landlord's top secret formula for arriving at a square footage price. Restaurant owners often view tenant improvement money as a free gift when doing a build-out. This can seem like a huge amount of money when a landlord is offering up $20 a square foot for a 3500 square foot space or $70,000 of "free" money.

If you've ever remodeled your own home, you know that whatever budget you set will be exceeded and whatever time frame you commit to will be expanded. Multiply that experience times ten, and that's the headache you will get with a restaurant build-out. If you are even considering starting from scratch, we recommend you look at existing restaurants first.

Chapter Summary-Key Points

* The landlord is not your friend.
* Landlord approval will require a personal financial statement, consent to credit check, and tax returns. He will also want a menu and business plan in most cases.
* Biggest failures to plan for in the lease negotiation are: exit strategies, lease transferability, and experience clauses.

* There are multiple ways to overcome a strong personal guarantee demand, including a diminishing guarantee, a fixed guarantee, or a removal at the end of a fixed term.
* Tenant improvement money, or TI, is not free money—you are charged back in the rent at very high rates.

The Restaurant Business Plan

There are entire books written on the art of writing a business plan, and it's an important subject. As the competition for the best restaurant sites heats up, landlords are increasingly requesting a formal business plan even if you are taking over an existing restaurant. Whether or not your landlord requires the plan, it's a key exercise for restaurant operators to map out their expectations for the business. The old adage that if you fail to plan, you plan to fail can be a reality for those that don't commit to long- and short-term goals for their business. At the same time, we have seen some of the most grandiose business plans result in the most spectacular restaurant failures. Our clients have provided everything from complex business plans perfectly bound that include fifty pages of projections to one-page documents with misspellings.

In our experience, there is a correlation between business plans with the highest numbers of pages and the greatest level of failure. The guys that sell restaurants would say that the thicker your business plan, the worse the business idea in practice. Before crafting your business plan, we recommend you spend time in the industry and understand the basic concepts of table turnover, menu costing, food costs, labor costs, marketing, and advertising. Don't view your business plan as an exercise to impress someone. Instead, use it to fully flesh out the concept of your restaurant. Finally, if your restaurant business plan does not include a menu, you don't have a restaurant business plan.

It's that simple. The menu is the single most important prerequisite for a restaurant and will be required by the landlord.

This is an actual story from our experiences; only the names have been changed.

> A recent MBA grad and former general manager of hotel restaurants wanted space for his new sandwich shop. He sent us a sixty-eight page business plan that created projections ten years into the future and an expansion plan for the business into franchise concepts. This complex business plan crashed our computer as well as the landlord's. The Small Business Administration was wowed, and he got his startup money. What the business plan failed to do was make any sense.
>
> The projections estimated top line sales and added on growth by year. In the first year of opening, the plan was to do $500,000 in volume from a restaurant with an average price point of $8.50 with 70% of the business done at lunch Monday through Friday (without major catering). That's 260 days of operation. Since the lunch period covers a two-hour period and the restaurant seated only forty-five people, simple math would reveal the flaw in the business plan. At 226 average tickets per day, 70% handled during lunch is 158 diners. The two-hour lunch window, if the restaurant were completely filled, would have to turn the tables 3.5 times. The size of the restaurant and the fact that they were a 100% dine-in precluded them ever getting to this volume.
>
> Before your business plan gets too grandiose, do the basics and figure out based on average price how many people you will have to serve in the prime hours you are open and whether you can even fit enough bodies into the seating available to do this number.

There are multiple audiences for the business plan, and depending upon who receives yours, the plan may need modification. Overall, however, the business plan is meant to accomplish one goal, which is: clearly articulate your restaurant concept along with its short- and long-term goals. This should be accomplished in a well thought out and meaningful way to demonstrate the validity of your concept. The end use could include any of the following:

1. A landlord deciding whether you have the experience and background to run and operate a successful concept in his space. He also wants to compare your concepts to his existing restaurants.
2. A bank, lender, or other financial institution that is deciding whether to loan money on the business.
3. A seller deciding from your plan whether to accept an offer for some level of owner financing.
4. Partners or investors you may need for capital or assistance.

Although you need to tweak the end product slightly based on the audience, here are the elements of a very straightforward business plan that should cover most restaurant needs. Include in general terms what will happen under new leadership. This is important to the landlord or someone investing because there's an established business in this location that is either succeeding or failing. He wants to know what you are changing.

Restaurant Description

Start with a clear, well-defined description that is not too wordy. This would be your thirty-second commercial or snapshot of your restaurant if you were asked what your business is about. You should have this at the tip of your tongue for anyone who asks, "Hey, what do you do?" This should answer who you are, what you do, and why. Here's an example if you were acquiring Mario's Italian Pies:

Sample Restaurant Description

Mario's Italian Pies is a pizza restaurant rooted in tradition. Mario's makes their dough and sauce daily using spices that create great taste. Combined with fresh vegetables and high quality meats, quality is the hallmark. The cheese is a blended mozzarella shredded every day. By the slice or by the pie, Mario's Pizza serves the best pizza in town.

This section of the business plan should also include:

- Business goals and objectives
- Brief history of the business
- List of key principals

Continuing with our example for Mario's Pizza, here are the next elements of the business plan.

Business Goals and Objectives

Under new leadership, Mario's Italian Pies will accomplish the following:

- Continue the Italian-American menu featuring great pasta and pizza that lives up to the promise of quality and fresh ingredients daily but increase sales at a rate of 3% annually and improve gross margin by 2 percentage points.
- Introduce a premium draft beer selection along with the current range of coffees, sodas, bottled water, and soft drinks. Alcohol sales at a 70% margin will grow to 15% of sales in year one.
- Provide excellent service in a casual and fun atmosphere.
- Increase sales through a focused marketing plan driven by business relationships and strong marketing skills of the new principals.

The next element might include how you will be different from existing competitors. This demonstrates that you have considered the competitive set and how you will get market share from them.

Differentiation

The location, size, and wood-burning ovens at Mario's offer a unique opportunity to differentiate and become the neighborhood casual Italian restaurant of choice. Mario's, under new leadership, will create an inviting place to relax, socialize, eat, and order takeout. The new leadership will offer additional incentives to increase business, such as:

- Clean, professional environment offering attentive service.
- Food and drink specials for dine-in and carryout throughout the week.
- Creative menu offering standard pasta as well as specials of the day.
- Increased delivery orders and increased food to go through effective neighborhood targeted marketing.

Brief History of the Business

Mario's Pizza has been established in this single location for more than seven years. Sales have steadily grown at a rate of 2.5% per year until the last two years, when they have remained stagnant.

Résumés of Principals

Mario's will be under the management of Mario Vincente and John Smith. Mario has more than fifteen years of food service and hospitality experience. John Smith has a business and marketing background along with financial services experience. Both operators will work in the business on a daily basis. John's expertise will be used to leverage all marketing and promotional efforts. Mario will manage the kitchen and front of house staff and ensure food quality. Both have strong education, experience, and knowledge they will use to grow Mario's.

The restaurant owner should be able to describe the industry outlook and define critical needs of the existing market. You should also identify your target market with a general profile of your targeted customer. Here's the Mario's Pizza example.

Market Outlook and Competition

The industry outlook for the pizza restaurant has remained flat in the prior three years except for takeout and delivery, which has experienced growth rates of 12% or more each year. The three-mile radius surrounding Mario's Pizza is heavily comprised of office buildings with workers ranging in age from twenty-five to forty-five and young married households. For that reason, the target market for the restaurant will focus on twenty-five- to forty-five-year-olds for dining, takeout, and delivery sales.

Mario's Pizza competes with three other pizza restaurants within a two-mile radius. Only one does any takeout and delivery business, and Mario's had not taken advantage of this lucrative opportunity. Mario's is estimated to have a 12% market share now, which can be improved to 16% with an aggressive growth strategy in takeout and delivery sales.

Products and Services (Sample Menu)

The next section of the business plan should include the menu. This is always a requirement of the landlord.

Business Structure and Hours

Landlords want to know your business structure and whether you are already incorporated. They want to know your hours to make sure you're not proposing a nightclub for their space (open 5 p.m. to 2 a.m. Wednesday to Saturday is a dead giveaway).

Example: Business Structure

Mario's will operate as an LLC in the state of Georgia. The LLC is established as Hot Pies, LLC. The partners in the business are John Smith and Mario Vincente.

BUSINESS HOURS	
Monday through Friday	11 a.m. to midnight
Saturday and Sunday	11 a.m. to 11 p.m.

Hours are designed to accommodate lunch throughout the week for office workers and neighborhood businesses. We will serve dinner and deliver until 11 p.m.

Marketing Plan and Promotional Strategy

This is probably the most important element of any business plan. It is often the most underdeveloped when we receive restaurant business plans. If your background is chef or kitchen driven and you don't understand how to market, here are a couple of options. One, don't open a business until you have acquired some expertise. Two, hire someone who does. No matter how good your food is or how great your restaurant looks, none of that matters if you can't get people in the door. Know and understand who you are targeting, whether this property is appropriate for that clientele, and how you're going to reach them. Your broker will be able to give you demographics to tell you whether they live in the area you're purchasing in.

Sample Marketing Plan and Promotional Strategy for Mario's

Target Market

Mario's target market is the twenty-five- to forty-five-year-old casual, urban professional single and married households.

Marketing and Promotional Strategy

Mario's will use the following promotional strategies to grow the volume:

- Extensive advertising campaign in the surrounding three-mile radius and zip codes:
    - Door hangers offering pizza delivery specials.
    - Dine-in offers to raise awareness of location and new ownership.
    - Special coupon offers.
    - Direct mail targeted campaigns in Val Pak or similar piece.
    - Initiate a delivery strategy to a targeted business network.
- Leverage new operating principals' background in the food services business.
- Seventy businesses located in the three-mile radius will be targeted with:
    - Sample delivery to office buildings to drive relationships and orders for the important lunch business.
    - Fliers on cars.
    - Direct e-mail program with offers for the day.

  - Expanded options including Internet, fax, and phone options for delivery. This will lead to one hundred business lunches delivered per week (average ticket of $10 plus delivery and tax).
- Cross-market pizza delivery with video stores offering "Pizza and a Movie" with cross-couponing between the two businesses.
- Business card drawings for repeat business for lunch giveaways once a week.
- Leverage proximity to nearby campus and offer student specials/loyalty campaign for takeout, delivery, and dine-in.
- Leverage radio station media by delivering free pizza in return for on-air exposure.
- Charity tie-in to breast cancer foundation. Mario's will host an annual event to benefit this important cause. A public relations campaign will be used around this effort to maximize exposure for the business in its efforts for this cause.
- Relaunch of existing Web site and social media marketing to drive online buzz about new ownership and menu.

Financial Projections

The last portion of the business plan is the most critical to most parties, particularly investors or banks. Anyone purchasing an existing business should rely on the last year's data and then forecast from this starting point. Modify their current expenses, including salaries, to reflect your own operational plan. Pay close attention to these elements, which the landlord will likely zero in on.

1. *Gross sales and rate of growth.* Be careful to use estimates in keeping with the industry. If you outperform the industry, that's great news. However, if you forecast to perform at a 15% annual increase when the National Restaurant Association is forecasting 2.5% annual growth rates, you'll look naïve and inexperienced. Landlords, potential investors, and banks are attuned to restaurant results.
2. *COGS or food costs.* Use the existing numbers or the high side of industry estimates you've already learned for this forecast. Be consistent, with the understanding that higher food costs are associated with fine dining and meat-intensive industries and lower food costs are associated with fast casual.
3. *Advertising and marketing expense.* If you are showing growth in sales, you better show growth in ad spend. You cannot achieve better results than the year before if you are not pursuing some improved sales and marketing strategy.

Sample Business Plan Financials

Fill in the statement below to arrive at an analysis of projected income from the operations at the designated location for the first two years. The best source of information for the plan is from the existing business. If that's not available, prepare your business plan using what you have learned already about common cost elements (food costs, rent, and labor costs). In the course of your search, you've seen multiple profit and loss statements, and they will begin to look very similar.

Here's a description of each financial element of the business plan. The appendix also includes a blank version of this document for your use.

1. *Gross sales.* Top line sales (exclusive of sales tax) that you are forecasting for the business go on line one. Use the reality check math on this. Using the average price of your restaurant meal, how many do you have to serve in a day to reach these sales? How many do you have to serve in an hour? Do you have that capacity? If you are forecasting turning over your table five times during lunch to reach this number of sales and the industry average is 2.5 times turnover, this is not realistic. If you're using the former owner's numbers, increase it by a conservative 3% for year one just because you're the new guy.
2. *Cost of goods sold.* These are the food and alcohol costs for the restaurant. Sometimes this is broken out between alcohol and food costs for your own purposes. We do not recommend you break this out for a landlord who doesn't like high alcohol percentages.
3. *Gross margin.* Deduct COGS from sales to get your gross margin. Again, if you are buying an existing business, these numbers should all originate from their P&L statements.
4. *Expenses.* Enter your expenses line item by line item. Make sure the rent is the same amount you've agreed to with the landlord.

Apply a reasonableness test to your data. Make sure the sales increases are not overly aggressive. Don't vary too much from the prior years. You want to be sure you can defend the document you've created and no one can argue with using last year as a baseline. Below is a sample business plan using the same data we looked at in the chapter on business valuation. We added an additional year as a forecast for a simple business plan for presentation to a landlord.

Business Plan Forecast

A	B		C	D	
Year		**2010**	**% Change**		**2011**
Gross Sales	$	695,652	3.88%	$	722,643
Cost of Goods	$	287,390	3.09%	$	296,270
Gross Profit	$	408,262	4.43%	$	426,348
Expenses					
Accounting	$	1,650	6.06%	$	1,750
Advertising	$	17,900	3.35%	$	18,500
Amortization	$	6,000	0.00%	$	6,000
Auto Expense	$	12,000	0.00%	$	12,000
Bank Charges	$	11,500	0.00%	$	11,500
Depreciation	$	14,055	0.00%	$	14,055
Donations	$	1,500	-100.00%		
Insurance	$	6,825	5.71%	$	7,215
Insurance Auto	$	1,200	0.00%	$	1,200
Ins. Health	$	3,000	-100.00%		
Interest	$	9,250	-1.62%	$	9,100
Maintenance	$	6,700	-2.99%	$	6,500
Office Supplies	$	2,350	6.38%	$	2,500
Owner's Salary	$	31,800	10.06%	$	34,999
Rent Facility	$	55,600	10.61%	$	61,499
Repairs	$	8,165	0.43%	$	8,200
Salaries	$	133,629	8.51%	$	145,001
Supplies	$	6,000	8.33%	$	6,500
Tax	$	6,500	0.00%	$	6,500
Tax Payroll	$	22,000	2.27%	$	22,499
Telephone	$	3,496	0.11%	$	3,500
Travel/Entertainment	$	1,500	0.00%	$	1,500
Utilities	$	42,000	0.00%	$	42,000
Water	$	1,200	0.00%	$	1,200
Total Expense	**$**	**405,820**		**$**	**423,717**
NET INCOME	**$**	**2,442**		**$**	**2,631**

A business plan is a critical tool, but the average restaurant owner acquiring a business that's doing less than $3 million in sales should be able to put a complete business plan into eight to ten pages. If your business plan starts hitting the twenty-page mark, consider another industry, like accounting.

That being said, every would-be restaurant owner should sit down and do a business plan to establish a baseline model for the business. Make sure that every element of your restaurant is thoughtfully considered. Part of the process of the business plan is to proof your own ideas and get you to consider elements you may not have thought about, like target market, potential market share, hours of operation, and more.

This is an actual story from our experiences; only the names have been changed.

> Evans Judges contacted us for a 1500 square foot space in a high-end Atlanta suburb for a barbeque catering business. He didn't want to spend more than $1500 a month in rent, and he wanted to be in a good shopping center. To add to his request, he also wanted to be able to park and operate a towable barbeque smoker in the parking lot. Finally, he didn't want to operate during any retail hours. We explained that his expectations were going to be very difficult to satisfy. He was quite adamant in pushing forward on a search and said if we found what he was looking for, he was ready to go.
>
> After spending hours online and riding out the suburb where he wanted to be located, we found eight potential sites. After calling the landlords and working with them, we eliminated all but two sites. Because of the economic conditions, we were able to actually locate a very good shopping center that would meet every single criterion except retail hours. The landlord suggested a negligible five-hour requirement for retail hours.
>
> We put forth a letter of intent, and the landlord caved on everything but five hours of operation. We received the lease for review, and at that point, he said, "I'm not doing it. My business plan doesn't support retail hours, and I just can't." We explained that the next best option we located that would accept him as a tenant was $1000 more a month in rent ver-

> sus five hours a week that cost $160 in payroll, so his business plan response didn't make economic sense. Ultimately, he admitted that he was spooked by reviewing the lease and seeing what a commitment he was taking on.
>
> Do your business plan up front and understand you are taking on grown-up responsibilities. If you're not ready to do it, don't waste the broker's time, the landlord's time, and the landlord attorney's time.

What you should not do is waste a lot of people's time for an idea you have not fully come to terms with yourself. Preparing a business plan in-depth will keep you from falling into that trap. Write the plan, review it, and update it monthly to measure against your success. This is a long-term roadmap to guide your success and will help you keep your eye on the ball. If you are seeking investor financing, bank financing, SBA financing, or even owner financing, a business plan will be required. The next chapter takes you through the opportunity to finance your dream. These lenders will be looking closely at the plan you put together.

Chapter Summary-Key Points

* The elements of a restaurant business plan should be:
  - Restaurant description
  - Restaurant goals and objectives
  - Market outlook and competition
  - Menu
  - Restaurant structure and hours
  - Marketing plan and promotional strategy
  - Financial projections

* Financial projections most important to landlords and investors are:
   - Gross sales and rate of growth
   - COGS or food costs
   - Advertising and marketing expense
* Apply a reasonability test to your projections. Can you seat enough people to do the volume you're projecting without catering? How will you accomplish a 12% sales increase in a marketplace predicted by industry experts to grow at a rate of 2.5%?

Financing Your Dream of Owning a Restaurant

The most difficult part of buying a restaurant always comes down to how you pay for the acquisition. There are really only two ways—your money or other people's money. Restaurants are notoriously difficult to collateralize and leverage. The contributory reasons for this are:

- Failure to maintain accurate books and records.
- Off-the-books income.
- Failure to appropriately recast to meet SBA standards. The net profit per month with add-backs, divided by the loan payment per month, must be 1.25 or higher.
- Inability for cash flow to satisfy the debt load.
- Extremely tight credit markets for businesses without real estate or inventory to collateralize.

SBA Loans

There is a great deal of misunderstanding in the industry regarding SBA loans, or Small Business Administration loans. The first misconception is that the SBA makes loans. That is not true. The SBA does not lend money. Instead, it insures against risk for banks in the event of a bank default. That amount is as high as 90% guarantee to as low as 75%. That being said, the SBA inserts itself in every stage of the process and must approve the loan package in order for the deal to fund.

The second misunderstanding is that SBA guaranteed loans offer good rates. They do not. The rates we see are generally on par with other commercial rates in the marketplace while the fees are much higher. The SBA fees surrounding the loan package can amount to 5% of the loan price, which is very pricey. That's $15,000 just to write a loan for a $300,000 restaurant.

The last big misunderstanding regarding the SBA guaranteed loan program is that any deadlines committed to by the bank will be met. The SBA is a government entity. Their Web site may quote a timeline of thirty to ninety days, but the clock doesn't start ticking until they have a complete package, and as the package goes from administrator to underwriting, the amount of items still "needed" seems to grow exponentially. At the point you finally get a final package, it's usually time to start all over again because the initial information is now sixty to ninety days old and is no longer valid for the loan.

A typical SBA guaranteed loan is generally sold to the restaurant buyer like this: "Of course we do SBA loans. It's very simple. It's very fast. It's very easy as long as you have all the paperwork. It's so cost effective for business lending." What they should say is, "It's a joke. We don't really loan on restaurants, but I'm going to pretend I do so I can have another loan application in my inbox and prove to my boss I'm doing the work. I'm going to jerk you around for ninety days so you can stay on my leads sheet and then tell you the loan can't be approved."

In recent years, with the tough lending market, we have seen a number of brokers come on to the scene that on a fee basis will shop your loan. They often collect an up-front fee for a loan that has a 0% chance of loan approval based on SBA standards. The SBA is inflexible in its guarantee program, so if the following conditions aren't met, they will not approve the loan for funding. That being said, many unscrupulous lenders will work with you on packages, collect a *nonrefundable* up-front fee ranging from $2500 to $5000, and then blame it on someone else when the loan can't be approved.

This is an actual story from our experiences; only the names have been changed.

> Two young business partners approached us on a yogurt franchise resell established for ten years. The current owner purchased the business from the original proprietor two years earlier. This was a good store with strong financial results that had weathered the test of time. In the initial meeting, the partners said they were getting an express SBA loan for the purchase. We told them the business wouldn't qualify since we had only two years of tax returns (the length of time owned by the current seller). They insisted they had been to the bank and were assured that with their financial background and a business established for more than ten years, they could finance. We asked them to call the bank and tell them clearly that only two years of tax returns were available in the hope that they would learn earlier, rather than later, that the financing wouldn't happen.
>
> We would not write the contract with the financing contingency since in our experience it wouldn't qualify, but they were fine with this, as they were confident in their lender. We set the closing for forty-five days in the future, as the bank assured them it was an express loan that granted an answer in thirty-six hours. If you check the SBA Web site, it is true they state they will respond in thirty-six hours after they have a full package.
>
> As the weeks rolled on toward closing, several things occurred. First, the lending broker they engaged to shop the loan for the best rate collected a $4500 nonrefundable fee from the buyers. Then the fun paper trail began. The lender wanted the tax returns, the 941 tax payment returns, the sales tax returns, the payroll records, the P&Ls with recast add-backs, the franchise agreement, the lease, and the firstborn child of the seller (not really, but almost). We patiently provided every item and had the buyers' initial documents stating their due diligence was complete. The buyers also signed and paid the fee to attend the franchise training, taking time off from their jobs to go to the ten-day franchise instruction.

> Six weeks later and only a few days before closing, the buyers called, in shock, to say the bank just told them the loan was denied. The bank admitted they were confused because the business was established for ten years but had only two years of tax records. It would not qualify. The lending broker refused to refund their $4500 fee; it was finally negotiated down to half the amount. The buyers were on the hook to move forward or lose their escrow money along with the bank fee, time, and the money paid for franchise training. We wrote an extension to the contract, and they scrambled to get loans on other assets and made the closing. They still work with us to find businesses, and now they trust our advice.

Here's what you need to know about SBA loans. Most of this can be found online at www.sba.org, but the ever-optimistic loan officer will simply ignore these requirements and wave you on through the line. If the following conditions cannot be met, the loan will not be funded. Remember that, and when someone says, "Give me an up-front fee," you should run, not walk, to the door.

The SBA program will not approve a restaurant with less than three years, thirty-six consecutive months, of profitable operation. This means:

- The business with twenty-eight months will *not* be approved.
- The business with two years of profitability and one year of losses will *not* be approved.
- The business that has existed for ten years but with only two years of records available for the current owner will *not* be approved.
- The business that operated for three consecutive profitable years except for the current year *may* be approved.

The books and records required will include both the tax returns and profit and loss statements. This means:

- If two business entities (two different locations operated by one company) are commingled on the tax return, the loan will *not* be approved.
- If the profit and loss statements are available without tax returns, the loan will *not* be approved.
- Again, if you have less than three years of both documents, the loan will *not* be approved.

Other SBA Fun Facts Your Lender May Forget to Tell You

1. The SBA will not approve any loan unless the owner is committed to finance at least 10% of the purchase price even if conditions one and two are met.
2. The SBA program requires that you collateralize the purchase with a second mortgage on your home. This is not negotiable in any circumstances we have seen. If you refuse to pledge your home for collateral on your business acquisition, don't try this route for borrowing.
3. The SBA program also requires that they lien the furniture, fixtures, and equipment.
4. The SBA program requires a minimum amount of business experience.
5. The SBA will require a business valuation based on four components:
    - Real estate, if any. Typically there is no real estate in restaurant purchase.
    - Furniture, fixtures, and equipment, if any. Generally speaking, there are furniture, fixtures, and equipment in restaurant acquisitions.
    - Inventory, if any. Perishable inventory is not considered in the business valuation, which is 95% of all restaurant inventory.

- Goodwill, meaning the business value to the new owner.

6. The SBA requires that that net profit per month with add-backs divided by the loan payment per month must be 1.25 or higher.
7. Key person life insurance is usually required. This can take up to six weeks to obtain.
8. For real estate deals, an appraisal and an Environmental Phase One are required at the applicant's expense. The broker and the buyer cannot order these; only the bank can.
9. Both the spouse and the applicant's credit history will factor into the loan approval.
10. Lenders insist on the seller and buyer both signing IRS Form 4506-T to protect against fraud. Both the seller and buyer face IRS trouble if the tax forms are false.
11. A business plan will be required by the lender as part of the SBA process.
12. The applicant for the loan must be a legal resident of the United States.
13. The credit score of the applicant must normally be above 650, and you cannot have an arrest record.
14. The applicant for the loan must have direct management experience to be approved in most instances.

For restaurants, remember, there's usually no real estate. The inventory doesn't count in the value since it is perishable versus a lumberyard or a furniture plant or many other businesses with hard economic value associated with the physical inventory assets. Furniture, fixtures, and equipment value as a percent to the total are very low; thus, when restaurants are valued on cash flow, they must be evaluated on cash flow or *goodwill* in SBA terms, the business value to the new owner.

In short, SBA secured lending is not an easy path to restaurant financing. The procedures and costs associated with obtaining an SBA or conventional loan are very complex. This is far more difficult than a residential loan the buyer may be familiar with. A business plan will be required, three years of cash flow projections are needed, and multiple forms will be required, lost, submitted, and resubmitted before this loan will ever pass the finish line.

This is the specific SBA rule language: "If the amount being financed minus the appraised value of real estate and/or equipment is greater than $250,000 or if there is a close relationship between the buyer and seller, the lender must obtain an independent business valuation from a qualified source." For restaurants priced over $250,000, this is almost always the case and another reason why financing a restaurant through the SBA is a near impossible feat.

If the amount is above $250,000, the lender will charge you to bring in a qualified source to do an independent evaluation. The following list represents some of the SBA guidance on a qualified source for the business valuation:

1. A licensed CPA that performs the business valuation in accordance with the SSVS published by the AICPA.
2. Accredited by a recognized organization. These are individuals that meet the following criteria :
    - Accredited senior appraiser (ASA) accredited through the American Society of Appraisers
    - Certified business appraiser (CBA) accredited through the Institute of Business Appraisers
    - Accredited in business valuation (ABV) accredited through the AICPA
    - Certified valuation analyst (CVA) accredited through NACVA

An appraisal from one of these qualified sources will cost in the neighborhood of $2500 to $5000. That's the first of the fees you'll encounter in the process. Based on these requirements, it's easy to see why SBA lending and restaurants don't often belong in the same sentence.

However, in an impossible to understand turn of events that makes sense only to the federal government, in its infinite wisdom, the SBA will fund startup franchises with no books and records and no track record. To take a look at the SBA's stunning results in that category, historical summary SBA loan portfolio data shows the following results:

Franchise Loan Failure Rates and Charge-Off Rates by Year

	LOAN FAILURE RATE	LOAN CHARGE-OFF RATE
2009	13.4	2.0
2008	10.8	1.2
2007	9.0	1.0
2006	6.9	.3

Source: Coleman Report – www.colemanpublishing.com1

401(k) Financing

It is possible to finance a business using your own 401(k) assets through an employee stock ownership plan. An employee stock ownership plan is a form of a 401(k) plan set up for your own C-corp. The employee stock ownership plan purpose is to purchase the shares of your own C-corp. This structure is designed to get cash from a 401(k) or IRA into a corporation without the normal tax consequences of converting your 401(k). Some of the benefits include:

- *Bank of yourself.* You are investing in yourself and your business. This is a debt-free way of starting your business.

- *Improves cash flow.* The program does not place debt servicing requirements on your new business, which improves cash flow.
- *Tax deferred growth.* Capital appreciation and growth of the business is tax deferred for the retirement plan.
- *Penalty free.* This eliminates many of the prohibited transaction problems when funding a business using retirement funds.
- *Combine with other funding.* 401(k) funding, traditional, and SBA lending can be combined on a single purchase.
- *Increase retirement deferrals.* 401(k) plans have much higher contribution limits, so you can build your retirement plan.

The actual process consists of four basic steps. The lending firm takes care of this for you. They begin by creating a C-corp, or C-corporation. After that, they establish an employee stock ownership plan. Then they roll money into the employee stock ownership plan from an IRA or former employer's 401(k). Then they use that money to purchase the shares of your newly created C-corporation. This places the cash inside of the business to be used to acquire the business. All of this has the impact of drawing funds from your retirement to acquire a restaurant without the tax penalties and consequences if you simply cashed it out. Firms exist for the conversion of these assets, which include most of the following activities to make sure the conversion happens within the boundaries of the law and there are no tax consequences.

- Setup of C-corp
- Filing of state articles
- Filing for corp EIN with IRS
- C-corp bylaws

- Setup and operating guide
- Stock certificates
- Meeting records (initial and annual)
- Banking authorizations for checking account
- Creation of 401(k) plan documents
- Filing of 401K EIN
- Favorable determination letter from IRS
- Complete set of plan documents with all necessary forms and guides
- Assistance and guidance in the rollover of current plan to new self-directed plan
- Assistance and guidance in setup of checking account
- Unlimited pre- and post-setup consulting for plan setup and operation

Personal or Commercial Lending

Financing your restaurant purchase through ordinary personal loans or commercial loans is simple enough if you have assets to secure the loan. Often this can be land or an investment home or other property outside of your personal residence that you are comfortable pledging as collateral on a business loan. It can also be stock accounts or other asset accounts. If you have good credit and history with a bank combined with substantial assets that are not liquid, obtaining a bank loan should be simple enough. Remember that when these assets are pledged, the bank or lender may take this collateral if you default on the loan. This is something to consider if this is the family farm with no debt that's been part of your heritage for more than three generations.

Owner Financing

Owner financing is an increasingly popular way to obtain a restaurant. Owners understand that they are taking a huge risk, so be prepared for the same scrutiny of your personal financial situation that you would encounter in a bank loan. The seller may want any or all of the following:

- Personal financial statement
- Current credit report or consent to credit check
- Background and experience résumé
- Personal references
- Lien on furniture, fixtures, and equipment at time of closing so the seller can repossess
- Personal guarantee on the note
- Lien on personal assets (land, home, commercial property)

There are many benefits to owner financing, including the lack of fees. This is a larger savings than most people anticipate. Without a lender, there's no one collecting between 2% and 3% on the loan, which can add up to big money. Favorable interest rates are another bonus. Generally—though not always—an owner will finance his restaurant at far better rates than that available on the open market. Interest rates are a reflection of risk, so market rates on restaurants are high. There is a high level of simplicity in executing the transaction with owner financing. Rather than chasing documents for three months, the deal is accomplished by the closing attorney simply preparing a standard note in addition to the closing documents.

There's a very quick time to closing since there's no waiting on bank approval. Lastly, and most importantly, there is now what we term "skin in the game" by the seller. This aids the buyer since the seller is now, to a certain extent, investing in your success.

Investors

We often hear of investors that are going to help in the purchase of a restaurant. The reality is that everyone seems to have someone that's willing to invest in his dream until push comes to shove and the actual dream has to be funded. We have seen countless people who experience huge disappointment when their investors back out at the last minute, so here's some advice. Prepare a business plan. Decide on the level of investment you need. Seek your investors. When you locate them and they say, "I'm in," require that they escrow the funds at that point with an attorney. You're going to have to be able to prove ability to purchase to look at most restaurants, so the money's going to have to be available up front. If they won't commit early and then tell you to "Let me know when you find something and I'm in," then they will not commit when it's time to put the money in play. Here are both the advantages and pitfalls of investors in your business:

Advantages

- The investors know you and your concept. They are willing participants, so you bypass credit checks and personal guarantees.
- Investors often want their payout in equity, so the interest rate is either favorable or nonexistent.
- The path to purchase is quick when the money's readily available and you're in line to acquire a location.

Disadvantages

- The distance between the idea and reality is huge. Investors are under no contractual obligation to give you money, and you bear the risk that they'll pull out of the deal prior to closing (unless you've secured the money up front).

- It's hard to do business with friends, and most investors are friends or acquaintances. A failed concept with a loss of capital will destroy a good friendship or send shock waves through a family.
- Because they invest early in your dream, you're on the hook to take a lot of their advice, like it or not. Expect phone calls saying the risotto was runny and the hostess was hateful on your cell phone.

The bottom line on all lending is that other people's money comes with strings attached and consequences for nonpayment. Nothing in life is free, especially not capital for your restaurant dream.

Chapter Summary-Key Points

* The SBA (Small Business Administration) does not make loans. They guarantee risk by other lenders and have strict requirements that can usually not be met by a restaurant.
* Never pay a broker a fee to shop a loan for a restaurant.
* Alternate forms of financing that are real opportunities for restaurant funding are 401(k) conversions, owner financing, and investor financing.

The Top Ten Reasons Restaurants Fail and the Top Ten Reasons They Succeed

You've absorbed hundreds of pages dedicated to the purchase of a restaurant. You've examined your own reasons for getting into the business and decided that despite all the war stories, the warnings, and the risk, this is the business for you. Here's what you need to safeguard to ensure your success. The guys that sell restaurants have a unique view into the operations because we're there when you buy and we're here when you sell. Here's why restaurants fail. Avoid these pitfalls. It's not rocket science. There are ten things you can identify, plan around, and execute against.

The Top Ten Reasons Restaurants Fail

Lack of Capital

Everyone predicts success at a much faster rate than it actually occurs. This is true for franchise and non-franchise restaurants, takeover of existing restaurants, conversions or rebranding, and startup restaurants. Restaurants fall victim to a rate of sales they cannot achieve or a growth in expenses they fail to control. These two elements, alone or in combination, lead to restaurant failures.

A new owner of a restaurant should prepare with approximately 10% of the purchase price in operating capital even if he is buying an existing business that is doing well. This is operating capital, over and above any capital you need for any planned improvements. This is the line of credit to adjust for the peaks and valleys of restaurant cash flow. The average restaurant takes between eighteen and twenty-four months to operate in the black from startup. A restaurant undergoing a change in ownership should plan on a dip in earning, slide in sales, and some risk.

You'll need thirty days of operating capital, or some people prefer to have three months of fixed expenses. As a rule of thumb, that usually works out to approximately 10% of the purchase price. A buyer purchasing a restaurant earning $200,000 on $1.8 million in sales purchased for $475,000 should have nearly $50,000 in the bank at startup. Considering that his rent would normally be 8–10% of sales (or about $12,000–$15,000 a month) and other fixed costs (water, power, et cetera) might be another $3000–$5000 or so, then you can see that three times fixed costs is approximately the same number ($45,000 to $50,000). Scale this back as you become used to the business and understand the ebb and flow of sales and profitability, but to ensure success you must have money to operate.

This is an actual story from our experiences; only the names have been changed.

> Jerry purchased Okay Café with the intention of rebranding immediately to a new concept. He had enough in the bank for the purchase price and 10% operating capital but dramatically underestimated the cost of conversion. By the time he added up the signage expense ($14,000), menu costs, POS changes, Web site reinventions, and printing costs for the new name, he had eaten through half his available capital to convert the business. Sales dropped because a new identity was associated with the business, and worse yet, he hadn't retained any money to advertise and market his concept change. He was left without operating capital and began bouncing checks and robbing one account to pay another.

> Ultimately, he resold the restaurant and took a loss on the acquisition because he didn't have funds on hand to last out the cost of conversion plus the buildup of sales under a new name.

Failure to Create and Execute a Marketing Plan

Too many restaurants launch or change hands with no plan to drive sales and traffic into the door. "If I build it, they will come" is a movie myth. It doesn't translate in real life. A transition in ownership will be felt by the regulars. Make sure you have thoughtfully considered how you will retain existing business and grow new business. Get a calendar of events for the prior year and make sure they are on the books for this year. Introduce a loyalty club or simply introduce yourself to the regulars and tell them an appetizer is on you. There is no excuse for failing to put together a marketing plan.

Failure to Launch

Restaurant buyers come into the game with some preconceived notion of what it will be like to operate their own business. Sometimes it's close to their idea, but more often it's not. The successful owner must roll up his sleeves, commit to the process, and engage with his team and customers if he is going to succeed. Above all, he must give the purchase and the restaurant a chance to succeed. There will be plenty of times that you second-guess your decision and your family and friends will join in the chorus of "What were you thinking?" Stay true to your long-term goal, commit to the process, and before you know it, running your own business becomes second nature. It's not for the faint of heart.

This is an actual story from our experiences; only the names have been changed.

> One of the shortest ownership stories in our history occurred with a young man, an ice cream shop, and a rainy day. The

buyer worked on the deal for several months. He developed a business plan to add small breakfast items and coffees to an ice cream shop menu, attended a trade show, and was seemingly ready to go. He conducted due diligence and even extended the closing a couple of times waiting on landlord approval. Closing day arrived, and the purchase was transacted. The seller was on hand to train for two weeks.

Following closing, both parties went to the store and started the training. The seller called us at 3 p.m. with the remarkable news that the buyer had walked out. The area experienced severe afternoon thunderstorms and rain. Business was terrible (normal in the midst of summer rain for an ice cream shop), and the buyer looked at the seller, threw him the keys, and said, "I can't do this. You can keep it."

We contacted the buyer, who said, "It's not for me. I don't want it." We got the closing attorney involved to work the details of a quit claim and relist of the store so we could sell it again. Neither we nor the seller ever heard from the buyer again.

Absentee Ownership

The number one reason brokers end up with listings is the all too familiar quest to make money without actually doing anything. Owning a restaurant is not a hands-off business. Late night TV and Internet ads are full of get rich quick schemes that don't require any effort, and they all work just about as well as an absentee ownership situation. There's no free lunch.

That doesn't mean that after enough years of ownership and management that you can't put people in place to run this business, but do not acquire a restaurant and expect to have it serve as your own personal passive cash cow/happy hour hangout where you can walk in and say, "This is my restaurant," without true oversight.

Lack of Execution by the Numbers

Certain basics have to be right. If you can't deliver food and drink within a reasonable time period to waiting customers in a clean environment, you will fail in this industry. You face too many competitors that all want a piece of the marketplace and extended market share to fail on the basics. The good news is that the basics are not that hard. It requires that a good manager break down the menu, understand the costs, understand the prep work involved, and expedite food to the floor. If you don't have this knowledge, you can acquire it from experienced kitchen staff anywhere. Included in the required execution is financial execution. All the background and experience in the world won't be enough if you can't read a profit and loss statement and understand what's working and what isn't.

Focus on keeping your kitchen staff and your bar staff running efficiently to keep your cash flow going. Replace your waitstaff as needed, as they are the most expendable, least dependable, and most available staffing.

Cleanliness deserves its own mention here. The kitchen, dining room, bathrooms, parking lot, floor, ceiling, and walls must be clean. This doesn't take skill. This takes attention to detail. You will destroy your reputation overnight with a less than excellent ("A" in most states) health score. Cleanliness is not a negotiable element of execution. It is essential.

Lack of Industry Knowledge and Experience

The restaurant industry does require specialized knowledge. It is barely conceivable to those who've spent a lifetime in this industry that someone without experience would make a huge investment in acquiring a new restaurant. Yet every day novice buyers enter the restaurant business and, without any way to predict why or how, succeed spectacularly. We have seen remarkably qualified and experienced restaurant operators fail miserably while someone who enters the business from a corporate background thrives. There's no rhyme or reason beyond the individual determination to learn the industry and get it right. The buyer with little experience understands his flaws going in and may have a better understanding of the risk. The buyer who comes from a restaurant background often overestimates his own abilities and ends up in trouble.

Failed Partnerships

Partnerships are like marriages; at least 50% end up before a judge. Finding a compatible business partner is a difficult task, and we have seen every version of partnership failure you can imagine take place within restaurants. The problem with partnerships is that each party wants something different from the business, and rarely does this align with the other partner or partners. A non-operating partner is looking for passive cash flow, so he's looking at every expense to nickel and dime the store into profitability. The operating partner is feeling unappreciated, and if he's doing all the work, he sees no harm in lifting a few dollars before they actually make it onto the books. The minority partner who drops in every weekend to drink and eat, which creates a hit to the comps line, wants the glory of saying he's an owner without doing any work. Ultimately, every partner or owner wants the sum total of more than the business can actually deliver, and at the point that the pie isn't large enough, the conflicts break out. That's where we come in to perform a valuation and sell the business.

Failure to Grow or Adapt

Restaurants that don't adapt to the changing marketplace end up stagnant. Once you have the basics under control, stay current by visiting other restaurants, joining associations, and reading restaurant news. The Internet has introduced an entirely new way to stay current. Follow the foodie blogs for your area. Join the social networking sites and make sure you're reading the online reviews of your restaurant to see what your clients are saying. Then introduce changes a few at a time. The time honored tradition of specials in a restaurant offers the ultimate opportunity to test something before it ever finds a permanent space on the menu.

Shock to the System

The flip side to reason eight, failure to adapt, is reason nine—shock to the system. This is the buyer that buys an existing restaurant and then immediately changes everything about it. He shocks the staff, the regulars, the suppliers, and the kitchen and the waitstaff into a state of crisis where nothing can be delivered on time since no one knows what they are doing anymore and then calls us to say, "What was it you sold me? This restaurant isn't working."

This is an actual story from our experiences; only the names have been changed.

> A buyer relocating into our market bought a seafood concept in an upscale suburb. The restaurant was well established in the neighborhood. The new owner took over and literally within days had ripped out the bar, uprooted the booths, converted everything to table seating, changed the menu, and reopened.
>
> His regular customers along with his staff were shell-shocked, and the service and sales quickly reflected this. The kitchen didn't know the menu. The waitstaff didn't know or push the specials. Within a week, he was calling to ask, "What happened? These are the sales and profits you represented." The answer? This isn't the same restaurant anymore. Go slowly unless you aren't buying the original cash flow.

If I Build It, They Will Come

The final reason for failure is all the money spent on building restaurant monuments. This is most typical with chefs. The top chefs of the world spend millions of dollars on fabulous restaurants, but they have the time, money, and investors for the projects. The problem is that we often see typical restaurant owners operating in smaller environments hiring everyone from restaurant architects to interior designers only to blow their budget getting the restaurant open. This leaves them in the same position as those owners that buy without sufficient capital. They have no money left to create the buzz that is required to launch a restaurant.

While these ten reasons sadly reflect actions that lead to failure, there are ten traits we see in successful restaurant owners over and over again. It doesn't take all these traits to succeed. A good combination of any of these elements combined with basic business skills will equate to success in this industry.

The Top Ten Reasons Restaurants Succeed

Great Food

It all comes down to the food. With great food, many other elements are simply overlooked or forgiven by a customer seeking what only you have to offer.

Restaurant Owners with a Passion for the Business

An owner without prior experience but a determination to succeed can overcome the obstacles and succeed when buying an existing restaurant. Purchasing an existing restaurant with a bankable cash flow is easily managed by someone with good management and financial skills.

This is an actual story from our experiences; only the names have been changed.

> One of our first sales was to a consultant ready to leave corporate America. He played in a small band on the weekends and decided he wanted his own pub. He ended up buying a sports bar. He had no experience but a strong desire to succeed.
>
> He called the first week to say he was having a problem and needed some help. According to him, the regulars liked him so much they were buying him shots. He said by the end of the night, after three or four shots, he couldn't remember his name, much less count out the till and shut the place down. We offered our suggestion, which was to have his bartender ring the shot at full price and tell the buyer he was having a Jagermeister (or some other dark) shot. The bartender was to pour his shot from a special bottle under the bar that was actually flat Coca-Cola. He thought this was brilliant and decided that would be his strategy. Not only did he avoid getting drunk, he earned a nice profit on the shot. We hung up the phone shaking our heads and wondering if this guy was going to make it. Six years later, he's going strong. Business is up every single year of operation, and he still reminds us that we kept him sober year one. You can't predict success in the restaurant and bar business.

Restaurant Owners that Can Read People as well as a Profit and Loss Statement

The restaurant business is a people business. Whether it's in hiring or walking the floor, successful restaurant owners can key into the body language and conversations happening on the floor to identify problems. Chain restaurants set standards for managers to walk up to tables and ask if everything is all right, but half the time this canned question is delivered without a real connection to the customer that says, "I really want an answer." Good operators approach the table, survey the situation quickly, size up that Sally the server hasn't delivered bread or a refill on the drink, and talks to the customers. Owners tuned into people know how to find those traits in the people they hire. They know how to find the loyal producer to turn out food from the kitchen along with the sales-focused waitress in order to drive revenue tableside.

Creative Restaurant Owners Know How to Sell, Sell, Sell

Good restaurateurs are strong sales and marketing leaders, and it's a key reason for their success. They look at their restaurant or bar as a place to gather, and they begin inventing events and reasons to bring more people together. The tired old sports bar that relies on karaoke and trivia nights will get nothing in the way of market share while the savvy operator that puts together a monthly St. Practice Day on the seventeenth of every month creates an event complete with Irish beer and food that gives his clients a reason to come.

Getting traffic in the door is only half the equation. The other half is driving sales while the customer is in the restaurant. Good operators look at their waitstaff as salespeople. They offer incentives to upsell the customer on the special, sell gift cards, appetizers, desserts, and more. They get customers to sign up for e-mail marketing, text marketing, and more. Sales are the vital lifeblood of the business. Without growth in sales, profitability will begin to be eroded by rising costs.

This is an actual story from our experiences; only the names have been changed.

> Our client operates a franchise wing concept in the suburbs. He's a former beer salesman who has a knack for bringing people together. When he bought his restaurant originally, he relied on the franchise advertising plan and marketing materials. As time went by, he saw little innovation or change, so he put his own talent to work. He always has an event or "reason to visit" happening at his store. While the other stores

plug along with 1% increases to flat business, his top line sales grow 8–9% a year along with his profits.

In an inland location as far from the shore as you can reach, he's developed a crawfish festival once a year that draws thousands. He puts together e-mail marketing, text marketing campaigns, and paints signs in his windows that communicate "We're having a party and you don't want to miss it." The result is a sports bar/franchise wings environment that packs them in night and day. Without following the franchise model, he sets his own vision for success and wins.

Restaurant Owners that are Active and Engaged with their Customers

Owners that remain in the kitchen are setting themselves up for failure while those that are on the floor interacting with their clients are lining up success. Listen to your client. Ask the question "Is everything okay?" and listen to the answer. Savvy operators can take the pulse of the room and figure out which waitress is more concerned with text messaging her boyfriend than taking care of tables. If you're hidden away in the office or kitchen, it won't happen.

Restaurant Owners that Live and Die by the Numbers

The restaurant business is a numbers business. Well-operated restaurants run by these statistics without fail. If you choose to enter the business because you're a great chef with a passion for food, that will only get you through about 15% of what's required to run a great restaurant. Here are the parameters you must manage to succeed.

Food costs must be controlled to be successful. As a percent-to-sales, there are specific ratios that should be managed if you want financial success. The food cost ratio will range higher for gourmet restaurants (more expensive cuts of meat and higher quality food). It's also higher in franchise concepts (especially when prepackaged franchise food is the only thing you can buy) and restaurants high in meat (steakhouses). Food cost should normalize for restaurants at approximately 35% for fine dining, 32% for American casual, and around 29% for pizza or Italian concepts. If the food costs exceed these numbers, there is no mystery here. One of three things is happening:

1. Food is being wasted. Food is a perishable item, and the inventory must be ordered and maintained based on the turnover of the product on the menu. If the kitchen staff is ordering the food and you're throwing out meats and vegetables, this is profit leaking from your store.
2. Portions are too large. Americans overeat in general, and some kitchen staff fail to place the correct food portion on the plate. Weigh, measure, or provide visual cues for correct portions.
3. Food is going out the back door. This may be related to item number one where the kitchen team orders too much and then, since it's going to go bad anyway, takes it home. This becomes a habit when their grocery bill is zero and your food costs are escalating. Running a kitchen by the numbers means managing the food cost.

The second number to control is alcohol costs. Alcohol is one of your highest profit and highest theft areas. Inspect what you expect here and maintain your costs. If you don't know how to manage this element, there are firms that will come in and weigh and measure. They will instruct your bartenders in an appropriate pour and make sure your money isn't being wasted.

Labor costs as a percent-to-sales is another number to manage. Labor should not exceed 25% of sales. If it does, you will be running a losing operation. Managing the schedule and gross payroll cost is simple fifth-grade math. Make sure the prep team is working when they should be and that extra staff is not on hand when they aren't needed.

There's a number associated with your sanitation score, and it needs to be 100 or so close that it's negligible. There's no excuse in the restaurant industry for failing to meet the minimal measures for inspection. The state itemizes what they are looking for. If you fail to manage into this number, your customers will leave. They will forgive a night of sloppy service, a long wait, or a hostess with an attitude. They will not forgive you for failing the grade on a health inspection. If these numbers are managed, the rest is easy.

Restaurant Owners that Train and Develop Long-term Staff

In the beginning, most owners spend more time than they wanted getting the operation right, but eventually they recognize they have to develop long-term staff that functions on their terms in order to succeed.

Restaurant Owners that will not Settle for the Status Quo

Restaurant owners that are always learning are talking to vendors and reading Web sites, blogs, and restaurant magazines. Good operators are on a quest for knowledge. They learn from this quest when something is a passing fad versus a trend that's here to stay. Knowing the difference allows them to stay ahead of the marketing curve. Good owners constantly reinvent their marketing, their menu, their processes, and their restaurant over time. They show up on local media doing interviews. They embrace new ideas like social media marketing or text marketing even if it's totally different from the direct mail campaign they've run for the last five years. They attend food shows and ask a vendor what's happening in the industry, and then they lead instead of following.

Restaurant Owners that Hire Expertise if they Don't Have It

Lots of good restaurant owners are great in the kitchen or great with the books, but when it comes to other areas like marketing, advertising, or public relations, they are lost. The successful restaurant owner knows how to identify both his strengths and weaknesses and will seek out and pay for professional expertise to supplement his skills.

Restaurant Owners that are Independent Operators

The best operators aren't poll takers. They don't need the safety net of other's opinions or partners to succeed. They are intrinsically risk takers and are willing to take the lumps when they fail as well as the applause when they succeed. Good operators dust themselves off and come up with the next great idea instead of hiding out after their last mistake.

Chapter Summary-Key Points

* The top ten reasons that restaurants fail are:
    - Lack of capital
    - Failure to create and execute a marketing plan
    - Failure to launch
    - Absentee ownership
    - Lack of execution by the numbers
    - Lack of industry knowledge and experience
    - Failed partnerships
    - Failure to grow or adapt
    - Shock to the system
    - If I build it, they will come mentality

* The top ten reasons that restaurants succeed are:
    - Good food
    - Passion for the restaurant business
    - Restaurant owners that read people as well as they read a P&L
    - Creative restaurant owners that know how to sell, sell, sell
    - Restaurant owners that live and die by the numbers
    - Restaurants that train and develop long-term staff
    - Restaurants that will not settle for status quo
    - Restaurants that will hire expertise they don't have in house
    - Restaurant owners that are independent operators

You Own a Restaurant-Now What?

You read this book cover to cover and finally took the plunge. You own a restaurant. Now what? Any new restaurant owner should spend some time with paper and pencil putting your own plan together. Begin by understanding what you purchased. If you bought a well-oiled machine spitting out cash in six figures that is running at the top of its metrics, the answer for the first one hundred days is to make no major changes until you fully understand the business.

If you bought an asset sale that requires a brand new identity, there is a whole list of work to accomplish. Somewhere in the middle may lie a franchise that is performing on average with the rest of the stores. Here's an exercise to develop your hundred-day plan so that post-closing you don't resemble the proverbial deer in the headlights but instead are concentrating your efforts where you can gain the most value for your investment. Here are the essentials for your first one hundred days.

Secure Your Money, Your Inventory, and Your Business

Lock Down Key Employees

Employees are vital to your business. Get to know the employees on the floor to understand which ones are trustworthy, which are loyal to the business, and which need to be replaced. Wait at least ninety days before you start terminating anyone unless you want to frighten most of your staff. An exception to this is any employee that steals. Catch him, fire him, and do it quickly to make an example before others start to think they can steal too.

Lock Down your Physical Property with Security and Key Changes

Rekey your business. Change the alarm codes and change the Web site pass codes to cameras (if you're under electronic surveillance). Change your Web site passwords and any other authorization codes with vendors. You don't know how lax the last owner was about security and who still has physical or virtual keys to the place.

Secure Your Sales and Create a Revenue Pipeline

Promote Your Business to Create a Pipeline of Secure Sales

This is the lifeblood of your business. Make sure you know every event on the calendar for the next ninety days. If there are no events, get busy putting them together. Just because you're new doesn't mean the loyal crowd for the bar doesn't expect the annual Halloween bash to happen again. If you don't promote in the first ninety days, expect business to fall off. Don't get stranded wondering why sales are down—plan for your success. You need a well thought out, targeted, and effective promotional plan. Start with what the business did last year and layer on to this. If you don't know what you're doing, seek a mentor in the business, hire a consultant, or call up a beer supplier and he can help you out.

Marketing

The day of closing you should already have business cards printed with your name. They should be in the hands of everyone you know. You're in the restaurant business now, and it's a people business. Tell everyone you know that they need to try your restaurant. Do not treat them to free drinks or dinner when they are there. One client we had did this and went out of business feeding the masses.

This is an actual story from our experiences; only the names have been changed.

> Marketing isn't giving it away. Our buyer had never been in the restaurant business as an operator but waited tables in college and loved dining. He bought a seafood concept that had very good food in an affluent suburb. After the closing he invited us to dinner. We accepted and had a great meal. He didn't bring the check. We asked the waitress who said it was "on the owner." Since our policy is not to accept meals from our operators, we quickly told her to print the check and gave her a credit card.
>
> We brought other business to his restaurant (group meetings and nights out with friends). Each time we faced the same dilemma. We had to force the issue to pay full price. A friend told us months later that he barely knew the owner but each time he visited the restaurant, his meal was heavily discounted. Before long, the owner was calling us to sell his restaurant. His sales were down, and his profit was off. We told him he needed to stop giving away freebies to the world, and he said, "I just want them to come back." We told him that when you give the food away, two things are going to happen. First, those that want a free lunch will keep coming back expecting it for free. Those who are uncomfortable with the idea will stay away. Ultimately, you have to be comfortable with the restaurant business and allow the food and service to stand for itself. Invite your friends and family to your restaurant but require them to pay.

Web site

Make sure your Web site is functional and up-to-date. Make sure you know how to monitor web traffic and how to get e-mail addresses from the system so you can continue to market.

E-mail Marketing and Text Marketing

Figure out how to get e-mail addresses or text message numbers from all your customers. Run a monthly contest with your waitstaff so the person with the most contacts turned in gets a payout. It is critical that you connect with your customers frequently. E-mail and text messaging are instant, easy, and inexpensive ways to do it.

Gift Card Marketing

Gift cards are a very important part of the restaurant business. They are also a huge source of cash flow, as the money is paid at the point of purchase and doesn't affect you until the card is redeemed. With only about 35% of all gift certificates converted, this is a huge moneymaking opportunity. If the restaurant you bought doesn't have the ability to issue and replenish electronic gift cards, there are plenty of vendors available online. Call one today.

Online Reservation System

Make sure you have an online reservation system. There are operators like www.opentable.com that operate this service seamlessly for you. Your goal is to make your restaurant accessible for booking tables twenty-four hours a day. In this digital environment, it's critical.

This is an actual story from our experiences; only the names have been changed.

> Everyone loves to say they know the owner. One successful operator we know gives his card to everyone saying, "This is my cell number. Call me and I'll get you a table." That particular cell phone never left his side and was linked directly to the restaurant reservation system. By creating the sense that the caller got moved to the front of the reservation line, his restaurant stayed full.

Secure Your Costs with Strong Controls

Food Cost

Along with labor, this is your single largest expense. Understand who is doing the food ordering, what he is ordering, and how he handles the inventory process very early in the game. Cost of goods sold expressed as out-of-control food costs are the major drain on any restaurant owner's profit and loss statement. You should have an ongoing food inventory sheet for the freezer and dry goods. That old adage that you "inspect what you expect" pays off in food costs. If you don't oversee the process of ordering, prepare for mistakes, and before you know it you have food costs spiraling out of control.

Create or review the prep list for the kitchen with levels required for each day of the week. Make sure someone is prepping only this amount and no more and no less each day.

Alcohol Costs

Secure the alcohol inventory separately. You should have a separate bar inventory sheet. If you don't want to do the inventory yourself or pay an employee, hire a service to handle this for you. There are firms like Bevinco that specialize in profit management and alcohol control. You can outsource your alcohol inventory to them at reasonable rates of return to you in savings on lost alcohol costs.

Energy Costs and Waste

Create an opening and closing checklist and spot check these each day to make sure they are correct. Are the heavy power users going on into sleep mode or turned off to maximize energy savings? Are the condiments being filled before everyone leaves at night so everything starts full in the morning and the staff isn't scrambling at lunch and turning tables away? Does everyone understand how the cash and credit card transactions are handled at each night's closing? Traffic is predictable. Table count is predictable. Your POS system and the historical records of the POS system are a treasure trove of information you need to build a process around transactions.

Go through the existing operations manual in detail. If there isn't one, get busy. Write a clear blueprint for the operations of your business. Most people can't operate a new car without a manual but try to operate a business without one. If the prior owner didn't have an operations manual, maybe that's why you got such a good deal. If one exists, bring it up-to-date. This should be a complete picture of everything going on in the business, a "Your Restaurant Guide for Dummies" so that if you're hit by a bus someone knows how to keep the business running. Make sure there's a copy held electronically and in paper form with your attorney or someone offsite.

Secure Your Regulatory Compliance

Labor

No one likes the level of government bureaucracy, and the level of compliance required seems to grow exponentially each year. On the other hand, compliance is required to stay in business, so understand the law. The federal government requires posting of the following:

* Equal Pay for Equal Work Act
* EEOC—Equal Employment Opportunity Act
* Fair Labor Standards Act (FLSA) minimum wage poster

The state you're living in has its own set of additional labor laws and postings that are also required. A good broker can provide you with links to most Web sites, or visit your Secretary of

State online and search under "starting a new restaurant business" for almost everything you need.

Food Service

Virtually every state now has some version of ServSafe®, an industry certification that must be completed by someone onsite at all times the restaurant is open. Check with your state restaurant associations (see list in the appendix) to find classes held in both Spanish and English. In addition, you'll have to comply with health department rules and inspections, standards related to the disposal of fats, oils, and greases, as well as fire inspections (sprinkler, extinguisher, and Ansul hood system) related to the containment of fire.

Alcohol Service

Restaurants have an entire regulatory bundle associated with the sale and service of alcoholic beverages. Most states require a liquor bond or alcohol or dram shop insurance policy. Most states will require that you attend a class before an alcohol license is issued to you or your place of business. Quickly make sure there's a 100% compliance with ID, as state officers do check and send underage-appearing officers into restaurants to enforce against underage drinking. Do not let your business be placed at risk for serving someone underage. You must have a zero tolerance policy on carding those for drinks. If you observe someone on your staff failing to card or potentially selling underage patrons, immediately fire them. There are commercial mystery shopping services that employ youthful-looking guests to test your servers. If you have any doubts, hire a service.

Secure Your Books and Records

Bookkeeping

Even if you are a certified public accountant yourself, outsource the bookkeeping and accounting for the first one hundred days. You need to keep your eye on the operation. Start having your financials produced beginning day one. You don't want to wait until the paperwork piles up to figure out which end is up. You need a monthly profit and loss statement to be certain the business you bought is the same business you're still running. If sales are taking a dive or profits are off the mark, the answers are in your P&L.

Payroll

Make sure you have a payroll service or accountant in place to handle payroll. Nothing makes an employee angrier than a screw-up on a paycheck. This is a simple process that should be outsourced.

Secure the Existing Business by Maintaining, not Changing

Status Quo

Virtually everyone that buys a restaurant from us has great ideas for improvement, and some of these will drive sales. However, in the first one hundred days, unless sales are in the tank and you bought assets only, our advice is to wait it out. Introduce specials to see how people respond to your Grandma's lasagna dish before you pull every other Italian dish off the menu. You have a loyal customer base that's been coming for years that doesn't like change. If you serve Grandma's lasagna as a special for three weeks and get no repeat orders, you have your answer.

Until then, leave the menu alone. Ask your customers as you are getting to know them what they like and what they don't. Be prepared for more information than you need and to listen carefully to a diverse range of opinions before making changes.

Don't rearrange the floor space in the first one hundred days. We sold a restaurant to a guy that insisted what the place needed was pool tables. He had to pull out half his seating to get two pool tables inside. He called us to sell the place after sales went down by 50% in the first month. Simple math skills would have shown him what a bad idea this was. Eight tables seating four people that turned 2.5 times a night were uprooted so he could replace them with two pool tables that earned $1.25 an hour. Which sales do you want? An average of $35 in gross sales per table (times eight tables) turned 2.5 times a night producing $700 in sales or a couple of pool tables that get you $1.25 a half hour per game and whatever beer they drink in that time—maybe $100 a night. Crunch the numbers before you make a change. Unless what you are doing is adding sales without subtracting any, put it off until you know the business better.

Staff

We've already talked about it, but it bears repeating. Very few loyal employees will leave in the first ninety days. Even if your brother is a top chef in waiting, it's best to get the lay of the land before you pull the firing card on loyal people. Someone that doesn't make a good first impression may turn out to be your most loyal and productive employee in the long run. Exceptions were noted already. Someone stealing from you or serving alcohol without verifying legal age needs to go.

Cleaning

Despite the early advice to leave everything status quo, that does not apply to cleaning. A new owner should clean and clean and then clean some more. Get the windows cleaned. Clear out the clutter underneath the hostess stand. Clean out the coolers. Look up at the ceiling tile, and where there's a single old, dingy brown spot from a leak of ten years ago, pull it out and put in a new one. An entire box of ceiling tiles won't cost you what a single table's sales earn when someone looks up and sees that brown spot. Paint the bathrooms (even if it's the same color) to freshen them up. Clean the carpet. Clean the baseboards. If there are curtains hanging in the restaurant, either burn them (who hangs curtains anymore?) or take them down and clean them. Polish the floors. Install new lightbulbs. People who have been coming for years won't know what's different, but they'll sense a positive change.

Logo Merchandise

You're excited about your business, and you should be. But before you go out and buy a lot of preprinted product with your logo on it, buy just a few things for yourself. In our experience, unless you're in a highly touristy area (think beachside), then t-shirts with the restaurant logo on them are costly and a huge opportunity for theft without a great deal of return on investment. That doesn't mean you might not want branded merchandise to sell down the road; just wait out your first one hundred days to be sure.

Secure the Ongoing Operation of the Business

Maintenance Contracts

You had initial inspections on the business, but in the first one hundred days you need service contracts to make sure everything keeps running smoothly. This preventative maintenance will head off a crisis situation on a ninety-five degree Friday afternoon when the HVAC goes out. Without an existing service contract, no one knows who you are and won't return a call for service until they've handled their regulars. Don't be pennywise and pound foolish. Restaurant equipment will fail at the worst possible time. You just spent a lot of money on this restaurant, so the least you can do is protect the ongoing assets with a maintenance schedule. Do it in the first one hundred days so you don't have to worry about it in the next one hundred. This may include any or all of the following:

- *Fire systems.* This isn't the fire department-required inspection; it's for the sprinkler inspection and annual fire extinguisher inspection.
- *HVAC contract and inspection.* Get on a contract so that when the HVAC goes down, someone can be called immediately that will show up. Preventative maintenance will catch most problems, but restaurants use immense amounts of cooling and it needs to be maintained.
- *Kitchen equipment.* Get someone on the hook that you can call when the fryer goes down, the seal on the cooler breaks, or whatever else. Again, you don't want to be stranded on a holiday weekend with a key piece of equipment down. In the restaurant business, weekends and holidays are critical, and you can't wait until Monday. You need someone that will come immediately.
- *Plumber and electrician.* Make sure you establish a relationship with both a plumber and electrician for the same reasons.
- *Hood inspection and cleaning.* Companies will steam clean your hood on a contract. Do it.
- *Grease trap cleanout.* This is required by law in most states, so set it up for a quarterly service or whatever's required by either your lease or the health department.

- *Pest contract.* Make sure there's never a chance for rodent problem by securing a contract up front.
- *POS provider.* Get on a first-name basis with your POS provider. You should have a contract in place with them and make sure you have a cell phone number. Trying to run handwritten orders to a kitchen that's only used to a POS system is a nightmare for the most experienced operator. You want someone on speed dial in the event your system goes down.

Secure Your Exposure

Lights, Camera, Action

Odds are the last guy maximized signage for the restaurant, but it doesn't hurt to ask. Get a copy of the local sign ordinance and have a lighting and sign person come out to take a fresh look. Most restaurant owners spend so much time inside their business that they totally forget to take a look from the curb. If you've maximized signage, can you do any more with lighting? If signage above your building is the best it can get, can you negotiate with the landlord for more room on a pylon at the road, even if it's temporary until he fills some empty spaces?

If you have outdoor seating, freshen up the tables with new umbrellas. This isn't a radical change but, like cleaning, will perk up the existing area and draw the eye. Use yellow where possible, as this is the most compelling color to the human eye (this is why road signs are yellow) and will draw people from the road to take a look. Often vendors will supply these free of charge if you allow the use of their logo. If you have space, add plants and twinkle lights. Again, this doesn't count in your signage but sets a visual standard you can see from the road.

Don't forget your windows as signage space. If you have standard plate glass windows in a shopping center, they are golden opportunities for signage. You can have them painted with upcoming promotions very inexpensively. Hire a window painter by looking online or asking someone else with painted windows for a recommendation. This doesn't count in your signage space for most ordinances. The same thing is true for your door signs. Does it highlight your logo? Are the hours painted, or do they consist of a dirty, hand-lettered sign? The doors are the first impression of your business. Put up a couple of topiaries for ambience and add twinkling lights. Make sure that first visual impression is one that says, "This restaurant looks good, and I can't wait to try the food."

That's it. You've gone from the first day of your search to your first one hundred days in business. After that it's up to you. You have joined a thriving industry that celebrates the most basic of human interactions, the breaking of bread. You are now a restaurant owner. We can't predict your level of success or risk of failure, but reading this book has armed you with more knowledge than the average buyer. Give us a call when you're ready for another location or you want to sell. After all, we sell restaurants; we wrote the book.

Chapter Summary-Key Points

* The first one hundred days are about securing your investment. There are ten elements you need to secure starting day one.
  - Secure your money, your inventory, your business.
  - Secure your sales and create a revenue pipeline.
  - Secure your costs with strong processes.
  - Secure your regulatory compliance.
  - Secure your books and record keeping.

- Secure your existing operation by maintaining, not changing in the first 100 days.
- Secure your ongoing operation.
- Secure your exposure.

Endnotes

Introduction

[1] Denise Roach, managing editor, *The* 2009 *Restaurant Industry Forecast* (Washington: National Restaurant Association, 2009), page 2.

[2] H.G. Parsa, John T. Self, David Njite, and Tiffany King, "Why Restaurants Fail," *Cornell Hotel and Restaurant Administration Quarterly*, Vol. 46, No. 3 (2005): 304.

Chapter 1

[1] H.G. Parsa, John T. Self, David Njite, and Tiffany King, "Why Restaurants Fail," *Cornell Hotel and Restaurant Administration Quarterly*, Vol. 46, No. 3 (2005): 304.

[2] Ayn Rand, *Atlas Shrugged*, (New York: The Penguin Group, 1999).

Chapter 7

[1] "The Lowdown on Franchising," USA Today.com, accessed February 4, 2010, http://www.usatoday.com/money/smallbusiness/strategies/2002/03–15-franchises.htm.

[2] "The Lowdown on Franchising," USA Today.com, accessed February 4, 2010, http://www.usatoday.com/money/smallbusiness/strategies/2002/03–15-franchises.htm.

[3] "A& W History," A&W, accessed February 4, 2010. http://www.rootbeer.com.

[4] Pricewaterhouse Coopers, LLP, "2010 *Franchise Business Economic Outlook.*" Prepared for The International Franchise Association Educational Foundation, December 21, 2009.

[5] H.G. Parsa, John T. Self, David Njite, and Tiffany King, "Why Restaurants Fail," (Cornell Hotel and Restaurant Administration Quarterly, Vol. 46, No. 3, 304–322 (2005).

Chapter 13

[1] "SBA Losses Climb 154% in 2008," accessed February 4, 2010, http://www.colemanpublishing.com/public/343.cfm.

Appendix 1

Business Brokerage Organizations

International Business Brokers Association (IBBA)
401 N. Michigan Ave., Suite 2200
Chicago, IL 60611–4267
Phone: (888) 686-IBBA (4222) Fax: (312) 673–6599
www.ibba.org

Arizona Association of Business Brokers (AABB)
www.azbba.org

California Association of Business Brokers (CABB)
www.cabb.org

Colorado Association of Intermediaries (CABI)
www.coloradobusinesses.com

Connecticut—New England Business Brokers Association (NEBBA)
www.nebba.com

Business Brokers of Florida (BBF)
www.bbfmls.com

Georgia Association of Business Brokers (GABB)
www.gabb.org

Illinois—Midwest Business Brokers and Intermediaries
www.mbbi.org

Kansas
www.kansascitybusinessbrokersassociation.com/

Maine—New England Business Brokers
Association (NEBBA)
www.nebba.com

Maryland—Mid Atlanta Business
Intermediaries Association (MABIA)
www.mabia.org

Massachusetts—New England Business
Brokers Association (NEBBA)
www.nebba.com

Michigan Business Brokers Association (MBBA)
www.mbba.org

Nevada Business Brokers Association (NBBA)
www.nbba1.org

New Hampshire—New England Business
Brokers Association (NEBBA)
www.nebba.com

New Jersey—Mid Atlanta Business
Brokers Association (MABBA)
www.mabba.net

New York Association of Business Brokers (NYABB)
www.nyabb.org

North Carolina—Carolina-Virginia Business
Brokers Association (CVBBA)
www.cvbba.com

Ohio Business Brokers Association (OBBA)
www.obba.org

Pennsylvania Business Brokers Association (PBBA)
www.pennbba.com/

Rhode Island—New England Business
Brokers Association (NEBBA)
www.nebba.com

South Carolina—Carolina-Virginia Business
Brokers Association (CVBBA)
www.cvbba.com

Texas Association of Business Brokers (TABB)
www.tabb.org

Vermont—New England Business
Brokers Association (NEBBA)
www.nebba.com

Virginia—Carolina-Virginia Business
Brokers Association (CVBBA)
www.cvbba.com

Mid Atlantic Business Intermediaries Association (MABIA)
www.mabia.org

Washington
Mid Atlantic Business Intermediaries Association (MABIA)
www.mabia.org

Wisconsin—Midwest Business Brokers
and Intermediaries (MBBI)
www.mbbi.org

Appendix 2

States Requiring Real Estate Licenses for Business Brokerage

ALASKA

Alaska Real Estate Commission
Robert B. Atwood Building
550 W. 7th Avenue, Suite 1950
Anchorage, AK 99501
Main Phone: (907) 269–8162
Fax: (907) 269–1066
www.commerce.state.ak.us/occ/prec.htm

ARIZONA

Arizona Department of Real Estate
2910 N. 44th Street, Suite 100
Phoenix, AZ 85018
Phone: (602) 468–1414
www.re.state.az.us/

CALIFORNIA

California Department of Real Estate
2201 Broadway
P.O. Box 187000
Sacramento, CA 95818
Phone: (916) 227–0782
http://www.dre.ca.gov

FLORIDA

Division of Real Estate
400 West Robinson Street, N801
Orlando, Fl 32801
Phone: (850) 487–1395
Fax: (407) 317–7245
www.myfloridalicense.com/dbpr/re/frec.html

GEORGIA

Georgia Real Estate Commission **or** Georgia Real Estate Appraisers Board
229 Peachtree Street, N.E.
International Tower, Suite 1000
Atlanta, Georgia 30303–1605
Phone: (404) 656–3916
Fax: (404) 656–6650
www.grec.state.ga.us/

IDAHO

633 North 4th Street
PO Box 83720 Boise, ID 83720–0077
Phone: (208) 334–3285
Fax: (208) 334–2050
Toll Free in Idaho: 866–447–5411
http://www.irec.idaho.gov/

MICHIGAN

Department of Commerce—Bureau
of Occupational & Professional Svcs.
Office of Commercial Services, Licensing Division
P. O. Box 30243
Lansing, MI 48909
Phone: (517) 373–0490
www.michigan.gov/statelicensesearch

MINNESOTA

Minnesota Department of Commerce
133 East 7th Street
St. Paul, MN 55101
Phone: (612) 296–2488
www.state.mn.us

NEBRASKA

Nebraska Real Estate Commission
P.O. Box 94667
Lincoln, NE 68509–4667
1200 "N" Street, Suite 402
Lincoln, NE 68508
Phone: (402) 471–2004
www.nrec.state.ne.us/

OREGON

Oregon Real Estate Agency
1177 Center St., N.E.
Salem, OR 97310–2503
Phone: (503) 378–4170
www.oregon.gov/REA/index.shtml

SOUTH DAKOTA

South Dakota Real Estate Commission
222 E. Capitol, Suite 15
P.O. Box 490
Pierre, SD 57501–0490
Phone: (605) 773–3600
www.state.sd.us/sdrec/

UTAH

Division of Real Estate
P.O. Box 45806
Salt Lake City, UT 84145–0806
Phone: (801) 530–6747
www.realestate.utah.gov/

WASHINGTON

Washington Department of Licensing
Business and Professions Division
Real Estate Program
P.O. Box 9015
Olympia, WA 98507
2000 4th Ave. W.
Olympia, WA 98502
Phone: (360) 586–6101
www.dol.wa.gov/business/realestate/

WYOMING

Wyoming Real Estate Commission
2020 Carey Ave. Suite 100
Cheyenne, WY 82002–0180
Phone: (307) 777–7141
www.realestate.wy.us/

Appendix 3

State Restaurant Associations

Alabama Restaurant Association
www.alabamrestaurants.com

Alaska Cabaret, Hotel, Restaurant & Retailers Association
www.alaskacharr.com

Arizona Restaurant Association
www.azrestaurant.org

Arkansas Hospitality Association
www.arhospitality.org

California Restaurant Association
www.calrest.org

Colorado Restaurant Association
www.coloradorestaurant.com

Connecticut Restaurant Association
www.ctrestaurant.org

Delaware Restaurant Association
www.delawarerestaurant.org

Restaurant Association Metropolitan Washington
www.ramw.org

Florida Restaurant & Lodging Association
www.frla.org

Georgia Restaurant Association
www.garestaurants.org

Hawaii Restaurant Association
www.hawaiirestaurants.org

Idaho Lodging & Restaurant Association
www.idahohospitality.net

Illinois Restaurant Association
www.illinoisrestaurants.org

Restaurant & Hospitality Association of Indiana
www.indianarestaurants.org

Iowa Restaurant Association
www.restaurantiowa.com

Kansas Restaurant & Hospitality Association
www.krha.org

Kentucky Restaurant Association
www.lra.org

Maine Restaurant Association
www.mainerestaurant.com

Restaurant Association of Maryland, Inc.
www.marylandrestaurants.com

Massachusetts Restaurant Association
www.massrestaurantassoc.org

Michigan Restaurant Association
www.massrestaurantassoc.org

Minnesota Restaurant Association
www.hospitalitymn.com

Mississippi Hospitality & Restaurant Association
www.msra.org

Missouri Restaurant Association
www.morestaurants.org

Montana Restaurant Association
www.mtrestaurant.com

Nebraska Restaurant Association
www.nebraska-dining.org

Nevada Restaurant Association
www.nvrestaurants.com

New Hampshire Lodging & Restaurant Association
www.nhlra.com

New Jersey Restaurant Association
www.njra.org

New Mexico Restaurant Association
www.nmrestaurants.org

New York State Restaurant Association
www.nysra.org

North Carolina Restaurant & Lodging Association
www.ncrla.biz

North Dakota Hospitality Association
www.ndhospitality.com

Ohio Restaurant Association
www.ohiorestaurant.org

Oklahoma Restaurant Association
www.okrestaurants.com

Oregon Restaurant Association
www.ora.org

Pennsylvania Restaurant Association
www.parestaurant.org

Puerto Rico Restaurant Association
www.parestaurant.org

Rhode Island Hospitality Association
www.rihospitality.org

Hospitality Association of South Carolina
www.schospitality.org

South Dakota Retailers Association, Restaurant Division
www.sdra.org

Tennessee Hotel & Lodging Association
www.thla.net

Texas Restaurant Association
www.restaurantville.com

U.S. Virgin Island Tourism Associations
www.virgin-islands-hotels.com

Utah Restaurant Association
www.utahdineout.com

Vermont Hospitality Council
www.vtchamber.com

Virginia Hospitality & Travel Association
www.vhta.org

Washington Restaurant Association
www.wrahome.com

West Virginia Hospitality & Travel Association
www.wvhta.com

Wisconsin Restaurant Association
www.wirerestaurant.org

Wyoming Lodging & Restaurant Association
www.wlra.org

Appendix 4

Alcohol Licensing Authorities by State

ALABAMA (CONTROL STATE)

Alabama Alcoholic Beverage Control Board
2715 Gunter Park Drive West
Montgomery, AL 36109
Phone: (334) 271–3840
Fax: (334) 277–2150

ALASKA

Department of Public Safety
Alcoholic Beverage Control Board
5848 E. Tudor Road
Anchorage, AK 99507
Phone: (907) 269–0350
Fax: (907) 272–9412

ARIZONA

Arizona Department of Liquor Licenses and Control
800 W. Washington, 5th Floor
Phoenix, AZ 85007
Phone: (602) 542–5141
Fax: (602) 542–5707

ARKANSAS

Alcohol Beverage Control
1515 W. Seventh Street, Rm. 503
Little Rock, AR 72201
Phone: (501) 682–1105

CALIFORNIA

California Department of Alcoholic Beverage Control
3927 Lennane Drive, Suite 100
Sacramento, CA 95834
Phone: (916) 419–2500

California Board of Equalization
450 N Street
Sacramento, CA 94279–0073
Phone: (916) 445–6464

COLORADO

Colorado Department of Revenue
Liquor Enforcement Division
1881 Pierce #108A
Lakewood, CO 80214–1495
Mail: 1375 Sherman Street, Denver, CO 80261
Phone: (303) 205–2300
Fax: (303) 205–2341

CONNECTICUT

Connecticut Department of Consumer Protection
Liquor Division
State Office Building
165 Capitol Ave
Hartford, CT 06106
Phone: (860) 713–6200
Fax: (860) 713–7235

DELAWARE

Delaware Department of Public Services
Alcoholic Beverage Control Commission
Carvel State Office Building, 3rd Floor
820 N. French Street
Wilmington, DE 19801
Phone: (302) 577–5210 Toll Free: 1–800–273–9500
Fax: (302) 577–8141

DISTRICT OF COLUMBIA

Alcoholic Beverage Regulation Administration
941 North Capitol Street, NE, Suite 7200
Washington, DC 20002
Phone: (202) 442–4423
Fax: (202) 442–4521

FLORIDA

Florida Department of Professional Business Regulations
Division of Alcoholic Beverages and Tobacco
1940 N. Monroe
Tallahassee, Florida 32399–0783
Phone: (850) 488–3227
Fax: (850) 922–5175

GEORGIA

Georgia Department of Revenue
Alcohol & Tobacco Tax Division
1800 Century Center Blvd., N.E. Room 4235
Atlanta, Georgia 30345–3205
Mail: P.O. Box 49728, Atlanta, Georgia 30359
Phone: (404) 417–4900
Fax: (404) 417–4901

HAWAII

Honolulu
Liquor Commission City and County of Honolulu
Pacific Park Plaza
711 Kapiolani Blvd, Suite 600
Honolulu, Hawaii 96813
Phone: (808) 523–4458 Toll Free: 1–800–838–9976
FAX: (808) 591–2700

Hawaii
Department of Liquor Control
County of Hawaii
101 Aupuni Street, Suite 230
Hilo, Hawaii 96766
Phone: East Hi: (808) 961–8218
West Hi: (808) 327–3549
Fax: East Hi: (808) 961–8684
West Hi: (808) 327–3550

Kauai
Department of Liquor Control County of Kauai
Lihue Civic Center
Mo'ikeha Building
4444 Rice Street, Suite 120
Kauai, Hawaii 96766
Phone: (808) 241–6580
Fax: (808) 241–6585

Maui
Department of Liquor Control
County of Maui
2145 Kaohu Street, Room 107
Wailuku, HI 96793
Phone: (808) 243–7753
Fax: (808) 243–7558

IDAHO (CONTROL STATE)

Alcohol Beverage Control Bureau (enforces distilled spirits laws)
Idaho State Police
700 S. Stratford Drive
Meridian, ID 83642
Mail: P.O. Box 700, Meridian, ID 83680–0700
Phone: (208) 884–7060
Fax: (208) 884–7096

ILLINOIS

Illinois Liquor Control Commission
100 West Randolph Street
Suite #5–300
Chicago, IL 60601
Phone: (312) 814–2206
Fax: (312) 814–2241

Springfield Address:
101 West Jefferson Suite 3–525
Springfield, Illinois 62702
Phone: (217) 782–2136
Fax: (217) 524–1911

INDIANA

Alcohol and Tobacco Commission
Indiana Government Ctr. South
302 W. Washington St., Rm. E-114
Indianapolis, IN 46204
Phone: (317) 232–2430
Fax: (317) 233–6114

IOWA (CONTROL STATE)

Iowa Alcoholic Beverages Division
1918 S.E. Hulsizer Avenue
Ankeny, IA 50021
Phone: (515) 281–7400 Toll Free: 866–469–2223
Fax: (515) 281–7385

KANSAS

Kansas Department of Revenue Alcohol Beverage Control
Alcohol Beverage Control
915 SW Harrison Street, Room 214
Topeka, KS 66625–3512
Phone: (785) 296–7015 Hearing Impaired TTY: (785) 296–6117
Fax: (785) 296–7185

KENTUCKY

Kentucky Alcoholic Beverage Control Department
1003 Twilight Trail, Suite A-2
Frankfort, Kentucky 40601
Phone: (502) 564–4850
Fax: (502) 564–1442

LOUISIANA

Louisiana Department of Revenue
Alcohol and Tobacco Control Office
8549 United Plaza Boulevard, Suite 220
Baton Rouge, Louisiana 70809
Phone: (225) 925–4041
Fax: (225) 925–3975

MAINE (CONTROL STATE)

Main Department of Public Safety
(Liquor, Beer & Wine) Licensing
Liquor or Beer & Wine
164 State House Station
Augusta, ME 04333–0164
Phone: (207) 624–7220
Fax: (207) 287–3424

MARYLAND

Office of the Comptroller of the Treasury
Alcohol and Tobacco Tax Bureau
Louis L. Goldstein Treasury Bldg.
P.O. Box 2999
Annapolis, MD 21404–0466
Phone: (410) 260–7314
Fax: (410) 974–3201

Montgomery County Dept. Of Liquor Control
16650 Crabs Branch Way
Rockville, MD 20855
Phone: (240) 777–1900

MD–Worcester County Liquor Control Board
MD–Worcester County
5363 Snow Hill Road
Snow Hill, MD–Worcester County 21863
Phone: (410) 632–1250
Fax: (410) 632–3010

MASSACHUSETTS

Alcoholic Beverages Control Commission
239 Causeway Street, Floor 1
Boston, MA 02114–2130
Phone: (617) 727–3040
Fax: (617) 727–1258

MICHIGAN (CONTROL STATE)

Michigan Liquor Control Commission
7150 Harris Drive
P.O. Box 30005
Lansing, MI 48909–7505
Phone: (517) 322–1345
Fax: (517) 322–5188

MINNESOTA

Minnesota Department of Public Safety
Liquor Control Division
Alcohol and Gambling and Enforcement Division
444 Cedar St., Suite 133
St. Paul, Minnesota 55101–5133
Phone: (651) 296–6979 **Hearing Impaired TTY:** (651) 282–6555
Fax: (651) 297–5259

MISSISSIPPI (CONTROL STATE)

Alcoholic Beverage Control Office
P.O. Box 540
Madison, Mississippi 39110–0540
Phone: (601) 856–1301
Fax: (601) 856–1300

MISSOURI

Division of Alcohol and Tobacco Control
P.O. Box 837
Jefferson City, Missouri 65102
Phone: (573) 751–2333
Fax: (573) 751–5399

MONTANA (CONTROL STATE)

Montana Liquor License Bureau
125 North Roberts
Helena, Montana 59620
Phone: (406) 444–0700 and (406) 444–6900
Fax: (406) 444–0750

NEBRASKA

Nebraska Liquor Control Commission
301 Centennial Mall South
P.O. Box 95046
Lincoln, Nebraska 68509–5046
Phone: (402) 471–2571
Fax: (402) 471–2814

NEVADA

Nevada Department of Taxation
(All beverage alcohol permits are regulated by each individual county)

Carson City
1550 E. College Parkway Suite 115
Carson City, NV 89706
Phone: (775) 687–4892
Fax: (775) 687–5981

Reno
4600 Kietzke Lane
Building O, Room 263
Reno, NV 89502
Phone: (775) 688–1295
Fax: (775) 688–1303

Elko
850 Elm Street #2
P.O. Box 1750
Elko, NV 89803
Phone: (775) 738–8461
Fax: (775) 778–6814

Las Vegas
Grant Sawyer Office Building
555 E. Washington Ave Suite 1300
Las Vegas, Nevada 89101
Phone: (702) 486–2300
Fax: (702) 486–2372

NEW HAMPSHIRE (CONTROL STATE)

New Hampshire State Liquor Commission
Robert J. Hart Building
Storrs Street
P.O. Box 503
Concord, New Hampshire 03302–0503
Phone: (603) 271–3134
Fax: (603) 271–1107

NEW JERSEY

New Jersey Department of Law and Public Safety
Division of Alcoholic Beverage Control
140 East Front Street
P.O. Box 087
Trenton, New Jersey 08625–0087
Phone: (609) 984–2830
Fax: (609) 633–6078

NEW MEXICO

New Mexico Regulation & Licensing Department
Alcohol and Gaming Division
725 St. Michael's Drive
P.O. Box 25101
Santa Fe, New Mexico 87504–5101
Phone: (505) 827–7066
Fax: (505) 827–7168

New Mexico Department of Public Safety
Special Investigations Division
6301 Indian School NE, Suite 310
Albuquerque NM 87110
Phone: (505) 841–8053
Fax: (505) 841–8062

NEW YORK

New York State Liquor Authority
Division of Alcoholic Beverage Control

Zone 1
State Liquor Authority
317 Lenox Ave.
4th Floor
New York, NY 10027
Phone: (212) 961–8385
Fax: (212) 961–8283

Zone 2
State Liquor Authority
80 S. Swan St.
Suite 900
Albany, NY 12210–8002
Phone: (518) 474–3114
Fax: (518) 473–2286

Syracuse District
State Liquor Authority
333 E. Washington St.
Room 205
Syracuse, NY 13202
Phone: (315) 428–4198
Fax: (315) 428–4201

Zone 3
State Liquor Authority
535 Washington St.
Suite 303
Buffalo, NY 14203
Phone: (716) 847–3035
Fax: (716) 847–3435

NORTH CAROLINA (CONTROL STATE)

North Carolina Alcoholic Beverage Control Commission
3322 Garner Road
Raleigh, North Carolina 27610–5632
Phone: (919) 779–0700
Fax: (919) 662–3583

NORTH DAKOTA

North Dakota Office of the State Tax Commissioner
Alcohol Tax Section
600 East Boulevard Avenue
Bismarck, North Dakota 58505- 0599
Phone: (701) 328–2702
Fax: (701) 328–1283

OHIO (CONTROL STATE)

Ohio Department of Commerce
Division Of Liquor Control
6606 Tussing Road
Reynoldsburg, Ohio 43068–9005
Phone: (614) 644–2411
Fax: (614) 644–2513

OKLAHOMA

Alcoholic Beverage Law Enforcement Commission (ABLE)
4545 N. Lincoln Blvd.
Suite #270
Oklahoma City, Oklahoma 73105
Phone: (405) 521–3484
Fax: (405) 521–6578

The Oklahoma Tax Commission
2501 N. Lincoln Blvd.
Oklahoma City, Oklahoma 73194–0004
Phone: (405) 521–4557

OREGON (CONTROL STATE)

Oregon Liquor Control Commission
9079 S. E. McLoughlin Blvd
Milwaukie, Oregon 97222
Phone: (503) 872–5000 Toll Free: 1 (800) 452–6522
Licensing: (503) 872–5124

PENNSYLVANIA (CONTROL STATE)

Pennsylvania Liquor Control Board
Commonwealth of Pennsylvania
Northwest Office Building
Harrisburg, Pennsylvania 17124–0001
Phone: (717) 783–9454
Fax: (717) 787–8820

PUERTO RICO

Luis Perez-Rivera
Director
Negociado de Bebidas
PO Box S-9024140
San Juan, PR 00904

RHODE ISLAND

Division of Commercial Licensing and Regulation
Liquor Enforcement and Compliance
233 Richmond Street, Suite #200
Providence, Rhode Island 02903–4213
Phone: (401) 222–2562

Division of Commercial Licensing and Regulation
233 Richmond Street, Suite 230
Providence, RI 02903
Phone: (401) 222–2416
Fax: (401) 222–2417

SOUTH CAROLINA

South Carolina Department of Revenue & Taxation
Alcohol Beverage Licensing Section
301 Gervais St.
P.O. Box 125
Columbia, South Carolina 29214–0137
Phone: (803) 737–5000
Fax: 803/734–1401
Beverage Alcohol Licensing: (803) 898–5864

SOUTH DAKOTA

South Dakota Department of Revenue & Regulation
Division of Special Taxes
445 E. Capitol Avenue
Pierre, SD 57501–3185
Phone: (605) 773–3311
Fax: (605) 773–6729

TENNESSEE

Tennessee Alcoholic Beverage Commission
226 Capitol Blvd. Building, Room 600
Nashville, TN 37219–0755
Phone: (615) 741–1602
fax: (615) 741–0847

TEXAS

Texas Alcoholic Beverage Commission
5806 Mesa Dr.
P.O. Box 13127
Capitol Station
Austin, Texas 78711–3127
Phone: (512) 206–3333
Fax: (512) 206–3449

UTAH (CONTROL STATE)

Utah Department of Alcoholic Beverage Control
1625 South 900 West
Salt Lake City, Utah 84130
Phone: (801) 977–6800
Fax: (801) 977–6888

VERMONT (CONTROL STATE)

Vermont Department of Liquor Control
Green Mountain Drive, Drawer 20
Montpelier, Vermont 05620–4501
Phone: (802) 828–2345
Fax: (802) 828–2803

VIRGINIA (CONTROL STATE)

Virginia Department of Alcoholic Beverage Control
VA ABC's Main Office:
2901 Hermitage Road
Richmond, VA 23220
VA ABC's Mailing Address:
Virginia Dept. of Alcoholic Beverage Control
P.O. Box 27491
Richmond, Virginia 23261
Phone: (804) 213–4413
Fax: (804) 213–4415

WASHINGTON (CONTROL STATE)

Washington Business License Services
Department of Licensing
P.O. Box 9034
Olympia, Washington 98504–3075
Phone: (360) 586–2784
Licensing: (360) 586–6700
Fax: (360) 586–1596

Washington State Liquor Control Board
3000 Pacific Avenue
P.O. Box 3098
Olympia, Washington 98504–3098
Phone: (360) 664–1600

WEST VIRGINIA (CONTROL STATE)

West Virginia Alcohol Beverage Control Commission
Enforcement & Licensing Division
322 70th St. S.E.
Charleston, West Virginia 25304–2900
Phone: (304) 558–2481 Toll Free: 800–642–8208
Fax: (304) 558–0081

WISCONSIN

Wisconsin Alcohol & Tobacco Enforcement
Department of Revenue
2135 Rimrock Road
Madison, Wisconsin 53713
Phone: (608) 266–2776
Fax: (608) 261–6240

WYOMING (CONTROL STATE)

Wyoming Liquor Commission
1520 East 5th Street
Cheyenne, Wyoming 82002
Phone: (307) 777–7231
Fax: (307) 777–5872

OTHER RESOURCES

Alcohol and Tobacco Tax and Trade Bureau
U.S. Department of the Treasury
http://www.ttb.gov

Appendix 5

Personal Financial Statement Form

Sample Personal Financial Statement

Name(s): ____________________

Street Address: ____________________

City: ____________ State: ____________ Zip ____________

Assets

Cash on Hand and in Banks $ ____________

U.S. Government Securities ____________

Accounts, Loans, and Notes Receivable ____________

Cash Surrender Value Life Insurance ____________

Value of Businesses Owned ____________

Listed Stocks and Bonds ____________

Privately Held Stocks and Bonds ____________

House (market value) ____________

Automobile Number ____________

Household Furnishings and Personal Effects ____________

Real Estate (other than house) ____________

Other Assets (itemize) ____________

TOTAL ASSETS $

Liabilities and Net Worth

Notes Payable $ ____________

Loan on House ____________

Liens on Real Estate ____________

Credit Card Debt (over thirty days) ____________

Other Liabilities (itemize) ____________

TOTAL LIABILITIES $ ____________

NET WORTH $

Source of Income

Salary $ ____________

Dividends and Interest ____________

Bonus and Commissions ____________

Real Estate Income ____________

Other Income ____________

TOTAL INCOME $

The undersigned certifies that he/she provided this information and it is true and correct.

Date: ____________

Signature: ____________ Home Phone: ____________

Appendix 6

Income Valuation Worksheet

Income Valuation Worksheet
Owner Benefit/Seller's Discretionary Earnings/EBITDA

A	B	C	D	E
Line Item	**Amount**	**Adjust +/-**	**Adjustment Reason**	**Adjust Expense Amount**
Gross Sales				
Cost of Goods				
Gross Profit				

Expenses

Accounting				
Advertising				
Amortization			Usual/Customary	
Auto Expense				
Bank Charges				
Depreciation			Usual/Customary	
Donations			Usual/Customary	
Insurance				
Insurance Auto				
Ins. Health				
Interest			Usual/Customary	
Maintenance				
Office Supplies				
Owner's Salary				
Rent Facility				
Repairs				
Salaries				
Supplies				
Tax				
Tax Payroll				
Telephone				
Travel/Entertainment				
Utilities				
Water				
Total Expense			**Total Adjusted**	

NET INCOME			**Owner Benefit**	

Appendix 7

Due Diligence Sales Audit Worksheet

	POS SALES	SALES TAX FILING	P&L SALES	ANNUAL INCOME TAX	P&L ANNUAL
January					
February					
March					
April					
May					
June					
July					
August					
September					
October					
November					
December					
TOTAL					

Appendix 8

Valuation Analysis Tool

A LINE ITEM	B AMOUNT	C ADJUST +/-	D ADJUSTMENT REASON	E ADJUST EXPENSE AMOUNT
Gross Sales				
Cost of Goods				
Gross Profit				
Expenses				
Accounting				
Advertising				
Amortization				
Auto Expense				
Bank Charges				
Depreciation				
Donations				
Insurance				
Insurance Auto				
Ins. Health				
Interest				
Maintenance				
Office Supplies				
Owner's Salary				
Rent Facility				
Repairs				
Salaries				

Supplies				
Tax				
Tax Payroll				
Telephone				
Travel/ Entertainment				
Utilities				
Water				

TOTAL EXPENSE	TOTAL ADJUSTED

NET INCOME	OWNER BENEFIT

Appendix 9

Landlord Background and Experience Template

Name
Address
City, State, Zip

____________________ is acquiring ____________________ Restaurant located at ________________________________.

____________________ has ___ years of food and restaurant experience in both franchise and independent concepts. He/she has held management and ownership positions in multiple restaurants with sales volume ranging from $_______ to $____________. His/her experience covers restaurant operations, hiring, expense management, food cost management, along with marketing and advertising.

______________________ will serve as the ____________ of ____________ Restaurant. His/her background includes the restaurants and time frames listed below. Excellent personal and professional references are available upon request.

EXPERIENCE

2009	Restaurant Name	Position
2006–2008	Restaurant Name	Position
2003–2006	Restaurant Name	Position
2001–2003	Restaurant Name	Position

Appendix 10

Business Plan Template

I. RESTAURANT DESCRIPTION AND VISION

This section should include:

- Restaurant description
- Business goals and objectives
- Brief history of the business
- List of key company principals

After reviewing this section you should know:

- Who the business is and what it stands for
- Your perception of the company's growth and potential
- Specific goals and objectives of the business

II. MARKET OUTLOOK AND COMPETITION TOTAL

- Define the restaurant industry and outlook
- Define the critical needs of your perceived or existing market
- Identify your target market
- Provide a general profile of your targeted clients
- Describe what share of the market you currently have and/or anticipate

After reviewing this section you should know:

- Basic information about the industry you operate in and the customer needs you are fulfilling

- The scope and share of your business market, as well as who your target customers are

III. MENU-DESCRIPTION OF PRODUCTS AND SERVICES

This section should include your menu, the centerpiece of your products and services.

IV. RESTAURANT STRUCTURE AND HOURS

This section should provide a description of how your company is organized (proprietorship, partnership, corporation, etc.), as well as operating hours.

V. MARKETING AND SALES STRATEGY

This section should:

- Identify and describe your restaurant market—who your customers are and what the demand is for your cuisine
- Describe your channels of distribution i.e. dine-in, delivery, takeout
- Explain your sales strategy, specific to pricing, promotion, products, and place (4 P's)

After reviewing this section you should know:

- Who your market is and how you will reach it
- How your company will apply pricing, promotion, product diversification, and channel distribution to promote your restaurant competitively

VI. FINANCIAL PROJECTIONS

This section should accurately forecast two to three years of sales and expenses along with expected earnings.